Adult Day Care

A BASIC GUIDE

Adult Day Care

A BASIC GUIDE

Sudie Maready Goldston

National Health Publishing

A Division of Williams & Wilkins

Published by
National Health Publishing
99 Painters Mill Road
Owings Mills, Maryland 21117
(301) 363–6400

A division of Williams & Wilkins

Printed in the United States of America
First Printing

Acquisitions Editor: Sara Mansure Sides
Copyeditor: Felice S. Li
Production Coordinator: Karen Babcock
Design: Sandy Renovetz
Compositor: National Health Publishing
Printer: Edwards Brothers

ISBN: 0–55857–001–2
LC: 88–063450

Dedicated to my mother, Corrine Casteen Maready,
who, when I was a child, taught me respect for older people
and to the memory of my grandfather,
William Nelson Casteen, who taught me to love them.

Contents

List of Exhibits

Preface

The unprecedented growth of our aging population has presented us with the demand for a wide range of social and health services to meet their burgeoning needs. These services must include a continuum of "in-home" services to respond to a societal development unique to our times: the need for daily care for frail adults who either live alone or are left at home alone while their families are at work. Adult day care came into being in response to this need and as a part of the necessary continuum. Providing a safe, caring environment during the day, it offers a desirable option which allows participants to continue to live in their own homes and communities.

The service has grown very rapidly, having begun essentially as a grass roots movement. As a result, most providers were forced to start and manage programs without a base of knowledge and experience to draw upon.

As the director of an early program, begun in Winston-Salem, North Carolina, in 1974, I felt deeply the lack of such information. Since our program was one of seven model programs in the state, I also had a sense of responsibility for sharing our learning experience with others, to pass along knowledge gained from both our mistakes and our successes. Miss Beth Barnes, the North Carolina Social Services Consultant for Adult Day Care at that time, and her superior in the department, Mr. John Tanner, were also recognizing the need to share this experience. In numerous conversations, we came to believe that a state-wide training program was needed. A committee was formed to develop a recommended plan for such training for presentation to the state. On the committee were Mr. Tanner, Elizabeth Knott, Adult Day Care Consultant (Social Services Department) for Wake County, North Carolina, Ms. Barnes, and myself. The committee recommended that a training curriculum be developed with two primary objectives:

1. To provide training for new and potential providers which would offer them the information gained by experienced providers. This part of the curriculum would include elements such as how to enlist community interest and support and how to start the program and develop budgets, funding, staff structure, etc.
2. To offer a second track of training designed to equip providers with specialized knowledge about needs of frail adults and to foster skills needed for programs to achieve the adult day care philosophy: helping participants to function at their maximum level of independence.

This track would cover such issues as program planning for functionally impaired adults, staff selection and development, and administrative issues, time management, use of community resources, etc.

The recommended training plan was shelved for several years due to unavailability of funds. It was revived in 1984, when the state allocated monies for a contract to develop the training curriculum and provide training sessions to try out and refine the curriculum. I was selected by the state to develop the training. I worked with a committee of providers and Social Services Workers representing divergent viewpoints to explore specific issues to be included in the curriculum.

The training manual was completed late in 1985 and training sessions were held in October of that year. Trainees responded favorably; the majority expressed a belief that the information would prove valuable to the field.

It is because of this positive response and because of my many conversations with other providers throughout the country that I have offered the manual for publication, hoping that it will be useful in helping to prevent costly mistakes and remedy deficiencies in adult day care management.

Adult Day Care: A Basic Guide is a "how-to" for both those considering starting an adult day care program and those presently engaged in operation of a program. The manual is not intended and does not attempt to answer all questions or solve all problems of planning and providing adult day care. Rather, it seeks to discuss the issues in ways which will help providers become aware of possible methods of problem resolution and be able to conduct questioning and research so that they can decide upon the directions most appropriate for their situation. All aspects of planning and program operation are discussed, from feasibility studies through site selection, board, staff and program development, and program administration. The concept and philosophy of adult day care are covered, as well as the needs and impairments common to frail adults. The manual is intended equally for the human services specialist who must understand the "business" side of the program, and the individual with a business, fund-raising, or public relations background who must learn more about the unique requirements of the service and the needs of frail adults. Thus the information included is that which is basic and which must be shared by all those involved in adult day care programs for the program to succeed.

Topics were selected in response to concerns voiced by the members of our advisory committee and by many administrators with whom I have discussed issues of adult day care provision. These administrators are the "pioneers" of the service, who have worked to develop a unique service and to establish and maintain high standards of provision. For this effort, all of us in the field owe them a debt of gratitude.

Acknowledgements

Work on this book has been going on for a long time, beginning with my first efforts to learn about the needs of frail adults in our society. In addition to drawing on knowledge gained in working with frail adults in a variety of settings, I owe much to the knowledge and assistance of others.

First, I wish to thank the State of North Carolina, which provided funds for initial development of the materials as a training manual for adult day care providers in the state.

A grateful acknowledgement is expressed to Ms. Jacqueline Paris, who in the role of Adult Day Care Consultant for the Social Services Department, State of North Carolina, during the period while the manual was being developed, provided technical assistance, support, and unfailing patience. These have contributed much to the finished product.

Appreciation is also expressed to the advisory committee who offered assistance during the early stages: Phyllis Latta and Amelia Fisher, Greensboro, North Carolina; Thelma Freeze, Concord, North Carolina; Suzie Kennedy, Shelby, North Carolina; Penny Williams, Durham, North Carolina; and Sarah Boyd, Salisbury, North Carolina.

Gratitude must also be offered to other individuals who provided support and advice: Gail Linker, Board of Education, Trenton, New Jersey; Betty Ransom, National Institute on Adult Daycare, National Council on the Aging, Inc., Washington, DC; and Ruth Von Behren, On Lok Senior Health Services, San Francisco, California. Also, to all members of the National Institute Steering Committee during my tenure as Chair-Elect and Chair: 1982–1986. Their knowledge of and enthusiasm for the service have done much to influence my thinking and build my knowledge about adult day care.

Special acknowledgement is due to Beth Barnes and John Tanner of the North Carolina Department of Social Services, whose persistence in keeping alive the need for training is largely responsible for the manual becoming a reality. Dr. Elizabeth Knott of East Carolina University, Greenville, North Carolina is another whose belief in the idea was instrumental in bringing this project to fruition.

Appreciation is also extended to my husband, Allan Martin Goldston, and my daughter, Diane Bauguess, whose hours of typing, proofreading, and provision of advice (sometimes unsolicited) provided support and helped to keep me motivated when the going became hard.

A heartfelt thank you goes to the frail and older adults who were participants in the adult day care programs in which I worked. Their love, friendship, and willingness to serve as my teachers made both that work and the writing of this manual tasks whose deepest meaning is an expression of gratitude to them for their role in my life.

A word of explanation and apology is in order for any content which may demonstrate bias on the part of the author. Careful research into available materials, plus conferences and conversations with many providers were conducted to make the materials as broad as possible. However, much had to be based upon personal experience, much of which has been gained in the State of North Carolina. Readers and users are invited and encouraged to re-construct any data to fit their own experience, needs, and location.

Sudie Maready Goldston
March 1988

Foreword

The book you are about to read should be required reading for all persons interested in beginning or modifying an adult day health center in their community. As a former administrator responsible for adult day care and a consultant to the Adult Day Health Care Network of San Francisco, I searched but could not find a comprehensive book on the multiple issues facing the brave who venture into adult day care. Sudie Goldston's *Adult Day Care: A Basic Guide* is one of the most useful and complete texts that has been compiled for adult day care planners and operators alike. In addition to creating a general source of information, Ms. Goldston has developed a clear road map to assist readers in getting from one element to the next.

Based on the projected increases in the oldest segment of the population and the advances in medical technology, there will be a growing need for community based long-term care service systems for the chronically ill. A key element in the network is adult day care which is projected to emerge in every community in this country. Adult day care in the United States has come of age! Since the late sixties when the first centers began providing service, the number of programs has grown to over 1,200. While the numbers have grown, adult day care is still unavailable to vast numbers of potential clients. A variety of problems contribute to this lack of adequate programs.

Many persons concerned with the well-being of older adults have never heard of this service, and many of those that have do not understand the term adult day care. Those who do understand and want to provide this service face many obstacles. Because of its complexity, many groups interested in developing the service have become frustrated and unable to proceed to completion. The interested parties find themselves faced by innumerable barriers representing the bureaucracy; namely, funding sources, zoning, insurance coverage, and agency turf. The existing establishment of senior services often reject the services as too difficult to develop and operate.

While for the user adult day care is a convenient, comprehensive one-stop opportunity to receive services, for the planners and developers it is a many-layered, complex service to provide. As one of my predecessors as President of the Board of the National Council on Aging, Ellen Winston, said several years ago, "Adult day care is a truly complex service which calls for great skill in day-to-day operations." Instead of a strict formula for developing these services, the author presents a framework. She begins by describing the types of populations served and goes on to offer different models and types of centers and organizational structures. Many of us who have been involved with starting and maintaining centers wish that this level of detailed information had been available to us many years ago. Chapters 3–10 include the answers to many of our questions about budgeting and financing, procedures and policies, evaluation, staffing, and board development. There is extensive detail on selection of space, director, staff, and consultants which presents the options available. The sections which may be the most useful for new centers or new directors are those chapters dealing with the target population, program planning, and working with the functionally impaired. Lastly, the section on community resources should be kept at the director's side for it will be a constant resource for survival. While I was Director of Geriatric Services at a hospital, I found that we had funding and in-kind contributions from over fifteen sources. Without this knowledge of community resources, both financial and human, our center and other centers would not have survived.

During the past twenty years I have read, reviewed, and heard dozens of presentations on adult day care. I myself have written, reviewed, and presented papers on the same subject. However, Dr. Goldston's book is the first that puts together all the pieces of the puzzle for beginners, as well as developers and managers of day care programs. I am sure that they will find it to be a trusted companion and resource as they proceed into the exciting and challenging world of adult day care.

As a co-founder of the National Institute on Adult Daycare some ten years ago, I said that I believed that the pioneers in developing adult day care were the most creative, determined service providers that I had ever worked with. As I have watched the hundreds of centers that have developed since then, I have not changed my mind. I am delighted that this book will now be available to help bring more of these creators into the world of providing this essential service.

Barbara Sklar
September 1988

1 Adult Day Care: A Working Knowledge

Introduction

To design an effective adult day care program, providers need to understand how and why the service evolved and in response to what needs. This chapter will discuss the philosophy behind adult day care, as well as whom it is meant to serve, what elements distinguish it from other methods of care, and how it relates to other forms of care within the care continuum.

History of Adult Day Care

Adult day care—in the form of day hospitalization—began in Europe and the Soviet Union as early as the 1920s. However, programs of day hospitalization, or "day care," designed specifically for geriatric patients, has been a more recent development.

The 1960s saw the first developments in the United States, when Dr. Lionel Cosin of Great Britain introduced adult day care as a part of his work with Cherry Hospital in Goldsboro, North Carolina. This program is still operating, but differs from the usual concept of adult day care: the participants are patients in the hospital but spend a part of each day in the day program. There they are engaged in training to develop skills to aid them in independent living after discharge. Special emphasis is placed upon use of community resources and activities of daily living.

Rapid growth of adult day care was stimulated when the State Department of Health and Mental Hygiene in Maryland issued a report concerning the purposes and requirements of the service for the aged. This served as official recognition of the need for the service. Programs had been developed in several states and the numbers increased when financial support was provided from offices of aging under the Older American's Act and in some instances, from Titles XIX and XX, beginning in the early 1970s.

The tasks facing early centers were numerous. Few persons involved had had prior experience with adult day care and they knew little about the concept and provision of the service. They had to educate themselves quickly about the appropriate population to be served, necessary components of care, and methods of service provision. Other immediate concerns included education of the public about the need for and availability of adult day care, participant recruitment, development of linkages with other agencies within the care continuum, and selection and training of staff.

Most centers received funds for start-up only, and thus their most pressing and time consuming task became the search for funds to continue the programs. Most early participants were unable to pay fees; the majority had fees paid from Titles XIX and XX. This meant that only those eligible under regulations of these funds—the low income elderly—were participants during this period. It would be some time before acceptance was wide enough to attract those in socioeconomic brackets who could afford to attend as fee-paying participants.

The availability of Title XX for even this degree of support decreased each year as more providers of other services became able to supply the required match for the funds and began to use monies which had formerly been allocated to adult day care. Adult day care was thus in competition with other essential services for the limited funds, causing some programs to be closed. However, during this period, programs began banding together and lobbying for allocation of funds to be used exclusively for adult day care. States in which this effort was successful were able to move forward in establishment of programs since the service was no longer in competition with other services. This had the effect of providing a degree of security for programs in those states.

Simultaneously, the development of standards for service quality was taking place. Early standards were adapted from day care standards for children. Using these as a model, some states developed minimum standards to be able to monitor quality of service and require that safety and comfort regulations be met.

Rationale for the Service

In spite of the difficulties encountered, adult day care continued to expand rapidly; numbers grew from a dozen centers in 1969–70 to more than 1,000 by 1984. This growth was in response to a realization that our present system of long-term care—mainly institutionalization of our frail elderly—is now and will in the future be inadequate to meet needs of this rapidly growing population. In addition, institutionalization is often inappropriate for many and is provided at great financial cost to the nation.

Costs for nursing home care grew from $1.3 billion in 1965 to $17.9 billion in 1979. If present policies and programs continue at that rate, the cost of nursing home care is estimated to reach $76 billion by 1990. The government now pays for more than half of nursing home care, primarily through Medicaid (Title XIX), with some costs borne by Medicare (2.1% of the total).

The number of older adults in our society is increasing at an unprecedented rate, faster than any other part of the population. In 1981 there were over 23 million older adults in the country; by the year 2000, the number is expected to increase to 32 million. It is obvious that, with a correlating growth in the number of frail elderly, and with tightening budgets, the financial resources to continue with any over-provision of care will not be possible. These facts will demand that alternative, less expensive methods of care be made available.

Belatedly, there is a growing recognition of the need to develop a comprehensive system of care for impaired adults who can be maintained in their own homes with the help of community-based services. Public policy has increasingly emphasized development of such a system, one allowing options for care, responding to individual needs, and providing care in the least restrictive environment consistent with needs and functional ability of the clientele. Adult day care is one component in this system, serving those adults who are unable to function at home without supportive services, but who do not need 24 hour care. It covers an existing gap between the more loosely structured services of senior centers and full-time residential care. More traditional services for impaired adults can be made part of adult day care. Adult day care programs should be coordinated with other services, such as senior centers, other in-home services, and hospitals and institutions.

Creating alternatives to institutionalization is critical both for our society and for our older individuals. Not only are financial costs for providing institutional care prohibitively high, but the cost of sacrifices in the quality of life may be even higher. For most older adults who have prized independence, enjoyment of life in later years means being able to remain in their homes and to function as independently as possible.

Adult day care provides the means to this independence for many frail older adults. A study conducted by Duke University (Duke Center for the Study of Aging and Human Development 1978) concluded that the adult day care centers in North Carolina were clearly serving a population of adults whose impairment level placed them at risk of institutionalization without enrollment in the programs. Most participants in the service express satisfaction with adult day care; many families of participants and health care professionals view it as an exciting alternative to entering residential care earlier than necessary. A study sponsored by the Virginia Center on Aging (Arling and Romaniuk 1982, 39) found that 61% of participants and 57% of families/caregivers reported improved outlook and mental well-being as a result of participants' enrollment in adult day care.

Most data available at this time supports the premise that enrollment and attendance in adult day care has a positive effect on the lives of participants in terms of maintaining life enjoyment and avoiding premature loss of independence.

Adult Day Care Service Definition

As a result of the rapid and fragmented development of adult day care, there are diverse models of service provision. This diversity has in some ways been beneficial: centers have been able to adapt services to meet local needs and to be flexible in planning programs adapted to the needs of participants. A less desirable result has been the lack of an accepted definition of the service, creating some confusion among government bodies responsible for enacting funding legislation. The existence of several methods of service all called "adult day care" has also caused a degree of confusion among other funders and the general public. Thus, diversity in the provision of adult day care has sometimes resulted in a lack of united support for the basic concept.

A growing recognition of the threat posed to continued growth of adult day care created by this confusion caused providers across the country to request the National Institute on Adult Daycare (NIAD, formed in 1977 as a constituent unit of the National Council on the Aging, Inc.) to formulate a definition which could apply to the varying models, but which would also speak to the essential principles upon which the service is constructed and to basic standards of provision of care. NIAD accepted the challenge as part of a greater challenge: to develop national standards for use by the field. The standards, including the definition, were published in late 1984.

The NIAD definition is as follows:

> Adult day care is a community based group program designed to meet the needs of functionally impaired adults through an individual plan of care. It is a structured, comprehensive program that provides a variety of health, social and related support services in a protective setting during any part of a day, but less than 24 hour care. Individuals who participate in adult day care attend on a planned basis during specified hours. Adult day care assists its participants to remain in the community, thus enabling families and other caregivers to continue caring for an impaired member at home (National Institute on Adult Daycare 1984, 20).

The definition, as formulated, sought to distinguish adult day care from other forms of care which may have some, but not all, of the components of adult day care and which may serve similar populations. While it is obvious that adult day care is easily distinguished from residential care, the difference from senior centers and other day activity centers is not so obvious at first glance. Major differences do exist, however, in the functional level of participants served and in the level of care provided. Adult day care participants should be those individuals who are *not* able to function in the more independent setting of a senior center. They need the close attention to their specific needs provided by adult day care based on individual plans of care developed within the program yet do not need to be in residential care, because they are able to function some part of the day within their home without constant attention.

Adult day care providers must possess a clear understanding of how the service is unique, where it fits within the care continuum, the characteristics of the population to be served, and these providers must demonstrate this understanding by their methods and the quality of service provided. These elements, when coupled with acceptance of the service definition and adherence to standards of care implicit within wording of the definition, will contribute greatly to growth and enlisting of public support for adult day care.

Supportive Data

Studies of the aging population indicate that about 90% of older people continue to function well, living lives which are full and independent. These studies also indicate that only about 5% of the older population is residing in a long-term care facility at any given time. This means that about 5% of the elderly population is in need of supportive services to enable them to continue living at home and functioning at their maximum level of independence. Other studies indicate that a large percentage (between 30 and 50 percent) of persons in long-term care facilities could have been maintained at home if they had had access to community-based services such as adult day care and other home-delivered services. A publication prepared by the National Institute on Aging (1980) states that 2.4 million persons aged 65 and older *need services to remain in the community, but are not in need of institutionalization.*

As mentioned earlier, there are indications that participants in adult day care have impairments putting them "at risk" of institutionalization. They suffer from a variety of disabling impairments. For example, as reported in the Virginia Center on Aging study, adult day care participants surveyed suffered from a wide range of health problems: 42% had arthritis or rheumatism, the most common disorder; 37% circulatory diseases; 37% cardiovascular disease; and 34% hypertension. Strokes and their aftermath, speech disorder and paralysis, afflicted 25%; cataracts or glaucoma 20%; and diabetes 12%. Most suffered from multiple impairments and were experiencing great difficulty with normal functioning. A sizable proportion, 59%, suffered from some cognitive impairment, ranging from slight dementia to severe memory impairment or loss.

An intensive study on 28 participants and 26 of their closest family members in the Levindale Treatment Program, Baltimore, Maryland, reinforces the Virginia results (Weiler and Rathbone-McCuan 1978, 112). All families considered that the adult day care participant was unable to function with only family assistance and that enrollment in adult day care was a last ditch effort to maintain the person in the home.

There are strong indications in both studies that the family perception was justified. Caregivers in the Virginia study indicated that care of a dependent member resulted in stress for the caregiver; 100% indicated that they had to make multiple life changes to provide the necessary care; 60% that they had less time for themselves; 52% that their activities and plans must consider the needs of the impaired individual; 48% that personal social activities had to be restricted. One-third reported psychological stress; 32% indicated that family disagreements had increased; 21% experienced disruptions in work patterns; and 17% reported that finances were taxed by the situation.

The Virginia study indicated improvement for both the caregivers and participants through enrollment in the adult day care program. As stated earlier, morale improved for 61% of enrollees, 19% showed improvement in health and social skills, 18% experienced some degree of rehabilitation, and 4% noted improvement in personal care skills. For caregivers there were also benefits: 57% reported improved mental health, 46% less worry about the participant, 50% more time for themselves, 25% more time for families and recreation. In addition, 25% were able to gain outside employment and 10% experienced improvement in their own physical health.

The research cited above confirms the need for adult day care, since individuals being served in programs like those studied have impairment levels which could otherwise result in their being admitted to full-time residential care. Studies also indicate that the service helps families to keep their impaired member in the home and results in improved function for some participants. Families and caregivers also appear to benefit from use of the service.

"Models" of Adult Day Care

In the 1980s, providers of adult day care across the country have attempted to focus attention upon commonalities of service provision among programs, in the interest of developing national standards and a generic definition of the service.

While some regulatory policies are applicable to any model, there are notable differences within United States government regulations. Under Title XIX (Medicaid), it is essential for the participant to need *active* health care services (i.e., medical, nursing, rehabilitative, or occupational therapies) in order to be eligible for adult day care funding. Title XX and the Older American's Act do not have this requirement for funding. Professionals in the field have struggled with classifying the service under different models, and most agree that there are no hard and fast dividing lines, but rather a considerable overlapping among the models.

As shown in Exhibit 1–1, early European models of adult day care can be classified according to their treatment emphasis—social work, psychiatric treatment, and occupational or physical therapy—and according to the source of development.

Padula (1983) outlines three alternative models (Exhibit 1–2). Padula believes that few centers fit neatly into these definitions, but that all models have certain basic services present.

Another approach is taken to categorizing service provision by O'Brien who outlines three levels of care (Exhibit 1–3). O'Brien sees these levels of care as giving a preventive orientation to adult day care services and believes that with the focus on prevention, the provider can place health promotion, detection, cure, and restoration on a continuum of care within a program.

Service provision in some states, usually those with primary funding from Social Security or Title XX funds, has traditionally been seen as oriented toward the "social model" or providing social services. Those states with most funding from Medicaid funds have leaned toward provision of more medical care services. However, as stated earlier, there are few centers which could be classified as limiting services to one model or the other; most programs provide services which combine some features of the two orientations. As more states have had their application approved for funding adult day care under the Medicaid waivers, the health care model has expanded. Some impaired participants receive specific treatments as mandated by their prescribed plan of care and required by Medicaid regulations. Services to other participants in the programs may remain as before, unless their condition necessitates their receiving more intensive health care services.

Exhibit 1-1 European models of adult day care.

Location	Type of Service	Provider
Social/Health centers	Social work; welfare services	Social day centers
Day hospitals	Physical therapy; medical services	Rehabilitation centers
Day hospitals	Medical services	Medical services; nursing home
Psychiatric hospitals	Occupational therapy	Psychiatric hospitals

Source: Weiler, P.G. and E. Rathbone-McCuan. 1978. *Adult day care: Community work with the elderly.* New York: Springer Publishers.

Auspices of Adult Day Care Programs

Adult day care has been developed by a variety of community groups and sponsors as an answer to a perceived need in the community. Its development has been largely a grass roots movement. The sponsors have ranged from churches and free-standing community groups to hospitals and state service agencies. They may be for-profit, nonprofit or public.

Private, For-Profit

For-profit private sponsorship is usually developed by an individual or an agency responding to a perceived need and is operated as a profit-making service. Many private programs are located in institutional settings such as nursing homes, rest homes, and hospitals.

The advantages of a privately sponsored program are that it often can provide a range of services on-site, and that equipment is often available for use by the program at little cost, helping to provide higher quality service at a lower cost. Frequently, management and staff both possess skills and training needed for planning and operating an effective program. The primary disadvantage of private sponsorship is that if the service motives become lost in the need to make a profit, the quality of the service may suffer. Also, participants are frequently reluctant to enter a program housed in the long-term setting, fearing that it is a first step toward institutionalization. There are many resources available to nonprofit organizations which profit-making centers may be unable to utilize, such as donations of time and money, widespread community support, and public funding.

Another setting for private, for-profit adult day care programs may be in the home of the owner. These are usually small (six or less participants) and called "adult day care homes." This concept originated in North Carolina, and other states have indicated an

Exhibit 1-2 Three Models of Adult Day Care.

1. Social:	Sometimes called psychosocial. Emphasis is upon socialization, while affording relief/respite for families and caregivers. No limits are set upon duration of service beyond those of natural increase of disability.
2. Maintenance:	Midway between social and restorative models in the mix of social and remedial components, types of participants, eligibility requirements, and duration of stay.
3. Restorative:	Offers extensive rehabilitative services for individuals who might otherwise require care in a skilled nursing facility, but who can be expected to improve within a stipulated time, at least to the point of needing a lesser level of care. Staff in this model is more likely to be composed of health care professionals.

Source: Padula, H. 1983. *Developing adult day care for older people, a technical assistance monograph.* Washington, DC: National Council on the Aging, Inc.

Exhibit 1-3 Three Levels of Adult Day Care.

1. Primary:	Services provided are nutrition, counseling, health teaching, provision of a safe environment, provision of adequate housing arrangements, periodic examinations, use of specific immunizations, and attention to personal hygiene.
2. Secondary:	Aimed at curing or arresting a disease in order to prevent complications from prolonged disability. Services include administering medications, blood pressure screening, diabetic screening, glaucoma screening, and selective examination for various diseases.
3. Tertiary:	Prevention of complete disability after the disease process becomes more stabilized. Services include retraining in activities of daily living, work capacities, necessary nursing services.

Source: O'Brien, C.L. 1982. *Adult day care: A practical guide.* Monterey, CA: Wadsworth Health Sciences Division.

interest in developing the concept, especially those with large rural areas such as Wyoming and Tennessee. They are required to meet essentially the same regulations as larger programs. These small programs have an advantage in that many participants respond readily to a family setting, feeling more comfortable than within larger centers. Operators are usually dedicated to the well-being of participants and are able to observe the needs of the individual in more depth than is sometimes possible in larger centers. But the small size can also be a disadvantage. The facility owner usually has difficulty showing a profit under existing schedules of payment for services from most funding sources. Consequently, the staff is small, sometimes limited to the owner with only part-time staff or volunteer help from family members or other interested persons. This limits the variety and scope of services and activities which may be offered. Professional contacts and opportunities for staff training are also limited by these factors.

Private, Nonprofit

Nonprofit private programs are usually begun by a group of concerned citizens within a community who became aware of a gap in available care and organized to begin an adult day care program to fill the perceived need.

These centers are usually managed by a governing body made up of interested citizens and are usually free-standing. This has the advantage of allowing the directors and staff to design the program to serve the specific population about which they have concerns and to exercise more flexibility in program policies and management. Among disadvantages of this method, members of the governing body are volunteers and often lack the skills necessary for implementing a successful program: understanding parameters of the population to be served, and knowing how to manage staff and obtain necessary funds. These problems can be overcome if planners use available resources to acquire needed skills and to overcome deficiencies in knowledge.

Public

Public programs are operated by social services departments, mental health centers, or other public social agencies. Participants served in these centers are usually already service recipients of the agency and the program is begun to provide a component of care recognized by the agency as missing from the care continuum.

Such public programs have an advantage over private in that, since participants already have a trust relationship with the agency, they are usually more willing to enroll in the program. Staff is often familiar with needs and characteristics of participants and space is available. In addition, other resources of the agency may be utilized by the adult day care program at a savings. However, the program may not be a priority of the agency and may be shortchanged in availability of funds and staff time if budget cuts must be made. The bureaucratic structure of some agencies is not conducive to offering a service with the flexibility and responsiveness to needs of individual participants desirable in adult day care. Furthermore, potential participants are sometimes reluctant to enter programs housed in public agencies, feeling that there is a stigma attached to receiving services from a social or mental health services agency.

Location

Basic philosophy and service of adult day care will not be altered substantially if the program is located in an urban as opposed to a rural setting, but planners should be aware of the advantages and disadvantages of each type of location and be able to adapt their program accordingly.

Rural Setting

There are usually well-established communication networks in rural neighborhoods, making it easier to spread word of a new service and to advertise program needs for funds, volunteers, or donations of equipment and supplies. In many communities there are also effective family and neighborhood helping networks. These can be utilized to find and recruit participants for the program. The components of these networks (families, neighbors, churches, social clubs, etc.) make up a larger percentage of the community than in urban areas and, by virtue of their personal interest in the program, will serve as good will ambassadors. Volunteers may also be drawn from the network.

The visibility of the program and lack of the intensive competition for funds found within more urban areas may make funding easier to obtain. Certainly, the fact that participants, staff, and members of the sponsoring body are well-known will be helpful in gaining access to government and other decision-making bodies to present the case for obtaining funds and other support for the program. Such informal resources in rural areas can be invaluable to adult day care. Careful planning will bring about a successful blend of formal and informal resources, important to all programs, but especially to those in rural areas.

A disadvantage of a rural setting is that rural centers will most likely serve a large geographical area, increasing problems of transportation. Additionally, many supplemental services needed by participants will not be available in rural areas. Providing access to these services will add to the transportation problem, if indeed the services can be found within easy driving distance.

Urban Setting

The advantages and disadvantages for adult day care in an urban setting are the reverse of those in rural locations. In an urban setting there is a greater pool of resources to draw from, and a wider range of adjunct services is more readily accessible. This enables providers to plan and carry out a diversified program which can respond more quickly and completely to the needs of participants. Transportation is still likely to be a problem, but programs may be able to utilize public or special means of transport. Colleges, training centers, and other professional educational organizations are frequently in close proximity and can be used to enrich programs and to obtain training for staff.

On the other hand, urban areas often contain a large number of community service agencies which compete for public recognition and support. Small, new programs may get lost within the system. Staff and governing bodies may lack personal contact with governmental bodies and funding sources, making it difficult to gain their attention.

Overall, there does not appear to be a compelling argument for either location as being vastly superior to the other. Planning must be adjusted to take advantage of available resources and to overcome disadvantages. The important point to remember is that there must be a realistic assessment of efforts needed to do the job, resources to be utilized, and need for the service.

Summary

Adult day care appears to be an idea whose time has come. As with any new service concept, it is undergoing a developmental period, with continuous efforts to refine and clarify what it is meant to be and whom it is meant to serve.

The fact that the service began as a grass roots effort (rather than as a planned governmental program) has been both its strength and its weakness. On the one hand, lack of definition and imposed limits have prolonged the developmental and classification process. But on the other hand, providers have been able to be flexible and creative in their service approach. It is true that the wide variation in auspices, location, funding sources, and treatment emphases has sometimes created schisms among providers. However, the common and unifying theme in adult day care provision has been and remains that of offering whatever services are needed and using whatever resources are available to help recipients increase or maintain their independence and improve their quality of life.

References

Arling, G. and M. Romaniuk. 1982. *The final report from the study of adult day care programs in Virginia.* Richmond, VA: Virginia Center on Aging, Virginia Commonwealth University.

Duke Center for the Study of Aging and Human Development. 1978. *OARS training program in techniques of adult day care assessment.* Durham, NC: Duke Center for the Study of Aging and Human Development.

O'Brien, C.L. 1982. *Adult day care: A practical guide.* Monterey, CA: Wadsworth Health Sciences Division.

National Institute on Adult Daycare. 1984. *Standards for adult day care.* Washington, DC: National Council on the Aging, Inc.

National Institute on Aging. 1980. *Our future selves.* Department of Health, Education, and Welfare, NIH Pub. No. 80–1096. Washington, DC: Government Printing Office.

Padula, H. 1983. *Developing adult day care for older people, a technical assistance monograph.* Washington, DC: National Council on the Aging, Inc.

Weiler, P.G. and E. Rathbone–McCuan. 1978. *Adult day care: Community work with the elderly.* New York: Springer Publishing Company.

2 Beginning Steps

Introduction

Organizing an adult day care program is a complex task, requiring hard work by a core group of knowledgeable individuals as well as support from the community. A group or individual must act as a catalyst, arousing interest in the concept and motivating key individuals to become involved. Recognizing the need for the service in their community, this group or individual must take steps to pull together representatives of the community who will support the idea and who will form the nucleus of the planning and development committee.

Assessing Feasibility

The first step in the development process is to locate individuals who represent the community in the area of adult services and to set up a meeting to discuss the feasibility of beginning an adult day care program.

The initial approach may be a phone call and/or a personal visit to the key individuals who will be asked to participate in the meeting. One should request a few minutes of their time, briefly discuss the concept in words which point out the need for and effectiveness of the service, and ask if they will attend an exploratory meeting and if they can recommend others who should be a part of the discussion. All agencies and groups who will be central to starting and operating an adult day care program in the community should be represented at the meeting. The list will be somewhat different in each community, but will usually include the following public and private providers.

Social Services Department

Mental Health Department

Public Health Department

Medical Association

Nurses' Association

Voluntary Action Center

Retired Senior Volunteer Program

Council of Governments/Area Agency on Aging

City and County Officials

Local Foundations/Funding Agencies/ United Way

Religious Leadership

Educational Leadership

Council on Aging

Senior Citizens' Center

Senior Citizens' Clubs

Recreation Department

Local nursing homes or rest homes

Hospitals

Each community will differ in its configuration of service providers and leadership, and care must be taken that community representation is comprehensive.

Meeting Agenda

There is likely to be little concrete action taken at the initial meeting, since its purpose is primarily for brainstorming and deciding upon the feasibility of further action. However, to create a climate favorable to subsequent positive action, it is imperative that the agenda be well thought out, and that those who call the meeting are clear about anticipated results. Convening such a meeting only to have everyone leave without any decisions being made is a waste of time and detrimental to future progress. Exhibit 2-1 outlines a workable agenda for this initial meeting.

If there is a consensus among the group that the need for a service does exist and is great enough to warrant further consideration, the next step is to put together a formal planning committee.

Formation of a Planning Committee

Planners of adult day care and other human services, in their commitment to providing quality services, often select committee membership from among persons who have experience and reputations in the field of human services. While it is certainly important that such individuals be included, it is equally important that the membership include persons in the community at large who possess other skills needed to achieve the objectives of the committee.

Planning and implementing an adult day care program requires skills in the areas of community leadership, business administration, and human services.

Community Leadership

In all communities there are individuals who are instrumental in shaping public opinion and who are able to wield influence to gain support for the adult day care program. Inclusion of civic, government, and business leaders will open many doors and will greatly increase the success potential for the adult day care committee.

Exhibit 2-1 The Initial Meeting: Need and Feasibility Assessment.

The following issues should be among those discussed at the inital planning meeting.

1. Is adult day care needed in the community? Is there a gap in the present continuum of services? For what population? Are there sufficient numbers of persons needing and likely to use the service to justify setting it up? What would these individuals require from the program?
2. Are there funds available and from what source or sources, public and private? What groups of groups of individuals are eligible for available funds? What is the time line and process for applying for funding?
3. Is the community likely to support a new program? How can this be determined?
4. What about housing for the program? Is there space available in an existing building which may house a service complementary to those already in the building? Is the facility in a desirable location, accessible to the population to be served and needing little renovation to meet regulations? Is it in a safe location? If an existing building is not available how feasible are the alternatives of building or leasing?
5. What about transportation? Is there a community transportation project which may offer transportation? If not, what are the alternatives, including lease of vans or having participants provide their own transportation?
6. What about staff for the program? How difficult is it likely to be to find qualified personnel?
7. What is the level of commitment among those present? Is it possible to recruit two or three who will serve as the nucleus of a planning and development committee?

Business Administration

Adult day care providers must recognize that the program must be viewed and operated in a businesslike manner. Therefore, the committee will need members who can make contributions in all aspects of sound business administration.

1. *General business management skills* to provide leadership, direction, coordination of effort, motivation, assessment, and evaluation.
2. *Planning skills* to analyze needs and resources for purposes of formulating both short and long range plans.
3. *Personnel management skills* to plan staff structure to fit program needs, staff recruitment, and selection.

4. *Financial management skills* to project costs and income to develop and manage budget.
5. *Fund-raising skills* to research and locate sources of funds; to make grant applications; to plan and carry out fund-raising events.
6. *Marketing skills* to plan publicity and promotion efforts; to serve as spokesperson for the program to the community; to help to gain community support.
7. *Legal skills* to explore local regulations and laws which will affect the program; to help to meet all legal requirements.
8. *Real estate knowledge* to select site and purchase, lease, or rental agreements.
9. *Construction skills* to select and modify site; for construction or renovations.
10. *Transportation knowledge* to arrange for transportation, van purchase or lease; to contract with transportation providers.

Human Services

The committee needs members who understand the concept and goals of adult day care, as well as the needs of the population to be served. These individuals must constantly keep the philosophy of the service before the group so as not to lose the ultimate objective: development of a program which addresses the needs of participants and their families in ways which will enhance their quality of life.

The committee will benefit from having members with expertise in the following professions:

Medical/health
Mental health
Social Services
Services to the Aging
Education
Recreation
People management
Home Economics
Communication

In addition to possessing needed skills, all persons serving on the planning committee must agree on the long-term-care needs within the community and agree with the philosophy and broad service goals of adult day care as an integral component within the care continuum.

It is probable that the permanent governing body for the program will be formed at least partially from among the planning committee membership. This increases the importance of structuring a broad-based planning committee which can make substantive contributions to the program's development as well as helping to form a bridge between the program's development phase and its implementation.

Ideally, some planning committee members will have talents or abilities in more than one field, and will be able to contribute in several areas. This will help to keep the committee at a size which is likely to be efficient, i.e., with no more than 10 to 12 people.

Committee Duties

Once the decision to develop an adult day care program has been made, a multiplicity of tasks faces the planning committee. Before any other action is taken, the committee should devote itself to the development of a detailed pl*an of work.* The plan of work ensures that all committee members know what they need to do and also establishes a time frame for the tasks, eliminating "dead time" between activities. Delays in the progress of a committee's work tend to reduce motivation.

Committee Orientation

Before work is begun, all members of the committee need to become thoroughly versed in the specific issues of adult day care: service philosophy and goals, methods of providing service, and characteristics of the population to be served and their needs. All members must understand that knowledge and acceptance of these concepts is fundamental to the success of the committee. Only by a strong commitment to these precepts will they be able to gain needed community support and to develop a program which will offer high quality care.

Several publications are available which will provide content for the orientation session. Many states have now published their own standards and licensure regulations, which are available on request from state human services departments or offices on aging. In addition, the publications *Standards for Adult Day Care* and *Developing Adult Day Care for Older People, a Technical Assistance Monograph* are available through the National Council on the Aging, Inc., 600 Maryland Avenue, S.W., West Wing 100, Washington, D.C. 20024.

Community resources may be interviewed to provide content for the orientation, or they may be willing to make a presentation. One can consult personnel from existing adult day care centers; adult day care consultants and consultants in the field of aging; county Departments of Social Services personnel; State Division of Social Services Adult Day Care personnel or personnel of other state agencies with responsibility for adult day care programs. In addition, planning committee members can plan to visit existing adult day care centers in other communities.

It is strongly recommended that participation in an orientation session be required as a pre-requisite for serving on the planning committee and, later, on the governing body. Orientation should be repeated periodically to refresh memories and to inform new members who join the committee.

Committee Structure

Either immediately after or before the orientation session, the committee will want to take steps to organize formally. Selection of officers and appointment of subcommittees are among the first steps. Officers should be selected not only for their leadership abilities (although these must be a major consideration), but for their commitment to the philosophy of adult day care and to the goals of the planning committee. In addition, they must have time available in which to carry out the duties of the position.

Community Needs Assessment

Needs assessment may take one of two directions. A comprehensive assessment to determine the total number of persons in the community needing adult day care, including all populations within broad parameters who may qualify to use the service, (for example, frail elderly, developmentally handicapped, orthopedically handicapped, those suffering from brain trauma, etc.) may be made. However, if this information is already available, or the decision has been made to serve a specific segment of the broad population, then the committee may elect to assess the extent of the need for only that group.

There are a number of methodologies available for use in assessing the need. Both the State of Maryland and the State of Kentucky have developed assessment instruments, which are available from their State Offices of Aging.

Most critically, the committee will need information not only about the numbers who may *need* the service, but also about the numbers who will *use* the service. Determination of this issue should be included as a part of the initial assessment process, and it is recommended that an active recruitment effort begin as soon as a projected opening date has been set (see Chapter 4, "Marketing the Program"). Depending upon the location and other variable factors, filling the center with participants may be a long and frustrating effort. Even in the planning stage, one may locate potential users of the service, making home visits and having them visit the center if feasible, and carrying out preliminary enrollment procedures. This will save time and effort for the program and is a partial solution to the problem of filling the center with participants.

Setting Program Goals

Since specific goals for the adult day care program will serve as the foundation upon which the program is built and as such will influence all decisions and actions to be taken by the planning committee, they should be developed early in the planning process. These goals will become part of the program operating policies (see Chapter 6). Study of state and national adult day care standards is a good starting point for the development of goals. Their formulations of adult day care philosophy and broad service goals will provide language for helping to frame goals which are specific to the program. A study of program goals and objectives from existing adult day care programs will be similarly helpful.

All members of the planning committee should take an active part in the goal-setting process, with input also invited from other appropriate sources: agencies who will be referring participants, regulatory agencies, funding agencies, potential users of the service and their families, and other community service providers which are a part of the continuum of care or which will be working closely with the adult day care program.

It is important that committee members agree on the language and intent of the goals as formulated, since there must be mutual understanding and dedication to objectives in order to achieve the desired outcome.

The goals and operating policies should have been completed by the time the program begins services.

Subcommittees and Their Tasks

With preliminary steps accomplished, the committee is ready to move into organizational tasks. These tasks are best undertaken by subcommittees whose membership is composed of individuals with the expertise and abilities needed to carry out the specific responsibilities of that committee.

The following list of subcommittees and their duties is relevant only to the period of planning and organizing the adult day care program. After the organizational process is completed and the program is implemented, the permanent governing body will begin functioning, with status of subcommittees changing to that of standing committees.

Organizational Subcommittee

The organizational committee will begin the process of meeting requirements for the program's becoming a legal entity. This will involve ascertaining incorporation procedures, writing by-laws, making application for nonprofit status (if applicable), registering the organization with local governments and fulfilling requirements of any local regulations which apply, and beginning steps to form the permanent governing body. It will be the responsibility of this committee to explore local and state requirements for becoming a legal organization and ensuring that these are met. *Necessary skills* for committee membership include legal, planning, business management, and financial.

Finance Subcommittee

The work of the finance committee may be carried out more efficiently if it divides into two areas of responsibility: 1) budget preparation and management and 2) fundraising. Such a division will require close collaboration between the two groups, with frequent meetings and exchange of progress reports and action plans. One group must not take action without the full knowledge and support of the other.

The budget preparation and management group will project costs by line item for the program start-up budget and project costs and income by line item for preparation of a first-year operating budget. The fund-raising group will make a comprehensive study of possible funding sources for the adult day care program; put together information needed for funding applications and making application; and plan and carry out fund-raising events.

Necessary skills include financial, fund-raising, business management, marketing, human services, and community leadership.

Personnel Subcommittee

The initial responsibility for the personnel committee is that of writing a job description for the director, making sure that program goals and objectives are kept firmly in mind. This will ensure that the person selected will possess the qualifications needed to achieve program goals as established by the planning committee. Recruitment and selection of the director may proceed once the job description is in place and program development is at a stage where staff leadership is needed.

A second duty of this committee is that of writing personnel policies. This may be begun by the subcommittee or be deferred until a permanent governing body is formed. In any case, benefits for the position of the director must be decided upon before filling that position.

Necessary skills include community leadership, business management, personnel management, financial, legal, human services, and planning.

Marketing Subcommittee

The marketing committee must make comprehensive efforts to inform the public about plans for opening an adult day care program and take steps to gain widespread community support for the program. Use of the media, speaking engagements, mailings, and personal contacts are among useful methods to keep the community informed about plans, progress, and needs.

Initial steps toward development of working liaisons with other community service agencies and organizations are among the duties of this committee. The committee will also accept any service inquiries which it may receive and refer them to the admissions committee.

Necessary skills include community leadership, business administration, marketing, public relations, legal, and human services.

Admissions Subcommittee

The admissions committee is responsible for developing admission policies which define the target population and carrying out pre-admission procedures with potential participants. The committee must be aware of the parameters of the specific population to be served by the program. It should design policies which encourage and allow to be admitted only those individuals who can be effectively served.

To obtain referrals of potential participants, the committee must establish contact with sources of referrals—service organizations and agencies, medical health care providers, and families—to inform them about the program, the admission criteria, and benefits to participants and families. In the course of this information process, referrals can be solicited. Follow-up to referrals received should be done either by phone or a home visit.

Many individuals who may need the service and meet admission criteria may be resistant to enrolling because of their lack of familiarity with the concept. It will be the task of the admissions committee to "sell" the program to participants and their families, educating them about the benefits of enrolling and attending. Contact should be made with sources of participant referrals: Social Services organizations and agencies, families, and senior citizens' organizations. Accomplishing this education effort requires that committee members be sold on the program themselves, understanding needs of the population to be served and ways in which adult day care has a proven record of meeting such needs.

Necessary skills include human services, marketing, communication, interviewing, and motivation.

Program Subcommittee

The program subcommittee should begin work on the certification and licensing process in conjunction with the director (once the position is filled). Some responsibility for developing necessary documents will be shared with other committees: the preparation of job descriptions and personnel policies with personnel committee; the preparation of facility requirements with the facility committee; the development of admissions policies with the admissions committee, etc.

Another major responsibility for the program committee will be that of developing program policies and deciding on the services to be provided by the center. Included within the policies will be a "statement of services." The committee must locate providers for any services which are to be provided by contract or purchase: e.g., meals, transportation, medical care, and therapies. Negotiations for contractual or purchase agreements should be carried out by the committee so that the services will be available when the program opens.

Necessary skills include program planning, human services, business management, personnel management, legal, community leadership, communication, and financial.

Facility Subcommittee

The Facility subcommittee will be responsible for deciding upon the most appropriate and affordable housing for the program. Research will determine whether there is an existing building which will accommodate program needs, or whether other arrangements, such as building or renovating, must be planned. Building a facility will require designing the building to accommodate the program services and activities; consultation with an engineer and an architect is recommended. Costs estimates and bids must also be obtained.

Committee members must familiarize themselves with certification and licensure regulations, local zoning regulations, program services to be provided, admission and operating policies, and other information needed to understand what will be required in the facility which is to house the program.

Necessary skills include real estate, building, engineering, financial, business management, and legal.

Transportation Subcommittee

The transportation committee should determine the most feasible and practical method for providing transportation for participants to and from the program and for program events. Methods to consider include existing community transportation systems for elderly and handicapped persons; public transportation; purchase and operation of a van or other vehicle by the day care program; and transportation by families. Several factors must be considered in the transportation decision, including parameters of the service area; availability of funds; availability of existing transportation services; functional level of participants; insurance availability and costs; purchase and maintenance costs for owning vehicles; effect on the program if the driver is not a member of the program staff; and staff costs.

Necessary skills include transportation, business management, financial, legal, planning, and human services.

Historian

It is important that one person or a small committee keep accurate and complete records of the planning and development process. The information will be invaluable in establishing credibility with funding and other support groups, and will be of continuing interest and benefit to future program planning and growth.

Documentation may include a pictorial history (slide or video) as well as written records of the planning committee. Copies of any newspaper publicity and other evidence of public notice or recognition should also be included. All documents and records from the planning period are of significance, and copies should be made part of the recorded history.

Necessary skills include marketing, legal, writing, and photography.

It is evident that some tasks of subcommittees overlap and that many of the same skills are needed on several committees. A part of the subcommittee organizational process should be an analysis of the skills and abilities of the committee members. The subcommittees should be kept as small as is feasible for the amount of work to be accomplished; careful planning may allow combining of some subcommittees without diminishing effectiveness or requiring too much time and effort from members.

Developing an Action Plan

Once the subcommittees are in place and have a clear understanding of their job descriptions, and before they begin their work, an action plan should be developed by each subcommittee. These should be coordinated into a master work plan for the total planning and development committee. Included in the subcommittee plan should be a statement of designated responsibility for each committee member and a projected date of completion for each task.

To design the action plan one must take the following steps.

1. Decide what must be done first. Set priorities.
2. Decide upon specific objectives or the desired outcome.
3. Decide what skills and knowledge will be needed to achieve each objective.
4. Decide what other resources will be needed and how they may be obtained.
5. Decide upon a target date for completion of each step and for completion of the full objective.
6. Decide who is responsible for each step.
7. Decide who is to be in charge of overseeing action and how accountability is to be required.
8. Decide upon the review and revision process.

As these decisions are made, the plan will be set up and tasks assigned to each individual on the subcommittee. Mechanisms should be in place for dealing with unexpected problems; the committee should envision the worst scenario and develop contingency plans for that situation.

Meetings of the full planning committee should be scheduled on a regular basis and should be held frequently during the organizational period, at least every two weeks. A method for calling meetings which are not part of the regular schedule should be established, so that major crises which call for action by the full committee can be handled expeditiously. Subcommittees will make reports at meetings of the full planning committee to inform them of progress, problems, and new directions. The greater committee will act upon recommendations and reports from each subcommittee, either approving decisions or asking for further research or planning.

Dissolution of the Planning and Development Committee

Throughout the work of the planning and development committee, organization of the permanent governing body should be ongoing. This process includes identification of officers, consideration of potential members, formation of an organizational chart and determination of the structure of standing committees. The organizational subcommittee will carry most of the responsibility for these actions.

Once the governing body is operational, any further work to be carried out in the planning process will be done at the direction and discretion of that body.

Those members whose contribution was intended for the developmental phases only may elect, or be asked, to remain on the board until the program is safely implemented, or to become a part of the permanent body. Subcommittees should merge into standing committees, with full reports of past actions, results, and future plans being conveyed to new members to ensure continuity of work in progress.

The membership of both bodies must make every effort to accomplish a smooth transition, always keeping the well-being of the adult day care program as the primary objective.

Reference

O'Brien, C. L. 1982. *Adult day care: A practical guide.* Monterey, CA: Wadsworth Health Sciences Division.

3 Budget and Funding

Introduction

Finding funding sources for start-up and operation of an adult day care program is a primary issue for those who develop and operate these programs. The relative newness of the service, together with recent reductions in governmental financing, make the search for funds by adult day care providers a never-ending task. Planners, developers, and operators of adult day care must recognize the challenge and educate themselves about likely sources of funds and how to obtain them.

A first step is the preparation of the program budget. For purposes of fund-raising and budget management, it is recommended that two budgets be prepared: a start-up budget and an operating budget.

Start-Up Budget

The start-up budget will include only those costs which will be incurred in the planning and development of the program, many of which will be one-time expenses. Categories to use in planning the start-up budget are outlined in Exhibit 3-1.

Cost estimates are not included here because prices fluctuate, and location and available resources will influence amounts which must be spent in each category. Cost estimates can be arrived at by investigation of the current market prices for items to be purchased, and by conferring with budget management personnel from other adult day care centers.

A careful analysis of the budget in light of proposed plans for the program will help determine the amount and quality needed for each item. For example, in deciding upon the phone system, ask: How many phones are needed by staff? Will these be accessible to participants or is there a need for an additional telephone in the program area? How many lines are needed? Should these be rotary lines, or will two or more separate lines suffice? Which is less expensive to install? To support over time? Is it more prudent to purchase phones or rent them? What kinds will best meet program needs?

In regard to kitchen equipment, ask the following: Are meals to be prepared on site, or catered? What will be needed for program activities: a microwave, stove, refrigerator, cooking utensils, other?

In regard to program equipment, decide: What will be needed for planned activities, for example, need the program purchase a kiln for pottery or ceramics, or can the

Exhibit 3-1 Start-up budget considerations.

1. *Facility acquisition.* Lease, lease/purchase, purchase, rental, or renovation of a facility to house the program.
2. *Equipment.* Office: desks, office chairs, typewriters, copy machine, file cabinets, etc. Program: tables, chairs, lounge chairs, sofa, bed, sheets, blankets, pillows, bookcase, kitchen equipment, tools and other equipment needed to provide program activities and services.
3. *Program and office supplies.* Although purchase of these supplies will not be a one-time cost, the initial purchase should be included in the start-up budget.
4. *Public relations.* Costs for publicizing the program: printing brochures, any paid media advertising, business cards, open house, flyers, etc.
5. *Telephone system*. Installation and purchase of telephones.
6. *Personnel.* Since it is recommended that the director be hired prior to opening, salary, benefits, and travel costs for this position should be included in the start-up budget. The amount should cover the time period from date of hiring to projected opening date.
7. *Miscellaneous*

program use one owned by the city or other organization? Will the functional level of participants be such that tools will be needed, such as a sewing machine, iron and ironing board, or carpentry tools? Will activities include laundry and clothing care? Are medical services to be provided which will necessitate use of medical equipment? What about personal care—is there a need for bathing equipment?

A reasonable projection of per item cost can be arrived at by breaking down each component of the budget in this manner.

Operating Budget

Items to be included within the operating budget will be those costs incurred in the regular and ongoing operation of the program. The budget committee decides the period of time for which projections will be made. Projections for an annual budget with cost accounting in monthly or quarterly increments is commonly used. Exhibit 3-2 outlines typical operating cost categories.

Again, assistance in making cost projections can be obtained by conferring with other adult day care providers, especially those who may have been in operation for a year or more. Planners should become familiar with local salary ranges and current costs for other budget items. Staff salaries and benefits are likely to be the single largest item

Exhibit 3-2 Operating budget considerations.

1. *Personnel* salaries
   Benefits: Insurance, Social Security, Workman's Compensation, vacations, sick leave, retirement.
   Staff Travel: Cost per mile for number of miles traveled. Per diem cost if program planning calls for out-of-town travel.
   Substitute Staff
2. *Facility* rental, mortgage payments, lease, or whatever costs are incurred for use of space.
3. *Utilities.* heat, air conditioning, electricity and/or gas.
4. *Telephone.* Regular monthly charges, plus estimated cost of long distance.
5. *Building and equipment.* Maintenance and repairs.
6. *Cleaning/housekeeping.* Services and supplies.
7. *Food.* Purchase or preparation of meals and snacks.
8. *Transportation.* For transporting participants to and from the center by whatever method is to be used.
9. *Travel.* Costs for transportation for additional travel and program events.
10. *Program supplies.* Crafts, activities, services (excluding food and transportation).
11. *Publicity.* All costs of ongoing public relations.
12. *Office supplies*
13. *Special program events.* Includes anything not done on a regular basis, such as tickets for cultural events, resource persons for educational events, etc.
14. *Staff development*
15. *Insurance*
16. *Miscellaneous*

on the budget: O'Brien gives the average percentage as 65%. The amount will depend largely upon the services and activities to be provided by the program and the level of staff skills needed to carry these out.

Transportation and food will be the next most expensive items. Research in the community must be carried out to locate and select the best options for provision of these items. Contractual arrangements often prove to be the most practical solution, but planners should consider the advantages and disadvantages of all available options.

In regard to transportation, contractual agreements may be the least expensive method. Such agreements free the provider from responsibility of ownership and maintenance costs for operating vehicles. On the other hand, the provider loses some control over the quality of transportation. In some instances this may be detrimental to the best interests of participants and to the achievement of program goals.

For food preparation, contractual arrangements usually prove to be the most satisfactory source, especially where the food provider is equipped to prepare therapeutic diets. Drawbacks to on-site preparation of meals include the costs of equipment necessary to meet health and safety codes and of hiring qualified staff. Planners must also consider the amount of time which must be devoted to food purchase and to planning and preparing meals. Furthermore, storage space for food takes away from available space for the program.

Planners will want to follow the same analysis process as that used for the start-up budget: look at each item in light of proposed program plans to determine the projected costs for the specific program.

Income Projections

Preparation of the operating budget includes a projection of expected income, i.e., sources of funds and amount expected from each source. Care must be taken to distinguish between funds in hand or firmly committed versus potential resources. Programs which open without sufficient operating funds may have to close if they have overestimated income from possible resources.

Examples of anticipated income include the following:

- Participant fees from whatever source, including Department of Social Services purchase, Medicaid, or private pay.
- Grants from foundations and other philanthropic organizations.
- Local government allocation from city or county.
- In-kind donations of space, transportation, food, equipment, etc.
- Church or civic group contributions.
- Individual donations.
- Local business and industry contributions.

Participant fees may be based upon the cost of care as determined by cost projections in the operating budget, i.e., total cost of care divided by the number of persons to be served in the program. Fees from governmental sources may be limited to a maximum rate which may be less than the actual cost of care. The difference between the amount of funds in hand or committed to the program and the amount budgeted for expenditures represents the amount which must be raised by the committee with responsibility for fund-raising.

Sources of Adult Day Care Funds

Few adult day care programs are self-supporting. The costs of operating the program are seldom covered by payment of participant fees, and most programs must find supplemental funds to meet costs.

Locating potential sources of supplementary funds should begin early in the development process, with a committee formed to assume responsibility for this task. A starting point is the local library, which will have materials listing foundations and other philanthropic organizations and information about their history of grant giving. The committee should look for organizations with a pattern of giving to services with similar purposes and goals as those of adult day care, and should also explore the potential for obtaining funds from local governmental sources.

Potential funding sources may be either public: federal, state, or local; or private: foundations, philanthropic organizations or individuals, United Way, churches or civic organizations. The committee may also elect to plan and carry out fund-raising events, either alone or in conjunction with other local service providers.[1]

Public Funding

Public funds come from a variety of sources and an exhaustive search will be necessary to learn about all possible sources.

Often, the major source of public monies is the state. Local Social Services departments or their counterparts serve as the funneling agency for these funds. If adequate information cannot be found locally about how to obtain any state funds which may be available, the searchers must contact departments on the state level. Medicaid and Medicare funds are available for adult day care in some states. Local and state agencies responsible for disbursement of these funds should be contacted to discover the potential for obtaining funding for adult day care.

Older American's Act monies are used in some states for provision of adult day care. Providers wishing to apply for these funds should contact the local area Agency on Aging or the state office for handling aging affairs. Whether or not funds are forthcoming from this source, the local office should be included in the community network which is involved in planning the service and should act in support of the program.

Other potential sources for state or federal funds are the Divisions of Mental Health, Mental Retardation and Substance Abuse and the Division of Services for the Blind. Support from these agencies may take the form of specific services to the populations served by them, such as special equipment and help with mobility training for blind participants, or counseling services for participants referred by local mental health departments.

In some locations, city and county officials have been supportive of adult day care programs and have been willing to provide funding as a part of the local budget. It is important for providers to enlist the support of these bodies early in the planning process and to keep them informed of progress by providing periodic updates and asking for advice and support. Any requests for funds should be carefully timed. The fund-raising

---

[1] Some funding sources enumerated will be available only to nonprofit agencies. Proprietary organizations must consult the source to determine their eligibility.

committee should become familiar with the city or county budget planning schedule and how to submit funding applications.

If funding requests are to be submitted, the committee should determine the most opportune time and request funds for a purpose which is most likely to be viewed favorably. A cautionary note: few programs have been successful in obtaining funds from local public sources for start-up expenses. Most programs which have been successful have demonstrated a track record of cost effectiveness and provision of a service which is meeting a proven community need before being considered.

Private Funding

With respect to availability of private funding sources, some adult day care programs are more fortunate in their location than others, having access to a variety of foundations, or other private sources. However, most communities have some such resources.

Committee research should focus upon philanthropic organizations: local, state, and to a lesser extent, national. Possibilities include foundations, the United Way, churches, civic groups, and volunteer organizations with a special concern for the populations being served by the adult day care program. Likely volunteer organizations are the American Association of Retired Persons, the National Retired Teachers Association, and the Retired Federal Employees Association.

Local businesses should also be considered. If they cannot contribute funds, they might consider contributing equipment or supplies.

Corporations. Soliciting funds from corporations may be difficult, since many funnel community support through the United Way. Still, some corporations do reserve funds for donating to services in which they might have a strong interest, and some service agencies have been successful in obtaining these through a carefully planned and executed approach. It will be valuable to make personal contact with the individual within the corporation who has responsibility for corporate giving. If the fund-raising committee has among its members an individual who is influential in the community and has access to these corporate representatives, the effort is more likely to meet with success. Many corporations are directed by individuals who are civic minded and want the organization to make a worthwhile contribution to the community. Also, if the corporation is a successful one, some funds are designated for charitable purposes as a tax shelter. Research will locate such companies in almost every community.

United Way. New organizations are not likely to receive funds from the United Way in their planning and developmental stages and before beginning to provide services. However, the national office of the United Way has placed concern for the aging among their highest priorities, making it advisable to establish and maintain contact with the local office in order to build a relationship which may lead to a favorable response for future requests for funds.

In some locales, organizations may ask that those who donate to the United Way specify that their donation be given to the program or agency of their choice. Thus, even if the adult day care program is not being formally supported by the United Way, one may in this manner mount a successful campaign to receive United Way funds.

Foundations. Careful planning and development of strategies for appealing to the priority concerns of foundations may gain funds for at least some aspects of program operation. The research process should eliminate those foundations that have shown no interest in programs such as adult day care or for populations similar to those served by the program. Instead, the committee should pinpoint those who have funded services for the aged or for impaired adults.

Some foundations with a strong tie to the geographic area in which the program is located may be interested in funding the program, even when such a service is outside their usual sphere of interest. Investigation will reveal whether there is potential for receiving funds.

The initial contact with foundations may be made by mail or by personal contact. Some foundations are receptive to having representatives of an organization meet with their staff to discuss needs and how well the needs fit into the foundation's concerns. If the contact is made by mail, a short letter of inquiry—including a statement of program goals, the problem which is to be addressed, and how the program fits into foundation funding goals—will result in a request for further information if the foundation will consider providing funds.

The format for funding applications varies somewhat among foundations, but there are certain components which are included in all applications. These elements are outlined in Exhibit 3-3.

Foundations are generally inclined to favor short-term funding for new organizations which are taking a unique approach to a problem with which they are concerned, or for ongoing organizations who add a new component of service or take a new and different approach. However, some foundations will consider multi-year funding if the organization can make a compelling case for the existing need and can gain sufficient interest from the foundation for helping to meet the need.

In-Kind Donations. All financial support need not be in the form of money. In-kind donations can represent sizable savings for the budget, and in some instances, be used to provide the necessary match for other funds. For example, Older Americans Act funds require a local match, a percentage of which can be in-kind.

In-kind donations can include staff salaries, use of space, equipment (transportation vehicles, office and program equipment), volunteer time (program consultants, therapists, medical professionals, program volunteers), and supplies (consumable program supplies, medical or office supplies).

All such donations should be properly documented with an assigned monetary value. Such documentation increases the likelihood that the donations will be accepted as an in-kind match. The documentation may also be used to demonstrate the degree of community support when applying for grants or other funds.

Exhibit 3-3 Grant proposal outline.

1. *Introdution.* In writing this section, the commmittee should attempt to build credibility for the organization. Tell who is involved, including members of the governing body and the credentials of the director, if the director has been hired. Planners should demonstrate how the agency has credibility in the adult care field. Include a statement of how the organization began, in response to what need, and what is unique about the service approach. Add any evidence of public support, such as newspaper articles, letters of support, etc.
2. *Problem Statement.* For this section, document the problem which will be addressed. Provide any available statistics which prove the need for the service. Demonstrate the connection between the problem and the concerns of the funding organization. Outline the specific service to be offered, along with a time schedule and a plan for obtaining future funding.
3. *Program Objectives.* For this section, state the goals of the program in quantitative terms, including what specific services are to be provided, for what number of people, within what time frame, and with what expected results.
4. *Methods.* Here, describe what methods will be used to achieve results. The committee should demonstrate knowledge of what is already being done in the field and how other services or programs relate to or complement the adult day care program. Do not present the service in such a way as to make it seem in competition with other services; rather, show that adult day care will fill a gap in the continuum of care in the community.
5. *Evaluation.* For the evaluation, state what the expected impact upon the target population will be. Include how effective the service is expected to be in solving the problem and in meeting outlined objectives. Track records from other adult day care programs may be used, if available.
6. *Future Funding.* A legitimate concern of foundations is that new programs will not continue operating once the foundation's funds are no longer available. The application must address this issue. Include a plan for meeting future financial needs, for at least 1 to 3 years.
7. *Proposed Budget.* Here, the program should be described in numerical terms. Costs should be broken down into categories: administrative, personnel, space, equipment, consumable supplies, transportation, materials, any overhead not covered in the above categories, miscellaneous. Be sure that all costs are reasonable for the service to be provided and are in line with other similar services.
8. *Summary.* This section could be placed at the beginning of the application as the introductory letter, or included at the end as a summary and wrap-up. The opening

Exhibit 3-3, continued.

paragraph should be designed to capture the interest of the foundation. It should prove immediately that framers of the application are knowledgeable about the service and the population of which they are speaking.

The amount of funds required should be stated up front, with evidence that what is asked for is consistent with the foundation's priorities and policies.

Individual Donations. In addition to donations of equipment or supplies, individuals may also be the source of monetary donations. The fund-raising committee should make efforts to let the community know that such donations are desired and appreciated.

Special approaches may be planned to publicize the need. Scholarships may be started in the name of individuals, with contributions by family and friends; or donations to the center may be requested by the family in lieu of sending flowers at the death of a program participant in order to provide a lasting memorial.

Churches and Civic Organizations. Many community civic groups and churches will demonstrate support for services such as adult day care by putting the program into their annual budget for a specific amount, to be given annually. The committee should establish contact with these organizations and make them aware of the need. Requests for scholarship funds to aid attendance of an individual participant is an approach which holds appeal for many such organizations.

In addition to asking to be included in the budget, a request may be made for assistance with a specific fund-raising event. Civic organizations may be very receptive to this method of providing aid. Or, groups within churches, such as Sunday School classes, may be asked to make donations of money or supplies on their own.

Fund-Raising Events. The committee may elect to raise some funds by carrying out special fund-raising events. These require a great deal of planning and hard work, but can be very successful, especially if they become an annual event which the public comes to expect and can be enlisted to support. The events serve a dual purpose: in addition to raising money, they also gain public attention for the program.

Once the decision has been made to hold such an event, the committee should take several preparatory steps: check local ordinances to make sure that such an event will be allowed; make sure that other organizations do not have similar events planned which will compete; try to decide upon a date which is not close to other major fund-raisers such as the United Way annual campaign; and search for a location to which large numbers of people travel or congregate, one near major intersections, shopping centers, etc.

Effective fund-raising events include golf or tennis tournaments, flea markets, ethnic fairs, bake sales, walk-a-thons or bike-a-thons, and auctions. The decision on which type of event to hold will depend upon what the committee feels will appeal to community interests, what will be different from other recent events, and how much money the program needs to raise from the event.

As much as possible, program participants should have the opportunity to be involved in some aspects of the fund-raising event. (These events should never be so frequent that they become the focus of a participant's daily activity or interfere with achievement of the individual care plan.) Handicrafts or other items made by participants make good sale items and demonstrate to the community the work carried out by participants in the program. One should be sure that any handwork included is of marketable quality.

A Fund-Raising Campaign

When substantial funding is required for an adult day care program, committee members should explore the feasibility of formalizing fund-raising efforts into a well planned and executed fund-raising campaign. A formal fund-raising campaign is very effective in raising funds and has the added benefit of keeping the program before the public, thus attracting potential participants while gaining funds. Such a campaign requires a large effort on the part of the Board or of the committee charged with the responsibility. Substantial preparatory work is necessary.

Feasibility Study

For a successful campaign, the Board, by its example and involvement, should motivate and enable the committee. If the Board does not demonstrate interest and support, there is little hope of success, and an effort of this magnitude should not be attempted. The potential for recruiting volunteers must also be explored, as well as strategies developed for bringing in community resource people who can attract other volunteers. There must be an analysis of what has worked in the past, what has met with success or failure.

Planning

Committees and volunteers must be organized so that they understand their roles and responsibilities and these are formalized. Individuals should be carefully matched with responsibilities so that they are able to discharge them successfully. All members of the committee must believe in the concept of adult day care and know enough about the program to be able to motivate others to contribute time and money. Different groups in the community—religious and civic organizations, businesses, merchants, professionals, the medical establishment, etc.—should be represented on the committee since they will be needed to reach the total community. Every individual on the committee should be a trusted member of the community.

Publicity is a key part of all fund-raising and should be planned as a part of the fund-raising campaign. It must be constant, informing the community about the upcoming campaign and the purposes of adult day care.

A time schedule for all campaign activities must be established and adhered to. Periodic progress meetings should be scheduled.

Implementation

Once the committee is set up and the campaign plan formed, the work of gathering funds will start.

In pursuing direct solicitation, each occupational group within the community should be approached by one committee member who has connections to that group. For example, a member of the medical community would be assigned to collect from that group; a teacher would work within the school system, etc.

In seeking large donations, an approach should be made to large business concerns with headquarters or offices in the community. Many corporations have community affairs departments which screen requests. Corporate giving practices are often influenced by the nature of the service. When presenting the request for funds the committee should emphasize how adult day care can benefit employees and the corporation by reducing employee stress and absenteeism related to the care of an older family member. Fund raisers should keep in mind that some companies provide adult day care payments or insurance as an employee benefit.

Other Suggestions

Before a large scale fund-raising campaign is started, it is a good idea to determine whether any permit or registration is required. Permit information should be available from the county attorney's office. Information regarding solicitation registration may be obtained from state solicitation licensing boards.

A large fund-raising campaign is a complex undertaking, usually directed by a professional fund-raising firm. However, a small scale campaign can be carried out without professional assistance. It is recommended that board membership include individuals who have previously participated in a formal fund-raising effort such as a capital fund-raising drive for hospitals or major churches. Someone who has chaired such a campaign would be invaluable on the board.

Summary

Ongoing fund-raising for adult day care programs should be accepted as a part of operational planning. The fund-raising committee must be a permanent one, composed of members who are willing to put forth the effort required and who possess the abilities to achieve the goal of keeping the program supplied with necessary funds.

Work of the committee should be carried out year round. A last minute scramble to raise funds when a deficit becomes apparent near the end of the fiscal year may result in the program closing due to lack of funds.

Research on potential sources of funds must be constant. The committee, in conjunction with the director, should be engaged in continuous planning to find unique and innovative approaches to service provision, with the purposes of continuing to improve services and of gaining the interest of funders.

4 | Marketing the Program

Introduction

The success of adult day care programs is often directly proportional to the success of their public relations efforts. All new organizations face the task of publicizing their services and working to build and maintain a positive image in the community. This task is somewhat more complex for adult day care than for some other programs. Because of the newness of the service, public relations efforts must include plans for educating the public about the objectives and effectiveness of adult day care.

Marketing Goals

Public relations efforts must be directed toward achievement of several broad goals.

Gaining Community Support

In the long run, survival of the adult day care program may be dependent upon support from the community. Support is evidenced by financial assistance, volunteer help, and donations of equipment and supplies.

Anecdotal evidence indicates that few programs can operate solely on revenue generated by fees paid for service. Local resources are the major source of on-going funds for many programs. Among these resources are service contracts, local government allocations, grants from United Way or foundations, and donations from private corporations and civic organizations.

The value of community volunteers and resource persons as a resource is immeasurable. They can help to expand the quality and variety of activities and services. And, serving as public relations ambassadors, they provide information about the program to the community and referrals of potential participants to the program.

There are many sources in the community which will provide donations of equipment and supplies once the program has been recognized as an important resource to the community.

Reaching Potential Participants

If the program is to receive inquiries from those in need of the service, information about the availability and effectiveness of the service must reach potential participants, their families, and those providing them with supportive services.

Developing Working Relationships With Other Community Service Agencies and Organizations

Becoming a vital link in the community network of services will enable the program to utilize resources of other agencies to broaden the range of services it can offer to participants and to obtain referrals of individuals needing adult day care.

Responsibility for Public Relations

Primary responsibility for public relations should belong to a committee whose members will work in conjunction with the director or other designated staff person to develop and carry out strategies to achieve the above goals. The committee should comprise members from the governing body or other body responsible for management of the program.

Committee Skills

All members of the committee must possess enthusiasm about the program. They must also be thoroughly educated on all aspects of adult day care, including whom it serves, its service goals, program services and activities, staff, costs, and benefits to participants and their families. Members should be carefully selected for the skills and knowledge they can bring to the work of the committee. Needed skills include:

Organization

Understanding and knowledge of the community

Communication

Speaking

Motivational

Creativity/originality

Decision making/good judgment

Analytical ability

Follow-through

Energy

The Director's Role

The director (or other staff member assigned to work with the committee) must possess many of the same skills as other committee members and must be able to work in harmony with the committee. The director will supply much of the necessary information and help the committee to set goals. Some duties will belong almost exclusively to the director, such as the development of working relationships with other community agencies. The director will serve as a training resource for seminars and workshops, and a large part of the process of educating the committee must be carried out by the director.

Committee Duties

The committee must develop a comprehensive plan for carrying out public relations for the program. In addition to achieving the broad goals outlined above, the committee will need to set specific goals for themselves, based upon needs of the program, budget and time factors, and resources available.

The Planning Process

There are three fundamental determinations to be made in planning a public relations campaign.

To What Audience is the Message Directed?

The most skillfully planned public relations effort will not succeed unless the people who use the service and those who will support it learn about its availability and become convinced that it meets a need. The primary audience for adult day care public relations includes potential participants, families or caregivers, management and staff of community service organizations and agencies, health care professionals, community leaders, funding bodies, and the general public.

What are Audience Characteristics?

Once the committee has decided which audience they are attempting to reach, they will need to evaluate the characteristics of the group. Ascertain the audience's values and attitudes, cultural values, ethnic background, economic background, problems and needs, lifestyle, media habits, and response to previous public awareness efforts. Groups to be reached will often vary widely in these characteristics. The committee should search for common denominators and tailor the message to reach the targeted audience.

What is the Message?

When the committee is confident that it has sufficient information about the audience, it will then need to shape its message based upon answers to analytical questions such as the following.

- What product is being sold? Should it be described primarily as health care, life quality, independence, social activities, freedom for the family, or other?
- What key words describe the product and will capture the attention of the audience? The committee might consider "quality," "effectiveness," "financial savings," "better care," "new opportunities," "growth potential," "social activities."
- What problems or needs of the audience can be resolved by use of the product? Likely choices include relief from worry and stress, end to loneliness, need for socialization, or time for the caregiver.
- What is the product's appeal to the community? Does it fill a gap in the care continuum, improve quality of care for impaired adults, supply freedom for caregivers to become employed, other?
- What attitudes on the part of the audience need to be affected or changed? These may include myths of aging, or acceptance of institutionalization as the expected method of care for impaired adults.

Methods and Strategies

Marketing efforts fall into three general categories: publicity, promotion, and public relations. There are no clear-cut boundaries among the three; for example, promotional efforts may receive publicity. All plans to "sell" the adult day care program will require use of a combination of the three methods.

Publicity

Publicity is the dissemination of information designed to make the public aware of the program. This method, more than the others, will require use of the news media. The committee must understand how the various news media can be best utilized, as well as becoming familiar with other publicity strategies.

Use of the Media.

News Releases. News releases are used to announce an event or a press conference, to disseminate news, or to inform the public about special program events. The release must be succinctly written and contain only essential information.

A news release should include the following. First, a short, snappy lead paragraph telling about the event. Think of this as the "how and why"; what is the purpose of the event, and why is it different from others. Second, a description of the complete event: time, place, date, and principal players. Third, supplementary information: where to go, any needed directions, costs, how to obtain tickets, etc. Finally, the name, title, address, and phone number of the person sending the release should be placed in the upper right hand corner of the first page.

The newspaper will decide if pictures are to be used. They may send a photographer or request pictures. Photos submitted must be sharp and clear. Black and white, 8 by 10 glossy are preferred. Names of persons in the photograph should be printed on the back. One should be sure to thank the newspaper and individual staff representative for any coverage. Free tickets of admission to paid events should be provided for reporters who attend.

Feature Articles. Feature articles must have a special interest message for readers. The committee should work with the appropriate editor of the newspaper, magazine, TV or radio station to plan how a story might be used to meet objectives of both the program and the publication. Lead time for feature articles will be longer than for news releases and should be confirmed with the editor. Articles slanted toward special events or holidays such as Easter or Mother's Day may catch the editor's attention for the human interest appeal. Trade or professional journals and agency and organization newsletter are among publications to consider when submitting such articles.

Public Service Programming on TV or Radio. Often called "public service announcements" or "PSAs," this is a resource available to nonprofit organizations; public service air time is mandated by Federal regulations for the use of these organizations. Possible formats for use of this time includes interviews, panel discussions, presentations on regularly scheduled programs, spot announcements (brief messages broadcast at intervals during the day), or human interest feature stories.

The amount of time and the schedule may vary from station to station, but all TV and radio stations make time available. In addition to using the free time, some stations will conduct interviews or other coverage which fits into their program or news schedule. This coverage may be available to both non- and for-profit programs when they have stories of general interest.

Information about how to get coverage and the procedures to follow may be obtained by a call to the local stations. When requests are submitted for time, a request for airing at a specific time could be included. This should be based upon what is known about the lifestyle of the targeted audience. A personal visit to the station to deliver the materials may gain more attention for the request.

To use PSA time effectively, one should accept suggestions from the station about format, content, and scheduling. They are the experts! Keep in mind that PSA spots usually last from 10 to 30 seconds. About 25 words can be spoken in 10 seconds.

Visuals are important for TV. Slides should be interesting and should demonstrate the message. They must be in focus. Check with the station program manager about the type of slides or video tape to use. One slide should be provided for each 10 seconds of air time. The total effect is gained by use of good visuals, well-written copy clearly read, and appropriate background music or sound effects. Both interviews and spot announcements can be pre-recorded or video taped. Submit all PSAs as far in advance as possible.

Type all copy on 8-1/2 by 11 white paper, double spaced, written on one side only. Type name, date, address, and phone number of the person submitting the information in the upper right hand corner. Give all facts (who? what? when? where?). Provide a biographical sketch for any person to be interviewed. Use simple, descriptive language. Write, re-write and re-write again to eliminate unnecessary words and to use only those needed to evoke the desired image.

Press Conferences. Press conferences are designed to announce news and should meet the following two criteria. They must announce something that is really new and which affects the community (not just something new to the program). The news must be of interest to all the media, not something which could be announced in a routine release.

If the committee decides to hold a press conference, it should first choose a convenient location, and set a time and date suitable for the media. Morning meetings may make afternoon papers and evening broadcasts; afternoon or evening will make the late news and morning radio and newspapers. The press conference should be announced three to four days in advance, or with as much lead time as possible. Announcements should tell: where, when, why. The name and phone number of a contact person should be given. The contact person should follow up with reminder phone calls the day before and prepare a press kit to hand out at the conference. The press kit should include the basic news release, any noteworthy comments or stories, photographs or slides, organization history or other literature, if relevant.

Paid Media Advertising. If funds permit and if circumstances warrant, some advertising in newspapers, trade journals, radio, and TV may be included in strategies for publicity. The format of the advertising should be designed to attract participants and their families. Consideration should be given to the kind of newspaper and TV and radio stations likely to be used by this audience. For example, stations which play hard rock music probably do not attract a large audience among older people.

Costs vary for the amount of time or space, circulation size, listening audience, etc. It is a good idea to run the advertisement for a short period of time first to determine the effectiveness of the advertising method.

Other Publicity Strategies.

Marquees and Buses. Many towns have marquees available to nonprofit organizations to display a message for a designated period of time. Businesses such as motels may allow their marquees to be used to provide a public service. Churches may also allow messages to be displayed on their marquees. Use of the advertising space on public buses is another strategy to consider. This may be free to nonprofits if not otherwise committed or may be available for a small fee. Research and observation will determine the feasibility of these methods.

Billboards. When billboard space is not rented, it can sometimes be used by nonprofit agencies for little or no cost. Information can be obtained from the company responsible for billboard rental.

Directory Listing. In addition to listings in both the yellow and white pages of local telephone directories, adult day care programs should be listed in other community directories of services. In most communities directories of information and referral services, senior citizens' organizations and services, health resource directories, and nonprofit organizations can be found. Chamber of commerce and business directories also list adult day care programs.

Promotion

Promotional efforts are those which foster a positive image and stress benefits of the service. Promotion may also be loosely defined as program advertising. Some publicity functions will overlap with promotional functions: PSAs, billboards, marquees, and paid advertising are examples of methods which serve both purposes. Promotional strategies include brochures, posters, flyers, an open house, and an opening announcement.

Brochures. As early as possible in the organizational process, the program should have a brochure printed. Those designing the brochure should be clear about the message they want to convey, such as attracting potential participants or increasing visibility for the program. The brochure should be easy to read, with the message succinct and well-written. It should include a brief description of the program and whom the program serves; enumeration of benefits to participants and families; a sketch of program activities and services; and the program name, location, phone number, and instructions for obtaining further information.

The brochure design should be simple and professional, with large headlines and a message which invites action on the part of the reader. Pictures or artwork which demonstrate the message are desirable. The color should be one which attracts attention and conveys life and hope. Dull, drab colors such as beige and black should be avoided. The major expense for printing brochures is the initial type-setting and artwork, so all paste-ups, negatives, and reproductions should be kept on file for future printing.

Posters. Should be well-designed and eye-catching. As with brochures, the wording should be succinct and planned to obtain the desired result. They should be posted in strategic locations, areas likely to be frequented by potential participants and their families:

public service agencies	YWCAs and YMCAs
banks	clubs
shopping centers	churches
beauty and barber shops	places of employment
grocery stores	hospitals and clinics
parks and recreational areas	medical and physician's offices

Flyers. Flyers are less expensive to print than brochures, so they may be distributed more widely. Door to door distribution should be used in neighborhoods with a large population of potential participants or their caregivers. In shopping centers flyers can be placed on cars or handed to shoppers. Permission may have to be obtained for this from shopping center managers. Churches and places of employment are good distribution points. In addition, consider direct mailings at strategic times. Flyers should be included in all outgoing correspondence and be used as envelope stuffers in mail of other organizations or businesses.

Posters and flyers should include essentially the same information as brochures, but couched in even briefer language. They should be punchy and to the point, while giving all pertinent information. The name of the organization must be included and should be in bold lettering.

Open House. An open house should be held as early as possible after opening the center and at regular intervals after that. While it is possible to hold an open house to allow the public to view the facility before the program opens, showing the program in operation makes a greater impact because guests can both view the facility and watch the program in action.

The event should be planned in detail. Program participants should be involved in planning and should understand what is taking place and what their roles are to be. Program events which lend themselves to the open-house may be ongoing while visitors are in attendance. The center should look warm and inviting, and all staff should be well briefed on how to greet visitors and respond to questions.

The invitation list should include public officials, representatives of service agencies and organizations, community leaders, families of present and potential participants, clergymen, senior citizens' clubs and organizations, representatives of funding organizations, business and professional organizations, and the medical community. Planning to make the open house an annual event, during anniversary or National Day Care Week, will help to keep public attention focused upon the program.

Opening Announcement. A mailed formal announcement of the center's opening is another method of helping to raise public awareness. The mailing list can be more inclusive than the invitation to the open house, going to all those with a potential interest in the program. These include organizations and agencies which serve populations similar to those in adult day care, such as nursing homes, domicilary care homes, and other adult day care programs; public institutions, such as colleges and businesses; and social organizations, such as garden clubs, fraternal clubs, and civic groups. The center should also request that the announcement of the opening (and of the open house) be placed in church bulletins, local newspapers, and any other publications which reach large groups of people. Banks, utility companies, and others who mail on a regular basis may consider including the announcement for nonprofit agencies in a mailing.

Public Relations

While the term "public relations" is commonly used to cover all aspects of marketing, for purposes of this discussion it will be used to describe the day-to-day effort to build supportive relationships in the community. In this context, some elements of publicity and promotion will be included.

Strategies to build the necessary linkages and relationships may include the following.

Board Memberships. Program board or staff members should serve on boards or advisory groups of other community organizations. Community leaders can be invited to serve on the adult day care board as representatives of their organization.

Speaking Engagements. Board or staff members should make the effort to speak in the community. All presentations should be well prepared and targeted for the specific audience. The speaker should be prepared to respond to any questions.

Slide and Video Tape Presentation. Audio/visual presentations of the adult day care program are excellent tools for educating the community about the service. These should be planned to demonstrate the effectiveness of the service, whom it serves, and with what purposes.

Support Groups. Support groups can be planned as a part of the program for families and caregivers of participants. These support groups also serve as a method for fostering good will and support. Both family members and persons serving as resources will become ambassadors for the program.

Educational Programs. Ministers, physicians, pharmacists, and other health care professionals can be asked to conduct educational programs in the center for participants. This serves a secondary purpose of enlisting their support for the program. Extending speaking invitations to influential individuals (politicians, public officials, agency heads, etc.) and small groups will also serve these purposes.

Presentations. Dramatic vignettes portraying life experience, rhythm band concerts, or other presentations for guests in the center or groups in the community (nursing homes, schools, churches, etc.) may be incorporated into the public relations plan. These methods serve a secondary purpose of helping participants to increase social skills.

Volunteers. Individuals and groups of volunteers can talk about the program in the community, helping to develop a positive image. Training and information about the program should be provided to volunteers, so that all reports will be accurate. Appreciation events for volunteers are also valuable public relations tools and should be well publicized.

Community Projects. Demonstration projects, exhibits, and other opportunities for joining with community groups in community events should be utilized to enhance the program's image and further develop relationships with other organizations.

Word of Mouth. Word of mouth can be the most effective method of promotion if the image portrayed is positive. Care should be taken that participants, families, and others in contact with the program receive satisfactory service and accurate information from everyone in the program, from the individual who answers the phone or greets visitors through efficient response to inquiries. Individuals who refer potential participants or support the program in other ways should have these contributions recognized by the program.

Information. Dissemination of information can generate support. Regular reporting of program results to professionals or agencies which refer participants, mailing of newsletters or a calendar of events to supporters, regular conferences with families and caregivers and reporting of program progress to financial supporters should all be used to build community awareness and favor.

Any favorable portrayal of the program is a building block in constructing the total image which is the goal of the marketing campaign.

Marketing Resources

In order to stretch the funds budgeted for public relations, the committee will want to take advantage of any resources which may be used at little cost. All committees have such resources, obtainable with research and planning.

For example, businesses retained by the center should be asked if it is their policy to give a discount to nonprofit agencies (if this is applicable). Since many do have such a policy, the program should make a practice of using businesses who give discounts. College and technical school classes in marketing, graphics, photography, video, and creative writing will sometimes take on projects which fit into their curriculum. Typical assignments in such classes include

- Planning an advertising campaign
- Putting together a slide/videotape presentation of the program

- Writing PSAs or press releases
- Doing art work for brochures, posters, flyers.

There may also be students who will take on a project for course credit. Local civic groups (Junior League, Lions Clubs, Civitan, Women's Clubs, etc.) may provide assistance with planning and carrying out the campaign, either as a group or as individuals. These groups may also have some funds which they will make available (to nonprofits) to help underwrite costs for a specific project, such as brochures, open house, or a fund-raising event. College or high school classes or clubs, Girl and Boy Scouts, and other youth groups may be recruited to help make and distribute posters and flyers.

Senior citizens' clubs, civic groups, or church groups, may put on or assist with a fund-raising project, such as a flea market, craft sale, sports tournament, walk-a-thon, or auction. It may be possible for for-profit agencies to get this help by building scholarship funds for those participants who would otherwise be unable to attend adult day care.

Other community organizations conducting fund-raisers may agree to have the center participate at no cost to the center. The program may be allowed a booth to sell their crafts at the Art Guild sale; sponsors of Bingo or other games may give a percentage of a night's profit in exchange for manpower; heart or stroke clubs with members in the center may be receptive to publicizing the program as a part of their public relations and to making a donation from receipts.

General Principles of Marketing

No organization is without public relations; the only decision to be made is whether it will, through careful planning and use of resources, ensure that all avenues are fully utilized to influence the public to act in support of the adult day care program. Exhibit 4-1 outlines the planning process.

All members of the public relations committee should participate in the development of the plan and accept responsibility for carrying it out. All members should be familiar with each phase of the actions to be taken; however, only a limited number of persons should be designated to speak for the group in public. All responsibility for answering questions and giving interviews should be referred to the designated persons. This policy prevents confusion and ensures that the information given to the public is consistent. Individuals selected for this responsibility should possess the necessary skills: ability to think on their feet, thorough understanding of the adult day care program, and good communication skills.

A technique the spokesperson will find helpful is that of cultivating acquaintances with key personnel at newspapers, radio, and TV stations. This will facilitate efforts to get attention for news submitted from the program. These persons should be kept

Exhibit 4-1 The planning process.

1. Look at what efforts are presently being made and analyze the success or failure of past efforts.
2. Decide upon short- and long-range goals of marketing: what specific results are needed and expected?
3. Identify obstacles to carrying out marketing plans.
4. Look at program resources available for marketing: funds, staff and committee time and skills.
5. Look at community resources which may be used to supplement program resources.
6. Develop an action plan to utilize all resources, one using a combination of publicity, promotion, and public relations methods.
7. Develop a time schedule for carrying out each step of the plan.
8. Assign responsibility for each task.
9. Design a system for evaluation, review, and revision of each step and of the total action plan.

informed of new developments and newsworthy events connected with the center. Care must be taken not to abuse relationships. Unrealistic requests should be avoided and appreciation expressed for any courtesies extended.

Summary

An effective marketing campaign requires great and continuing effort, reinforced by skills and ability. Since adult day care programs do not operate in a vacuum, but within a community upon which they are dependent for support, the effort must be made. Careful planning and sustained efforts pay well for the program. The results achieved in terms of financial aid, volunteer support, participant referrals, and use of community resources for the program are the foundation upon which the center will grow and improve, becoming a valuable asset in the community.

5 Documents and Records

Introduction

An essential component in any well-run organization is establishment and maintenance of an efficient records and document system. Such records are necessary to meet legal requirements, to provide information needed for assessment and evaluation of service delivery, and to serve as guidelines for planning.

New adult day care programs are faced with the need to develop necessary documents rapidly and simultaneously and create a record keeping system. The system should be as simple as possible while allowing the program to keep complete records and providing easy access to necessary information. The program may experience a period of trial and error before determining what methods best meet their specific needs.

The documents and records system for an adult day care program can be classified into four basic areas:

- Organizational
- Administrative
- Program
- Participant

Organizational Documents and Records

Included organizational documents are those required for formalizing the organization, meeting legal requirements, and maintaining all corporate records.

Articles of Incorporation

"Articles of Incorporation" is a legal document filed with the Secretary of State or an equivalent office within each state. Its purpose is to formalize the incorporation of the organization, making it a legally recognized entity. The incorporation process should be completed early in the formation stage.

The necessary forms may be obtained from the Office of the Secretary of State or from attorneys.

The following information is included on the form:

- Name of the Corporation
- Purposes of the Corporation
- Names and addresses of individuals forming the Corporation
- Legal address of the Corporation
- Plans for disposal of Corporation assets in the event of dissolution.

Care should be taken to make the statement of purpose a general, non-limiting statement, allowing room for future expansion of purpose or change in direction.

States require that the description of an organization requesting nonprofit status use descriptive language which is recognizable as establishing such status. Among accepted terms are: "educational," "charitable," and "benevolent."

It is generally wise to obtain legal advice in the writing of this document, unless those involved are experienced in such procedures.

By-Laws

Within the by-laws will be a more specific statement of the purposes of the organization. This document will be used as a guide for operation by the governing body and should be framed with this purpose in mind. Again, it may be wise to obtain legal advice to ensure that all legal requirements are met. Exhibit 5-1 lists elements that should be included in the by-laws.

Organizational Chart

The organizational chart is drawn to indicate lines of authority and communication within the organization and to define organizational structure. It is used to depict working relationships between the board (members, officers, and committees) and the staff; between the director and other staff members; and among staff members themselves.

The chart should show lines of authority between the following:

- Board chair to board
- Chair to committees
- Committees to full board
- Chair to director
- Board to director
- Director to committees
- Director to staff members
- Board to staff
- Staff to staff

Exhibit 5-1 By-laws components.

- Name of organization
- Organization purposes
- Number of members of governing body (i.e., Board of Directors)
- How members are elected
- Length of term of office
- Any limit on number of terms
- Duties of the Board
- Procedures for filling vacancies
- Schedule for holding regular meetings
- Procedures for calling regular or additional special meetings
- Number of members required to constitute a quorum
- Officers, standing committees, and their duties
- Length of terms of office, method of election and of replacement
- Procedures to meet legal requirements, including disposal of assets in the event of disbandment; and disclaimer of any profits accruing to members of the Board (if the organization is nonprofit).
- Revision/amendment process for the by-laws
- Date of adoption
- Signature of corporate secretary
- Corporate seal

The board and staff should become familiar with the organizational structure as outlined by the chart and abide by the lines of authority and communication depicted. An organization which fails to understand the value and use of the structure and to operate within proper channels invites chaos. For example, the chart will show that staff members should relate to the board through the director, with two exceptions. The first would be in cases of grievance resolution when the grievance is not resolved at the staff/director level; and the second in special circumstances when staff is invited to meet with the board to present special reports or to be recognized by the board. These exceptions should be noted in the personnel policies.

Board Manual

The board manual document should be designed as a working document for board members, providing them with information needed to understand the organization: how it operates and their role in the operation. The manual should be revised and updated periodically. Exhibit 5-2 outlines the board manual.

Program Philosophy Statement

Whether written or unwritten, all programs develop a philosophy under which the program operates. Organization and implementation of the program and adherence to a philosophy expressing the intent of the founders are facilitated when the founders have developed a well-thought-out statement of program philosophy.

The statement should answer questions like: What are we going to do? Why do we want to do this? What is the end result we hope to accomplish? The statement should talk specifically about this program, rather than about the concept of adult day care in general. It should define the program purpose, serving as the foundation upon which service delivery will be based and providing direction and guidance for management and operating decisions.

Program Policies and Procedures

"Policies and Procedures" is the action plan for the program, a translation of philosophy into performance. Exhibit 5-3 outlines the Policies and Procedures statement.

Contractual Agreements

The original of all contracts entered into by the organization should be included in this file.

- Rental or lease agreement for use of space
- Transportation contracts
- Contracts for provision of meals
- Insurance policies
- Any letters of agreement or memoranda of agreement with other agencies, such as social services, health, mental health departments, community colleges, churches, etc.
- Contracts with funding agencies.

Exhibit 5-2 The board manual.

The board manual should include:

- Copy of by-laws
- Organizational chart
- Program policies and procedures
- Statement of program philosophy and goals
- Current list of board members, addresses, and phone numbers
- List of standing committees and their duties
- List of any current ad hoc or special committees and their purposes
- Current budget
- Current financial report
- Minutes for most recent board meetings
- Job descriptions for board members and staff
- Personnel policies
- Informational materials, including program brochures, program history, current data relating to adult day care, etc.
- Operating procedures for the board

Exhibit 5-3 The "Policies and Procedures" statement.

The policies and procedures statement will include:

- A statement of program goals: what services will be offered and to whom, with what expected outcome
- Admission policies: who will be admitted to the program, and what criteria will define those to be served in the program
- Admission procedures: what enrollment process will be followed
- Discharge policies: what will be acceptable reasons for both planned and emergency discharges
- Program operating policies: how will the program be carried out
- Operationg procedures: what rules and regulations for program operation will be followed.

Administrative Records

Administrative records include all personnel, fiscal, program, and other internal records. Such records are used for planning, meeting legal requirements, providing information for funding applications, maintaining fiscal control, personnel records and program policies, and providing information needed to evaluate service delivery. Records should be carefully designed to contain all pertinent information, especially that which may be needed to submit reports to funding, regulatory, and other parties with a vested interest in the program.

Personnel Records

Personnel Policies. Personnel policies should be written early in the program development process. As the program becomes established, periodic review and revision will be necessary to reflect growth and change in the organization. The policies should state organization policy concerning personnel issues, or outlined in Exhibit 5-4.

The committee with responsibility for writing personnel policies should become familiar with federal and state laws governing employment to be sure of complying with those which will affect employment in the adult day care program. This legal informa-

Exhibit 5-4 Personnel policy issues.

Personnel policies should include:

- Staff rights
- Procedures to be followed in staff selection and promotion
- Staff responsibility to the organization
- Staff responsibility to participants
- Terms of employment (probationary period, job review process, etc.)
- Staff benefits (leave, insurance, raises)
- Classification of personnel
- Grievance procedures
- Causes and procedures for dismissal
- Requirements for notice of resignation
- Pay practices
- Staff development and training.

tion can be obtained from the United States Department of Labor, Wage and Hour Administration; the United States Social Security Administration; State Employment Security Commissions; and Local Health Departments.

It is recommended that the committee study models of personnel policies from other adult day care programs and other similar programs. This study will help to determine what has worked for other programs and to learn reasonable parameters for wage levels, vacation, leave time, and grievance procedures.

Orientation for new staff members at time of employment should include a review of the personnel policies, and all staff should be provided with a personal copy for their files.

Job Descriptions. Individual job descriptions must be prepared for each position to be filled within the adult day care program, both paid and volunteer. They will be used to ensure that all responsibilities in the program are assigned to the correct position, and to facilitate staff selection by allowing job applicants to be screened in light of the requirements for the position for which they are applying.

Each job description will include the following:

- Qualifications for the position (education and training, work experience, skills needed, personal characteristics)
- Lines of supervision and reporting
- Duties and responsibilities
- Salary range (except in volunteer jobs)
- Working schedule.

Individual Personnel Files. Individual files must be maintained for each employee of the program. When an employee leaves, the file should be relegated to a file for past employees.

Each file should contain the following:

- Employment application and/or resume
- References
- Medical examination report
- Copy of job description signed by the employee
- Records of salary, raises, promotions
- Records of work performance evaluations, corrective actions, or commendations
- Sick leave and vacation records
- Tax and insurance forms and records

- Records of participation in staff development and training
- Any other records necessary for the program, which might include record of professional licenses, and training in CPR or First Aid.

Fiscal Records

The fiscal records system within the Administrative Records encompasses all records which are necessary to establish and maintain fiscal control and accountability.

Budgets. Copies of both start-up and operating budgets, with projected income and costs should be included, to be used in fiscal planning and control.

Accounting Systems and Records. Many sources of funding for adult day care demand a high level of fiscal accountability, requiring that meticulous records be kept of all financial transactions.

The services of an accountant are likely to be needed to set up the required accounting system. If finances do not allow employment of a full-time accountant, a consultant may be retained for purposes of setting up the bookkeeping system, and providing assistance to the bookkeeper on an ongoing basis. A board member may have the skills necessary to keep the books.

Accounting records should include the following:

- Accounts Receivable: all sources of income, including participant fees, funds from funding organizations and agencies, donations and gifts, etc. Records should be kept of all billing for fees for service, whether or not they are paid.
- Accounts Payable: all administrative and program expenditures and receipts.
- Payroll Records: salaries, payroll taxes and deductions, payment of benefits.

Financial Reports. Regular financial reports should be prepared and submitted to the governing body, monthly or at least quarterly. These reports should reflect:

- Amount budgeted for income and expenses for the period
- Actual income and expenses (by line item) for the period
- Amount budgeted for income and expenses for the fiscal year
- Actual income and expenses for the fiscal year to date
- Explanation of significant deficits or overspending.

Tax Records. All tax records required by federal, state, and local tax statues should be scrupulously maintained. Tax offices should be consulted to learn what is required in the way of necessary documentation and tax payment procedures.

Tax records likely to be required include the following:

- IRS letter of tax exempt (nonprofit) status, if applicable
- Payroll taxes records
- Equipment amortization and depreciation records
- Records of any property tax
- Records of any taxes paid which are to be refunded and records needed to claim the refund.

Funding Records. Many funding organizations require specific records and documentation of expenditures as a part of the funding agreement. These may be additional to the financial records being kept or may require supplemental information. Policies of the funding organization should be clearly understood when a funding agreement is decided upon.

Internal Fiscal Procedures. Internal fiscal control and accountability procedures for the organization should be written down and adhered to as a part of the fiscal records system and for purposes of accountability.

- Procedures for expenditure of funds by the director
- Procedures for requests for funds by staff members
- Procedures for reporting expenditures by staff members
- Methods of documenting expenditures
- Procedures for use of petty cash funds
- Procedures for documenting receipt of funds
- Procedures for expenditures by board members.

Additional fiscal records should be kept by the organization if needed to ensure and demonstrate accountability. Advice from an accountant should be taken to decide what is needed by the specific program and required by terms of funding contracts.

Program Records

Program records cover planning and carrying out program services and activities.

Program Plan or Calendar of Events

This calendar should be prepared at least monthly and a schedule of planned events posted in the center. The plan will list:

- Activities and services planned for the period
- Staff member or volunteer who is responsible for the activity
- Where the activity will take place
- Any special arrangements, including preparations to be made, transportation arrangements, any unusual precautions or noteworthy demographics.

Safety and Emergency Plan

The Safety Plan is an outline of procedures and staff responsibilities to be followed in the event of emergencies. Copies of this plan should be kept in the permanent files along with plans for and records of fire and other safety drills.

The following emergency situations should be covered:

- Participant illnesses or accidents, either at the center or in transit
- Absence of the director or other key personnel
- Fire
- Bomb or other terrorist threat
- Severe weather, including extreme cold or heat wave
- Accidents or breakdown of the vehicle transporting participants.

The plan must be posted in the center, in several conspicuous locations. A floor plan of the facility must also be posted with exit routes clearly marked.

The staff must be familiar with all aspects of emergency plans. It should be impressed upon them that crises can occur at any time, so that they are prepared to deal with any eventuality. First Aid, Cardiopulmonary Resuscitation (CPR), and skills for transferring non-ambulatory participants should be included among required qualifications for all adult day care staff.

Volunteer Records

All activities involving volunteers should be documented. The program may elect to keep these records with personnel records. Included will be records pertaining to the following:

- Volunteer recruitment plans and efforts
- Volunteer policies
- Records of orientation and training
- Volunteer job descriptions and applications
- Documentation of volunteer time donated to the program
- Plans for and recognition of events carried out.

Supplies Inventory

Adult day care activities create a constant turnover in program supplies, making it difficult to keep a current inventory. However, a staff member should be charged with responsibility for keeping a weather eye on the level of supplies and replenishing them as needed. In addition, a record should be kept of supplies purchased, and at regular intervals this record should be compared with supplies on hand. This comparison will allow inventory control and facilitate replenishment.

A more formal inventory should be maintained of all equipment owned by the program. Each piece of equipment should have a control number assigned, and a master list should be kept with the permanent files. The cost of each piece of equipment should be included as a part of the inventory file. The program may choose to keep inventory records with fiscal records.

Meals Records

If meals are to be purchased, a daily count of meals consumed should be kept by the person in charge of ordering meals. This record will be used to compare with invoices submitted for payment of meals and will provide a record to be used in budget preparation and program planning.

If meals are to be prepared on-site, records of purchasing and other relevant information should be kept so that meal costs can be calculated.

Transportation Records

A daily log of miles traveled, number of persons transported, purchases of gas and oil, maintenance or repairs to the vehicle, and other pertinent information should be kept by the driver. A master list of participants to be transported each day should be kept on the transportation vehicle, with telephone numbers, name of responsible party, and any other information needed by the driver to help provide safe transportation.

Copies of this should be reviewed and updated as needed. Copies of meals and transportation transactions may also be included in the fiscal records.

Internal Communications

Memoranda from the director to staff or between staff members; copies of correspondence; and telephone logs should be included in the "Internal Communications" portion of the records system. Also included should be minutes and other records of staff conferences and meetings.

External Communication

Staff members should maintain a file of all correspondence relating to the program. This material is useful for verifying past actions and for future planning.

Records of Staff Development and Training

Staff development records should document the following:

- Staff development needs which have been enumerated or observed
- Gaps in staff skills which require training
- Records of all in-service training: who participated, topic, date, person providing training, cost.

Participant Records

Participant records should include all data and information about participants which is needed for planning and carrying out services.

- Application for service
- Emergency information: physician's name and telephone number, name and number of friend or relative, hospital preference, religious preference
- Medical form which should be updated annually
- Attendance and transportation records
- Functional assessment
- Service plan: goals of service, results of reviews and revisions, progress notes, progress assessment
- Record of participation in services and activities
- Actions taken: referrals to other agencies, special assistance rendered, family conferences
- Financial data
- Sign out forms
- Permission forms for emergency medical treatment, release of medical information, use of photos for publicity purposes.

Records should also be maintained on those individuals who have applied for admission to the program and not been admitted. Reasons for refusal of admission should be documented.

Past participant files should be kept on those participants who have been discharged or left the program, with reasons for discharge or decision to leave included as a part of the record. These records should be kept for a period to be decided upon by program management. Three to five years is recommended.

Complete and detailed information about participants enables staff to learn from past experience and to plan and carry out more effective service.

Storage of Records

A copy of all organizational records and documents should be filed at the legal address of the organization to insure retention and continuity through leadership changes in the governing body and administrator. All other documents and records should also be available at this address.

Records should be maintained with a filing system which allows easy access to any needed information. The system should be reviewed, with outdated materials discarded or removed to dead files, on a regular basis.

As with records of past participants, materials which may be needed for legal or other purposes should be kept for a period to be decided upon. Some state and federal tax and employment regulations require specific lengths of time for which some records must be kept. These time limits should be verified with the appropriate agency, to ensure that the record keeping system is in compliance.

While many records of adult day care programs are a matter of public record, it should be remembered that participant and some employee files must be maintained in a way which ensures confidentiality of sensitive information. Access should be allowed only to those individuals who have legitimate need for the information.

6 Operating Policies

Introduction

Organization and implementation of an adult day care program is facilitated when the founders develop a comprehensive statement of the program philosophy and of operating policies and procedures.

Program Philosophy

O'Brien (1982, 233) defines philosophy as "a system of motivating beliefs, concepts, principles, and values." All organizations develop a philosophy by which they operate, whether written or developed over time by habit and practice. Therefore, all adult day care programs should reflect upon the set of values and beliefs by which they wish their program to be operated and then articulate this philosophy in a written statement intended to serve as a guide for the board and staff.

The statement should be the foundation for all program goals and objectives as well as providing direction for management and operating decisions. The National Institute on Adult Daycare (1984) states the philosophy for the service in these words:

> The philosophy of adult day care is based upon the premise that adults should have the right to determine the type of care they receive, regardless of their age or frailty and that options should not be closed to them on the basis of limitations or needs. Adult day care programs allow for the combination of personal choice and appropriate care as the determining factors in service selection.
>
> Adult day care is a distinctive service in its approach and focus.
>
> - Adult day care approaches each person as a unique individual with strengths and weaknesses, yet with a potential for growth and development.
> - Adult day care assumes a holistic approach to the individual, recognizing the inter-relationships among physical, social, emotional and environmental aspects of well-being.

- Adult day care promotes positive attitudes toward the self-image, restoring, maintaining and stimulating capacities for independence while providing supports for functional limitations.

Adult day care reduces the isolation and prejudice often associated with the frail and impaired adult and ensures continued relationships with the community. It also enables the individual to maintain his/her role within the family structure and remain at home for as long as possible.

While families are the primary providers of care to the frail and impaired adults, they are seldom able to provide all of the needed physical, social and emotional support. Adult day care shares providing of the care while educating, counseling and supporting the caregiver. It seeks to create an atmosphere that enhances the value of human life and affirms the dignity and self-worth of an individual. The uniqueness of adult day care stems from its individualized approach and its ability to meet the individual's needs. It must, however, always be viewed as part of a larger array of community-based services that assist the frail and impaired adult to achieve the quality of life that makes living worthwhile.

The thoughts expressed in these words may be used by providers to frame the philosophy for their own programs. The statement should include additional ideas which reflect the unique approach to service delivery which will be taken by the program being developed. The statement must describe the spirit in which the service is intended to be provided. It should specifically articulate the following:

- What is to be done
- Why it is to be done
- The values which undergird actions
- Results which are to be accomplished.

If values and beliefs are set forth clearly and strongly to indicate how providers see their program, and if they are used as a basis for all management decisions, the program will reflect these beliefs in its daily operation.

Program Policies

The policies and procedures of an adult day care program are its plan of action, an explicit statement of what the program will do, what services are to be offered, to whom, and within what parameters. They should facilitate translating the philosophy statement into performance.

The policy statement should comprise eleven major sections.

Program Goals

Program goals outline what the program intends to do i.e., the objectives to be accomplished by the program. Program developers should examine the capability of their program as it is proposed, and decide upon the specific purposes the program can effectively address (Exhibit 6-1).
Developers may have these or other objectives in mind; it is important that providers be clear about which issues they intend to focus and state these succinctly within their statement of purpose. Failing to do so may result in a program which attempts to address such a broad spectrum of problems that it cannot be effective in solving any. Goals stated within the policies and procedures must be backed by a well-developed plan for accomplishment.

Admission Policies

To ensure that program purposes are acted upon appropriately, the population to be served must be well defined, with admission policies stated in a way that describes this population explicitly. Most state standards for certification and licensure require that admission policies be written as a part of the program policy statement and that they define who can be served in the program.

The policies should be specific to the program being developed and should be formulated with program capability in mind. The policy for admitting participants should speak to characteristics of the population to be served.

- Age requirements
- Requirements for participant self-care (feeding, toileting, etc.)
- Functional level of participants to be admitted (ambulatory/non-ambulatory, blind/sighted, continent/incontinent, etc.)

Exhibit 6-1 Suggested program goals.

Among adult day care program goals:

- Prevention of premature or inappropriate institutionalization
- Relief for caregivers of dependent family members
- Maintenance of functional level of participants
- Provision of medical and/or physical care for participants
- Provision of opportunities for growth and development of participants
- Rehabilitation for participants

- Limits upon numbers to be admitted with specific impairments (mental confusion, persistent wanderers, aggressive or violent behaviors, blindness, using wheelchairs, etc.)
- General restrictions upon admissions (those needing more care than the program is staffed for or is able to provide; those who cannot benefit from care; those who live outside geographical boundaries, etc.).

Admission Procedures

The Admission Procedures outline the process for making application for service and enrolling in the program.

- Making inquiry: number to call and contact person
- Applying for admission: filling out formal application
- Personal interview with staff member
- Visit to center
- Medical examination report
- Functional assessment
- Discussion and acceptance of program policies
- Completion of attendance, financial and transportation arrangements.

The procedures should also require a statement of why the applicant was accepted or refused admission into the program, including whether adult day care appears to be the appropriate service for the applicant; whether the program has the capacity to meet the needs of participants; and whether the present configuration of participants enrolled will permit acceptance of another participant with the functional capability of this applicant.

If participants are enrolled on a trial basis, this should be stated, along with the time line for making the decision for permanent enrollment. If admission is not possible immediately because present enrollment comprises participants with levels of impairment requiring maximum effort from staff, or for other reasons having to do with participant configuration, the applicant should be given the option of being placed upon a waiting list for the earliest possible acceptance. The policies should state whether applicants on the waiting list will be taken in order of application, or whether certain conditions will receive priority. If this is to be done, policy should specify what conditions qualify an applicant for priority admission.

Discharge Policies

Discharge policies should describe the process for determining whether the program continues to be the most appropriate care method for participants who are enrolled in the program.

- Reasons for routine discharge. These may include a need for more care than can be provided; behavior which has become unmanageable; or improvement in functional level to the point that adult day care is no longer needed.
- Reasons for emergency discharges. These may include communicable diseases which place other participants in danger; violent or abusive behavior which is uncontrollable; intentional or continuous disruptive behaviors; unmanageable wandering which creates danger for the participant and requires a disproportionate amount of staff time.
- Procedures for both routine and emergency discharges. These should cover notification method and length of notice which will be given (two weeks to one month is recommended for routine discharge). Circumstances of emergency discharge may not allow that notice be given, and this should be stated.
- Circumstances under which re-admission may occur. Re-admission should be considered if a person who was discharged due to improvement regresses to the point that adult day care is needed again; if a person who was discharged due to illness or unmanageable behavior improves to the degree that functioning within the adult day care environment is again possible, etc.

Withdrawal Policies

Withdrawal policies will state program expectations of participants and caregivers when they make the decision to withdraw voluntarily from the program.

- Length of notice which is expected
- Method notification is to take: written, verbal, or both.
- Any charge or penalty for withdrawal without proper notice.

Program Management Structure

The Program Management section is a brief outline of the governing structure of the program, including who is responsible for overseeing and providing the care for participants. It should include:

- Name of the organization operating the program. This may differ from the program name, especially if the program is a part of or operates under auspices of a larger organization. Families and participants have the right to know where final responsibility rests for provision and quality of care.
- Title of the individual who has responsibility for day-to-day management of the program.
- Outline of staff qualifications: medical personnel, social workers, therapists, aides, etc.

- Ratio of staff to participants which will be maintained in the program.
- Procedures for resolution of problems which arise during the period of enrollment.

Program Services

Program Services should state what services and activities are to be offered by the program and the terms of their provision.

- Food service and nutrition: meals, snacks, therapeutic diets, nutritional counseling, weight control.
- Arrangements for taking of prescribed medications
- Transportation: whose responsibility; geographic parameters for transportation to be provided by the program; any charge for transportation, if this is an addition to fee for service; transportation for field trips, shopping, etc.
- Insurance: what types are provided by the program (liability, accident, etc.)
- Social services: leisure activities, social interaction opportunities, community involvement, diversional activities, volunteer activities, etc.
- Health care: health supervision and monitoring; medical care to be provided on-site (nursing, blood pressure checks, health screening, medical examinations, etc.); training and assistance with activities of daily living; therapies to be offered (if there is to be a separate charge for these, this should be stated); physical exercise or activities
- Supportive services: service coordination; education; counseling; family support efforts.

Program Operating Procedures

Program Operating Procedures describe how the program is to be carried out.

- Hours and days of operation
- Holidays or other scheduled closings
- Weather or other emergency closings and procedures: will the program be closed when driving conditions are unsafe and if so how will unsafe conditions be defined; how unscheduled closings will be handled (notification of families, etc.)
- Participant absences: whether a charge will be made for absences; what notice is required for absences; what is program policy regarding frequent or prolonged absences and discharge (for example, if the participant is absent for two weeks, the program may elect to discharge the person, but place them on a waiting list if and when they wish to return).

- Accident or illness occurring at the center: what actions will be taken, who will be notified, etc.
- Medications: policies regarding participants keeping and taking own medications while at the center, safety measures which must be observed, etc.
- Storage of personal belongings: handling of valuables brought to the center
- Family visits: whether unscheduled visits are encouraged; any expectations of the program for family visits and participation in program events planned to include families
- Family conferences and problem resolution: expectations of the program toward family involvement in the formation of the individual plan of care and achievement of care goals
- Changes in days of attendance: either at the request of participants or by staff to have a participant benefit from an activity held on a day when the participant is not normally attending

Fees

Program policies should include a statement of the fee structure of the program and policies regarding payment of fees.

- Amount of charge for one unit of service (may be defined as one day, or in some programs as one-half day or as one hour)
- Fees to be charged for services not to be provided to all participants, such as transportation to and from the center, therapies, medical services, etc.
- Financial aid policies: how requests are to be submitted; criteria for receiving aid, etc.
- Method and schedule for billing
- Due date for fee payment
- Policies regarding non-payment of fees: Will service be continued? For how long? What actions will be taken to recover long-overdue fees?
- Policies for less than a full day of attendance if this is to be allowed.
- Policies regarding payment to hold space for a participant during a prolonged absence for vacation, illnesses, etc. Will space be held? For how long and at what charge?

Waiting List

The program should have an established policy for maintenance of a waiting list once capacity enrollment has been reached.

- Criteria for enrollment of applicants from the waiting list: Is the policy to be first-come, first-served, or will participant configuration at the time a vacancy occurs be considered in the decision? Will applicants in a crisis situation receive priority? If this is to be done, the program must clearly define what constitutes a crisis; included may be risk of institutional placement; discharge from a hospital conditional upon care being available; patient alone during the day in a situation which is potentially dangerous.
- Policy regarding application of past participants to re-enter the program: will they have the right to be placed at the head of the waiting list? How long can this position be maintained after they have left the program?
- Policy regarding an applicant being unable to enroll when they are notified that space is available: will they be placed at the bottom of the waiting list or receive the next available space?

Policy Acceptance

Program policies should include a statement to be read and signed by the participant and/or responsible party, signifying that they have read and agree to abide by the program policies as written.

The admission process should include a discussion of the policies between the participant or responsible party and the director or other designated staff member, with ample opportunity for questions or for clarification upon any point.

When there is indication that the policies are understood, the participant and/or responsible party should sign, indicating acceptance. The staff member representing the program should also sign; signatures may be witnessed if the program believes this to be desirable. The date of signing should be affixed.

Use of Policies

The policy statement as formulated should be used by the board and staff as the action plan for the center. All actions and decisions taken should be consistent with policies stated within the document. The statement may also be used to provide information about the program to potential participants, their families or caregivers, and other interested parties such as funding or regulatory bodies.

Each participant and the family or caregiver should receive a copy of the policy statement upon enrollment in the program. Another copy should be placed in the participant's individual file. Both copies should be signed by the participant and/or responsible party and by a program representative.

Copies of the policy document should be given to each member of the board and the staff immediately upon affiliation with the program. The material should be discussed in detail as a part of the orientation for both board and staff.

The board, in conjunction with the director and other staff as deemed appropriate, should conduct periodic evaluation and review of program policies and procedures to determine whether they continue to be an adequate and accurate statement of the intentions and plans of the program and whether the program is operating in accordance with the philosophy and program purposes as written. An annual review is recommended, with a suggestion that the process be included as a regular part of the annual evaluation of the program as a whole.

If, upon review, changes are decided upon which affect participants (fee structure, absences policy, discharge policy, hours of operation, etc.) care must be taken that participants enrolled in the program have the changes explained and are asked to sign a copy of the revised policy. All staff members must also be briefed on any changes.

Summary

All adult day care programs must have a policy statement, formulated and used as the action plan by which the program operates. Lack of such a statement places the board and staff in the position of having to make policy decisions each time a new situation arises. The policies also serve to provide legitimacy for decisions which will prove to be unpopular. A director without a written policy setting forth acceptable reasons for denying admission to an applicant or discharging a participant for whom service can no longer be provided is placed in a vulnerable position.

Providers must think through the circumstances of their program: staff capability, costs for providing care, location, amount of space, philosophy of the program, and other relevant factors and decide upon each policy and operating procedure in light of these.

It is unlikely that any two adult day care programs will have exactly the same operating policies, since most programs can and should adapt service delivery methods to the needs of the community and to the resources available to them. This potential for flexibility is a major strength of adult day care, allowing the service to be tailored to the unique needs of the individual and the community.

References

O'Brien, C.L. 1982. *Adult day care: A practical guide.* Monterey, CA.: Wadsworth Health Sciences Division.

National Institute on Adult Daycare. 1984. *Standards for adult day care.* Washington, DC: National Council on the Aging, Inc.

7 Program Evaluation

Introduction

Only by conducting regular, periodic evaluations of the adult day care program can providers know whether they are offering services as described within the program policies, whether they are serving the appropriate population as outlined by admission policies, and whether they are achieving desired program goals and objectives. (Appendix B of this Guide comprises a complete sample program evaluation.)

Funding and monitoring agencies will usually require evaluation of service delivery methods and program results. Even in the absence of such requirements, the continued growth and success of the program will depend in a large measure upon providers being able to understand the reasons for both successes and failures. Carrying out an annual, internal evaluation of both qualitative and quantitative issues and program components will help to provide this understanding.

Providers may find it helpful to anticipate evaluation criteria in the planning stages, as they are formulating policies and procedures.

Planning an Evaluation

Once providers decide to conduct an evaluation, a six-step process should be followed.

1. Decide upon specific criteria for the evaluation, i.e., what questions need to be answered.
2. Decide what information is needed to answer the questions.
3. Decide what individuals and groups have the needed information.
4. Design evaluation methods or instruments to be used to gather the desired information.
5. Determine how results will be analyzed.
6. Determine how results will be used.

These six steps are discussed in detail below.

Evaluation Criteria

Whatever the evaluation plan, the evaluation will be a search for information that will help ascertain whether objectives of the program are being accomplished. Objectives of the evaluation are discussed in Exhibit 7-1.

Data Identification

The evaluation plan should be designed to provide both qualitative and quantitative information. The following topics and lists of questions are suggested as useful measurements and indicators.

Direct Services

- How many participants have been served in the program over the period of time being evaluated? (This should be an unduplicated count.)
- What is the total number of service inquiries received?
- How many service inquiries have been processed?
- What services have been provided on-site by the program and to how many participants?
- What activities have been offered and how many have participated?
- How many interviews and home visits have been conducted?

Indirect Services

- What counseling services have been provided to families and caregivers? To how many individuals?
- What other supportive services have been provided to families and caregivers and to how many?
- How many members of the staff have engaged in outside training and development events? For how many hours? On what topics?
- Has the training achieved planned objectives for staff development? How has the program benefited? How has this been demonstrated in service delivery?
- How many orientation and training events have been provided on-site by center personnel, and to how many individuals? By outside resource persons and to how many?
- How have orientation and training events benefited the program and the participants?

Exhibit 7-1 Program evaluation criteria.

1. Measuring effectiveness of present service delivery methods
2. Analyzing the functional capability of participants who are being served in order to learn whether the program is serving the population described in the admission policies
3. Analyzing successes: What has been the functional level of participants who have either maintained or improved functional capacity while attending the program? What services and activities have been provided which appear to have contributed to the improvement? Can similarities be detected among participants who have shown improvement: Similar diagnoses at time of enrollment? Participation in the same services? Similar attitudes or support systems? Other?
4. Analyzing failures: What has been the functional level of participants who have failed to maintain or improve, or who have regressed? Are there similarities among this group: Similar impairments, attitudes, or support systems? Have the same services been provided? Were there gaps in needed services? Are there other commonalities?
5. Determining the number to whom direct services are being provided and the nature of the services. Are these figures in line with program goals as planned?
6. Determining the number of individuals to whom indirect services are being provided and the nature of the services. Are these in accord with program planning?
7. Measuring the role of adult day care in the total system of services being offered to frail adults in the community. Are participants being served who would lack necessary services without the program? Does the program offer a unique service and one which cooperates with other services in the system?
8. Measuring the impact of the program upon families and caregivers. Is the impact positive and if so, in what ways? What services contribute to this result? If negative, what is the cause for this result?
9. Measuring how efficiently the program is utilizing its resources: funds, facility, staff, board members, volunteers, supplies.
10. Determining whether all available resources within the community are being used to gain maximum benefits for participants.
11. Analyzing effectiveness of program administration: Is the governing body functioning in ways which fulfill its assigned role in support of the program? Is the director fulfilling expectations as outlined in the job description?

- How many orientation and training events have been held for board members? How many members have participated? How have the board and program benefited?
- How many volunteer recruitment efforts have been carried out?
- How many volunteers have been recruited? How many hours donated to the program? How have program and participants benefited?
- How many events have staff and board members engaged in with the objective of educating the public about adult day care? How many individuals have attended? Are there any measurable benefits for the program?
- How many public relations efforts have been planned and carried out for the purpose of getting referrals of potential participants or gaining financial support for the program? With what results?
- How many fund-raising events have been planned and carried out? With what results?

Program Performance

- How many participants moved into a level of care requiring less support?
- How many participants are maintaining functional level?
- How may participants would have to enter residential care unless enrolled in the adult day care program?
- How many participants for whom neglect (including self-neglect) or abuse has been prevented through enrollment?
- How many participants have had to move into a more intensive method of care?
- How many have left for other negative reasons?
- How many linkages (working relationships) have been established and maintained with other community agencies and organizations?
- How many service referrals to other agencies or service providers have been made and with what measurable benefit to participants?
- How many applicants have been refused admission to the program? For what reasons? Does this number reveal any commonalities of need which may indicate that the program should re-think its admission policies; that perhaps the program is not serving those most in need of adult day care?
- How many participants have helped in forming their own individual plan of care?
- How many families, caregivers, and professionals have participated in designing service plans?

- How many participants have accomplished goals of service plans?
- How many participants have been unable to accomplish goals?
- How many participants believe that their needs *are* being met by the program; how many believe that needs *are not* being met?
- How many families and caregivers state that their needs and those of their dependent member are being met; how many state that needs are not being met?

Program Impact

- How many families and caregivers have been provided respite and support by the program?
- How many family members and caregivers have been freed for gainful employment?
- How many participants have experienced positive changes from use of the service as evidenced by the following:

  development of or regaining social skills
  improved communication skills
  improved use of time
  improved family relationships
  improved use of community resources
  improved ability to make contributions to others and to the community
  improved self-esteem or sense of well-being
  improved health status, physical and/or emotional
  fewer unnecessary medical visits
  improved ability to care for personal needs

- How many families and caregivers have experienced positive changes from use of adult day care, as evidenced by the following:

  improved outlook on life
  reduced stress
  freedom of worry about participant
  more free time
  improved family relationships
  improved physical health

improved mental health

less work

freedom to become employed outside the home

Cost Effectiveness

- Does program have a planned annual budget?
- Are expenditures not exceeding budget per line item?
- Are costs per unit of care within budget projections?
- Does program operate within the budget?
- Do costs compare favorably with those of other similar services?
- Are financial resources adequate?
- Are procedures and practices in effect to ensure financial accountability?
- Does staff not have to spend an inordinate amount of time in fund-raising efforts?

Safety and Cleanliness

- Does program meet all certification and licensure requirements for health and safety practices?
- Is program in conformity with all local and state regulations and requirements for health and safety (if these are different from or exceed those for certification/licensure)?
- Does program facility meet public codes for health and safety?
- Are safety practices in effect?
- Is the staff trained in CPR, First Aid, and appropriate emergency measures?
- Are regular fire and emergency evacuation drills conducted?
- Are program supplies on hand when needed?
- Are supplies stored in a safe manner?
- Are medications and other potentially harmful substances safely stored and handled?
- Are storage areas adequate and is storage well-organized?
- Are services and activities planned and carried out with adequate attention to safety measures for participants?
- Are meals prepared and delivered in a manner which meets codes and prevents growth of bacteria?

Program Management

- Do board members carry out responsibilities assigned to them?
- Is the board supportive of the director, working to establish and maintain an effective relationship?
- Is leadership of the board available to the director when needed and responsive to concerns?
- Are board and staff relationships and areas of responsibility well-defined?
- Is the director in control of time and work responsibilities?
- Does the director function as the team leader, communicating well with staff members and helping to establish and maintain a team approach to service provision?
- Do staff members work together as a team?
- Are the numbers and skills of staff adequate and appropriate to provide services for the population being served?
- Do staff members utilize their time well and for the benefit of participants?
- Do staff members communicate well with participants and help to create a supportive environment?
- Is the staff well versed in service goals and philosophy; does it provide services in a way which supports these?
- Does the staff recognize the right of participants to function as adults and as autonomous beings, and does it act in support of these rights?

Evaluation Instrument

The evaluation instrument which the provider develops should be designed to obtain information about the foregoing issues as well as any others which may be deemed of importance to the program.

All questions should be framed to be as objective as possible and should not be phrased in ways which lead the respondent to believe that one answer is preferred over another. Questions should be worded to obtain data which is specific and measurable and which can be easily and accurately recorded and analyzed. This will be aided by use of fixed-choice questions, i.e., offering a selected set of possible responses from which to choose.

In addition to asking objective questions, program managers may elect to include a component which calls for more subjective opinions. This would include open-ended questions, with no limitations imposed upon either the length or method of answering.

Information from both objective and subjective methods may be useful to the program, providing the most complete picture of how the program is viewed. However, the subjective data will be more difficult to interpret and may be less useful in achieving the evaluation objectives.

The evaluation instrument should be designed with a separate questionnaire for each group which is to participate; each group will be asked to evaluate and provide information from its own perspective. Questions for each group will be framed with the differing perspectives in mind. Those designing the instrument should be aware of the characteristics of each group of respondents, in terms of education level, amount of time needed to respond, cognitive ability, and any other factors which may influence ability or willingness to fill out the questionnaire.

Rather than developing an entirely new instrument, the provider may wish to use an instrument which was originated by another human service agency, or one which has been modified or adapted for use by another adult day care program. Since it is of course difficult to find an existing instrument which will be perfectly suited to the purposes of the program, it is probably best to draft one, borrowing or adapting where feasible from an existing instrument. Obtaining several which have been used in similar programs to serve as models will be helpful. Careful study must be made in order to arrive at an evaluation instrument that will meed specific program needs. (See Appendix B for a complete sample evaluation instrument.)

Groups to Involve in Evaluations

To obtain complete information, the evaluation process should include all groups and individuals who participate in provision of the service, those who are affected in some way by its provision, and those who are in a position to evaluate the effects of the service upon participants. The following groups should be considered.

Program governing body/board members should participate in the program efficiency and management components of the evaluation.

Director should participate in all aspects of the evaluation.

Staff members should participate in all aspects of the evaluation.

Participants should help to evaluate direct services, indirect services, program performance, program impact, some aspects of program efficiency and management components.

Families and caregivers should evaluate indirect services, program performance, program impact, some aspects of safety and management.

Other care team members (physicians, nurses, therapists, mental health professionals, etc., who are not on staff) should evaluate program performance and impact components.

Department of Social Services and other monitoring agencies should evaluate program performance, program impact, some aspects of cost effectiveness, safety and management components.

Social service workers and others who have referred participants to the program and have been able to observe program impact should evaluate program performance, impact, and efficiency aspects.

Volunteers and other community resources persons should assist in evaluation of indirect services, program performance, impact, safety, and some aspects of program management.

Interpretation of Findings

Methods used to gather information in the adult day care program should allow for easy and accurate compilation and interpretation of data. Information from all sources should be compiled and tabulated, so that it can be measured and interpreted. Providers must be careful to measure outcomes with objectivity and lack of bias. If possible, the analysis should be carried out by individuals who are not involved with the program in a substantive way, enabling them to look at results without pre-conceived opinions about the program. Volunteers with skills needed for this might be recruited from among research personnel or organization such as the Junior League, etc.

The evaluation as carried out by the individual day care program is not expected to have the accuracy of a scientific research project; results should be interpreted with this in mind. Nonetheless, the information will be valuable to the program for achieving its own purposes. Findings should not be looked upon as either "good" or "bad" but should be used as a resource for learning what is revealed about specific services and methods of service delivery, what works best and under what circumstances.

The value of the evaluation is that of helping the program to analyze what it is doing, how it is being done, and with what results, so that this information may be compared with prior program plans and expectations.

Use of Results

Once information has been obtained and tabulated, a written report of the data should be prepared. This report will be useful to the program in many ways.

The report should provide analysis of successes and failures and under what circumstances these occurred. This information will enable providers to assess program performance and decide whether some change in direction or methods is indicated. For example, the program has a focus upon rehabilitation, but evaluation data indicates that those participants who have been admitted because of a perceived need for this service have not shown the degree of improvement expected in this area but that a high percentage of participants have been maintained at their present level of functioning. Now the program must examine whether its present focus should be changed or whether services must be adapted to better achieve rehabilitative goals.

By the same token, an evaluation can help providers build upon successful methods for purposes of planning for the future. The foregoing example applies: if success appears to lie in helping participants to maintain a functional level and in preventing further deterioration, it seems clear that the program as presently structured would be advised to focus upon the goal of maintenance.

Learning from past failures to overcome program deficiencies or inadequacies can also be facilitated by the evaluation. For example, participants are being admitted with problems of drug abuse, but the data reveals a demonstrated inability to absorb drug abusers into the program without detriment to the program and consequent failure to provide other participants with needed services. Providers must examine whether the program should continue to admit these individuals without some re-structuring of program staff and services. For another example, if data from families and caregivers indicates a need for more support than they are presently receiving, additional effort may be needed in this area of indirect service.

Program impact as measured by stated program goals and plans for the program can be assessed through the evaluation. The program has, for example, set a goal of serving a specific number of participants and the census has consistently remained below that number. Or, a goal has been to help prevent premature or inappropriate institutionalization for a number of individuals and this has not been accomplished. There must be intensive scrutiny of the data to learn why these goals have not been met and if the factors influencing these failures are subject to change.

Program efficiency can also be assessed. Does the data indicate that the program is utilizing resources to the maximum degree possible? Or is there evidence that actions could be taken to enhance effectiveness in this area? Is the cost of care as revealed by the data in line with other similar services, making it cost effective? Or is the service so expensive that it compares unfavorably with other services in this respect and will have difficulty proving its case for receiving funds based upon this criteria?

Providers can use evaluation information for purposes of marketing the program. The data should provide credibility for the program, demonstrating that the program is meeting an important community and human need, that it fills what would be a gap in the continuum of services, and that users of the service benefit in both measurable and intangible ways. If these claims are not backed by the evaluation data, providers must seek reasons why this is so and take remedial action.

The evaluation provides information requested by funders and monitoring agencies. These entities require hard evidence that claims made by organizations funded by them are factual. If the evaluation has been conducted in a manner which is objective and has been fairly interpreted, the data will be of use in proving the case for the service to these bodies.

A full report of the evaluation data and an interpretation of findings should be given to both the board and the staff. The report should be scrutinized by the board and its committees, in conjunction with the director, to learn implications for present service methods as well as for future planning.

Summary

Most adult day care programs are convinced that their programs are fulfilling a vital need in the community and to participants. This is usually an accurate assessment. However, believing that this is the case does not provide information needed to accurately assess program performance, efficiency, and impact. If the program is to remain flexible in its service provision, to be able to adapt to changing needs and to convince its supporters that it is accomplishing goals as advertised, it must be able to offer data which backs its claims.

A periodic internal evaluation supplies the information needed for these purposes and will, in addition, provide satisfaction to providers, helping them to know that they are continuing to work toward improvement of service quality.

8 The Facility

Introduction

The setting and physical plant for the adult day care program will influence almost every area of program provision, including program quality. Because of this, careful thought and deliberation must be given to selecting or building the facility to house the program. Although housing options may be limited by availability of suitable buildings or by the amount of funds on hand to purchase space, those who will make the decision should be thoroughly versed in facility requirements for the program in order to select options which will best meet those needs.

Facility Committee

The planning and development committee for the adult day care program should include a subcommittee whose specific responsibility is to conduct research in the community to locate suitable housing for the program. It will be the duty of this group to determine whether suitable housing is available in an existing building (and if so, what modifications or renovations will be needed to meet codes and certification or licensure requirements) or whether the best option is to build.

Committee Membership

It is critical that members of the committee understand the adult day care concept and how the program will operate. Only by having this knowledge will they be able to make decisions which will enable the program to operate effectively in the space selected or designed by them. Membership on the committee should be individuals who can contribute to the expertise needed and may include the following.

- The adult day care director or another person who represents the program provider point of view
- An architect or other individual skilled in space design who is willing to spend time learning about the program and its specific space requirements
- A builder or an individual who can evaluate structural soundness, electrical, plumbing, and heating systems in existing buildings or who can help to plan and build a new facility

- A real-estate broker or other individual who is familiar with community property values and demographics
- Public officials: qualified experts who can examine the facility (or plans) for safety and suitability and make recommendations for any needed changes to meet fire and safety codes, including fire marshalls, building inspectors, electrical inspectors, and health inspectors.

Committee Duties

The committee must first define the specifics of what will be needed, based upon program goals, parameters of the population to be served, expected numbers of participants, and services and activities to be provided. The factor of time must enter into this decision: Will the building or renovation schedule fit into the proposed program opening schedule? With these requirements in mind, the committee may decide to search for space in an existing building which can be modified to meet needs, or may decide to construct a new building. Either decision will entail commitment from members to stay with the project until the facility is completed.

The committee will need to schedule regular and frequent meetings, with some flexibility for additional meetings as needed. Each member should have specific responsibilities and assignments based upon his area of expertise, and should report results and findings to the full committee for action decisions.

Facility Requirements

As mentioned above, the facility committee must be knowledgeable about the requirements of its own program when selecting a facility. In addition, there are certain basic requirements—location, structure, indoor space, outdoor space, atmosphere—which must be considered when selecting or building a facility for any adult day care program.

Location

Safety is of primary importance when deciding upon the location of the center. Many older people, rightfully, have concern for their safety, and participants must believe that they are in a safe environment while in attendance at the center. The neighborhood must be one in which walks and other outdoor activities can take place without fear.

Demographic information and projections should also be factors which influence the site selection. Location in or near a neighborhood where the population includes large numbers of potential participants may help when enrollment begins, since residents may look favorably upon the opportunity to attend a program near home. Such a location may also help to simplify transportation arrangements, with families better able to transport their family member for short distances.

A further consideration regarding transportation is that of locating the program where participants can utilize public transportation, if possible. Accessible public transportation for those able to use it lessens the necessity for the program to own or lease vehicles.

Proximity to other community services which may be needed by participants is desirable as is closeness to facilities used for program services and activities, such as shopping and eating facilities, medical care providers, schools, and recreational programs and facilities.

Providers of adult day care should determine what the mood of a neighborhood would be toward having the program placed in the community. If there appears to be a lack of acceptance and support, or outright hostility, the program would be better off in another area. Carrying out public relations and educational efforts within the community may enlist support for the program; residents should be helped to recognize the program as a community asset and one which contributes to the quality of life in the neighborhood.

The decision to locate in any area will be dependent upon existing zoning regulations; these must be checked to be sure that such a facility is allowed under any regulations that apply.

Structural Requirements

In addition to safety of location, providers must consider safety factors in the building itself. To this end, members of the committee with the necessary expertise should examine the building being considered (or plans for constructing a new building or renovating an old one) to be sure that all systems will meet safety requirements.

Roof. In an existing building, the roof should be checked to be sure that it is safe and in good repair. It should show no evidence of leaks and should be constructed so that it drains well. The life expectancy of the roof should also be considered. Roof replacement is expensive and may require that the program be closed while replacement takes place, if this becomes necessary.

Exterior Walls. Exterior walls must be structurally sound. The committee should consider what maintenance costs are likely to be: if the outside is painted, how often must it be re-painted and at what cost; if the exterior is brick or block, is there any evidence of crumbling or other damage; are shingles or other siding in good repair and of materials which are durable, requiring little upkeep?

Interior Walls. Interior walls should be structurally sound, with no cracks or other indications of crumbling or water damage. Tests should be conducted to be sure that asbestos is not present in amounts which may be harmful. Ridding a building of asbestos is so expensive that a building where it is present may have to be eliminated from consideration, unless the budget will stretch to cover this cost. All paints should be lead-free and fire-resistant. Fire-resistant paint may be required in some areas. Codes should be checked for this stipulation. Wallpaper should be flame-resistant and in good repair.

Flooring. The floor should be sound and free from obstacles such as raised boards or thresholds. Any floor coverings should be in good repair and of materials conducive to easy movement for wheelchairs and for persons using walkers, canes, or other ambulation aids.

Electrical System. The electrical system should be in good repair and meet fire and safety codes or be in a condition which can easily be brought into conformity. The amount of electrical current into the building should be adequate for present program needs and should allow for future growth and expansion. Planners should ascertain that electrical outlets are adequate for program needs and in appropriate locations. Existing lighting should be adequate for those persons who are sight-impaired and should be of a quality which prevents glare.

Heating and Cooling. Heating and cooling systems should be in good repair, meet fire and building codes and be adequate for program needs. Temperature control is important in adult day care programs, since older and impaired individuals are subject to illness if they become either too hot or too cold.

A further consideration in this area is cost and power efficiency. Systems which are old are not likely to be efficient and will be expensive to operate and maintain, creating a constant drain on the budget.

Plumbing. Plumbing should be in good repair and adequate for program needs. Bathrooms must be in conformity with codes, be accessible to the handicapped, and be well-placed for convenient use by participants. Sinks should meet codes for the handicapped, and there must be at least one toilet for handicapped individuals. Doors into bathrooms should be easy to open and should not be the swinging kind, which can cause accidents. There should be no locks on the insides of the doors.

Indoor Space

The amount of available program space and its arrangement will influence the program in a variety of ways, affecting the size the program can reach, the kinds of services and activities which can be planned, and, to some extent, the level of care which can be provided. All of these factors should be kept in mind when viewing potential sites or planning the arrangement of space within a new facility.

The amount of indoor space must be adequate to meet certification and licensure requirements for the number to be served: national standards recommend 40 square feet per person, excluding halls and bathrooms.

Additional space should be allowed for staff offices and working areas. These should be convenient to program areas and have a vantage point from which entrances and activities can be kept under observation. Each staff person should have storage space for materials, records, and supplies needed to carry out specific responsibilities.

Program space should be flexible, adapting to varying activities. For example, the dining room may be used for crafts, the living room area may be used for small classes, etc.

The available space should be planned to include areas for both large and small group activities. In addition, there should be rooms or designated areas for individuals to withdraw from the group when they feel in need of quiet or they want to be alone.

In addition to regular program activities, space will be needed for special services and activities. This may include rooms for therapy sessions, if this is to be provided; a treatment room, if applicable; rooms for private counseling or family conferences; rooms for personal care activities (bathing, hair care, laundry, etc.); and a kitchen for snacks and preparation of meals if they are to be prepared on-site. Even if meals are to be catered, a kitchen is a valuable part of the program for participants to help plan and serve daily snacks and for program activities which involve cooking.

Planning space arrangement entails thinking through what services the participants will require, what activities are to be carried out, and, in light of these, how to best plan or utilize the space.

Traffic patterns should be such that participants are able to move easily about the center. They should not need to walk down long hallways to bathrooms, for instance. Isolation or quiet areas should be far enough from the activity area to ensure privacy and quiet, but situated so that staff is able to keep individuals occupying these areas under observation.

Entrances and exits should be easily accessible. Participants should enter the center in areas which are easily supervised by staff. Coat closets or lockers should be located near the entrance for easy storage of participants' personal belongings. Staff offices should be located close together to facilitate staff communication.

Adult day care programs rarely have enough storage space. Minimum requirements would be the following: one large closet for storing large items, several cabinets for craft items, a coat closet, kitchen cabinets for storage of food and cleaning supplies, and a locked cabinet for storage of potentially dangerous cleaning supplies, and a cabinet with a locking box for medications.

In addition to meeting fire and safety codes and ensuring the structural safety of the building, indoor space should be designed with safety precautions in mind. Planning should allow freedom from architectural barriers—hallways must be wide enough for wheelchairs and walkers. There should be no steep or narrow stairways. Ramps should have a gradual, gentle slope and have a surface which prohibits slipping and ramps and hallways should have handrails. Toilets must have grab bars or safety frames. All doorways should be wide enough to accommodate wheelchairs and walkers, and should be easy to open and to hold open while passing through.

Floors should be even. They must not be slippery, highly waxed, or covered by unanchored or easily moved carpets or other floor coverings. Any carpets used should be easy to walk on.

Outdoor Space

Outdoor space should be sufficient for outdoor activities, including walking. The area should be fenced or have other security measures which prevent confused participants from leaving. It should also be of a size which can be easily supervised by staff. The outdoor area should be planned to include smooth walkways, benches for resting or watching activities, recreational space, and, if possible, an area where participants may have a garden. Shady areas are desirable. If none are available, large umbrellas might be used to provide shade.

Atmosphere

The atmosphere within the adult day care program should be comfortable, relaxed, and homelike. Achieving this effect will involve recognition of the ethnic, economic, and cultural background of the participants to be served. What is homelike for participants in metropolitan New York may not be for those in rural Alabama.

Colors should be chosen for the effect desired. Warm and restful colors are suitable in resting areas and where quiet activities are to take place; brighter and more stimulating colors should be used in areas for activities designed to stimulate and motivate participants. Color combinations should be those which will both help to create a cheerful effect and which will contribute to participants' ability to see: a sharp contrast between objects and their background is important. Blue, green, red, or black on white, or white on bright colors are among the combinations which will achieve this. Other suggested combinations are red or yellow on green or yellow on red.

Furnishings should be arranged in groupings which invite participants to use them for the desired purpose: a living room arrangement for conversations and visiting among participants; tables and chairs arranged in easily accessible groups for handwork and crafts. Areas for carrying out work activities such as sewing, laundry, cooking, woodworking, etc., should be arranged so that the purpose is readily apparent and so that the equipment and tools needed for the activities are easily accessible to participants.

If the center does not have enough rooms to accommodate each activity in a separate room, the grouping or purpose may be indicated by furniture or equipment arrangements, by use of a screen, or by use of color coding.

Differentiating areas by use of color may be helpful in any case to some confused participants. For example: bathroom doors painted in a bright red or pink for women and blue for men will aid in easy identification. Another method for identifying space usage is by pictures. Bathrooms may have a large picture of a woman and a man on the respective doors, the kitchen may have a picture of people eating, etc.

Comfort considerations will include keeping temperatures at a reasonable level and in ranges which are safe in both summer and winter. Many older people lose much of their ability to feel heat or cold, but may suffer ill effects in temperatures which are much above or below the normal.

Humidity and air pollution are other comfort factors which should be controlled within the center. If smoking is allowed, it should be contained within a designated area and with proper safety and pollution control measures. The area should be constantly supervised by a staff member, especially for individuals who are confused or likely to be careless with smoking materials. Sand buckets should be placed for easy dousing of cigarettes. Clean air machines may be required to achieve the desired air quality. Participants who suffer from circulatory, respiratory, or allergy problems may be supersensitive to smoke or other air pollution and may become ill from exposure. Their needs will have to be considered when establishing smoking regulations. If humidity is excessive or the air is very dry, adjustments may have to be made by use of de-humidifiers or by humidifiers.

Noise levels are another consideration in establishing a comfortable atmosphere within the center. Excessive noise caused by loud or continuously ringing phones, loud typewriters constantly used within the program area, loud equipment (saws, sewing machines, mixers, etc.), and blaring radios or televisions must be controlled if there is any potential for their causing distress.

Placement of lamps and other lighting should be planned with the needs of older people in mind. The lights should be placed so as to shed the maximum amount of lighting upon any handwork, reading materials, etc., which they will be using. Glare from windows or doors should be reduced; curtains or blinds can be used for this purpose. Lighting should also be such as will contribute to the desired homelike atmosphere.

Facility Furnishings

All furniture should be chosen with the needs and functional abilities of participants in mind. Appropriateness for planned program activities is also a factor.

Sufficient furniture should be provided for the number of participants to be admitted. Arrangements and groupings of furniture should be such as will allow for freedom of movement by participants within the center. Walkers and wheelchairs take much more room for movement, and the number of participants who will be using these must be taken into account when buying and arranging furniture.

All furniture should be designed to promote independent use. Chairs should have arms to use for leverage and should offer support for rising. Participants should be able to sit comfortably with feet placed upon the floor or on a foot stool. Lounge chairs with foot rests should be made available for those who need to keep their feet elevated.

Round tables for dining and for work are preferred. If square or oblong ones are to be used, sharp corners must be placed so as to eliminate a hazard, or be covered with a padded surface. Table space for all participants to be served at the same time at meals is required, with at least one straight back or sturdy folding chair for each participant and staff member. There should be adequate table space for participants to be seated and to have ample elbow room and work space while eating or while engaged in program activities.

In addition to necessary furnishings, the center should display objects to support the homelike atmosphere and to stimulate sensory abilities of participants. Examples include a clock in each program room, mirrors, flowers and plants, magazine tables and racks, bookcases, piano, record player, radio, and TV if desired. (Care must be taken that these are not used as substitutes for programming, but are used in constructive, educational ways), sofa and chair pillows, footstools (care must be taken with these; they should be easy to see and sturdy enough so that they cannot be tripped over), comforters or throws for covering feet while sitting, calendars, and pictures. Magazines and books should be available, selected with consideration for the interests and reading and seeing ability of participants.

Program equipment should be selected to carry out planned program activities and may include such items as a sewing machine, iron and ironing board, laundry equipment, sewing tools, carpentry and woodworking tools, craft tools, outdoor grill, outdoor chairs, exercise equipment, and a kiln. Thought should be given to what activities will be of interest to and within the abilities of the population to be enrolled. Needs, such as for help with laundry, mending of clothes, etc., should also be included in program planning.

A stove and/or microwave and a refrigerator will be needed for program activities, whether or not meal preparation is to take place on-site. Other necessary kitchen equipment includes pots and pans, eating utensils, pot holders, a sink, a mixer, cooking tools, and dishes for food storage. All kitchen equipment should be chosen with safety features in mind. Pots and pans should have long handles and be sturdy and not easily tipped over. All equipment to be used by participants should be kept in good repair and should be stored in a safe manner. Heavy objects should not be stored overhead where they might fall and hit someone; knives and other sharp objects should be kept locked away; breakable objects should be kept to a minimum. Electrical appliances with automatic cut-off are recommended. Water temperatures are another safety concern: the temperatures for water to be used in both the kitchen and bathrooms should be within ranges not hot enough to scald or burn.

If nursing or therapies are to be provided on-site, equipment for provision of these must be included in center furnishings.

Additional equipment would include a telephone accessible to participants, at least one bed with sheets and pillows, mattress pad, rubber sheet, blankets, towels, wash-cloths, trash containers (with lids), bulletin boards, office furnishings and equipment, and a coat rack and lockers or other space for participants to store belongings.

Certification and Licensure Requirements

Before a final decision is made for selecting an existing facility or before plans are finalized for building, the county department of social services (or its equivalent with responsibility for overseeing certification and licensure of such facilities) must be consulted to ensure that all local and state building, fire, and safety codes are being met. If an existing building is not in compliance, consideration must be given as to whether it can be brought into compliance and at what cost. If the walls, electrical, or plumbing systems are worn out or in such bad repair that they will have to be replaced, the cost may be beyond what budgeted funds will allow, and the committee might be wise to continue the search for a facility not requiring such extensive repairs. Plans for a new building must also be approved to be sure that they will meet all codes.

In addition to seeing that all codes are met, the agency will determine whether the building (or plans) meet adult day care certification and licensure requirements. These will include having adequate space for the number to be served, adequate storage and meal preparation and serving areas, adequate toilet facilities, securely fastened floor coverings, handicapped accessibility, fire and smoke equipment as required, a sufficient number of exits, ample areas for resting, available telephones, and safe storage for potentially harmful materials.

The facility and grounds must also meet cleanliness standards established by local sanitation authorities: sanitary disposal of waste materials; appropriate sanitation measures for meal and snack preparation and serving; windows and doors screened; clean walls, floors, and fixtures.

Summary

As mentioned earlier, the selection and planning committee should be well versed in details of the planned adult day care program, its goals, the functional level of participants to be served, the number to be served, and what services and activities are to be provided. They must understand the philosophy of adult day care and the atmosphere which is desired. The program will not want to present an institutional appearance; rather, care must be taken to achieve the warm, inviting aspect which will help participants feel at home and function at their best.

With these factors in mind, and with knowledge of comfort and safety for participants and staff, the committee should work to establish a center which accommodates the program as well as one which promotes and enhances the quality of service provided.

Constraints upon achievement of these objectives must be recognized and allowed for. There may be a dearth of suitable buildings, shortage of funds, and difficulties in meeting safety and building codes. The committee will face challenges in developing solutions to overcome these shortcomings. Alternate solutions and readjustment of plans may be required often to produce the requisite features in the facility. These challenges are a part of serving on this committee and will require dedication from its members to achieve their goals.

9 The Governing Body

Introduction

No other single factor influences the success or failure of an adult day care program more than the degree of competency possessed by its governing unit. This unit may be called a board of directors, an advisory committee, or another name; it may consist of one person in an owner-operated program or of several persons in a formal and well-organized board structure. Whatever the body or structure, principles of sound management remain the same, and the responsibility for carrying out these principles rests with the governing body.

Factors in Board Design

Too often planners do not understand the importance of the role played by the governing body of an adult day care program. If inadequate attention is paid to the overall construction of the board, members may be selected who are not as knowledgeable about the service as they need to be. They may not understand the degree of hard work which must be put into beginning and managing the program. It should be kept in mind that the governing body determines program policy, is largely responsible for procuring program funding, and is legally accountable for the organization. Great care must be exercised to select members whose qualifications match theses tasks.

Before any members are selected, a design for the body in its entirety should be developed, much as any business would design an organizational structure. Those who are responsible for design of the structure should possess the following:

- A thorough understanding of the duties and functions of the governing body.
- A knowledge of the skills and abilities needed to carry out responsibilities.
- A knowledge of community demographics which will enable structuring of a board representative of the community (This is especially needed in a program which is to be nonprofit, since support of the full community will be needed if the program is to succeed.)
- A comprehensive understanding of the service of adult day care, so that members elected to the board will be supportive of the service philosophy and goals.

Functions of the Governing Body

In most instances, the adult day care board must be a "working board"; that is, it must assume a major share of the responsibility for certain duties which are critical to effective operation of the program. The full board assumes responsibility for major functions as outlined in Exhibit 9-1.

Board Committees

In addition to participating in carrying out broad functions of the board, each member should accept assignment to one or more committees where their special talents can be best utilized.

There are three basic types of committees.

Executive Committee

The executive committee is commonly empowered under the bylaws to act for the full board under two specific conditions. First, it may act for the full board between full board meetings. This allows for fewer meetings of the board and allows members to spend more of their available time carrying out committee assignments. It is in these assignments that much of the work of the board is accomplished. Second, it may take action in emergency situations when it is not feasible to convene a meeting of the full board.

Members include officers and chairs of standing committees.

Standing Committees

Standing committees are those responsible for the ongoing tasks of the governing body. The number and size of these committees will vary widely from one governing body to another. The following outline is a guide for understanding the work of the board and offers a method of handling tasks through use of committees. All boards will not find it necessary, nor will they have the personnel, to have so many committees. In instances where the program is owner-operated, for example, most of the work is likely to fall on the shoulders of a very few individuals. Whatever the make-up of the administrative system, organizing the tasks in the manner suggested below allows for more proficient management of duties.

Some of these suggested committees may have already been formed and working as a part of the planning and development process. However, since duties will alter somewhat once the program is in operation and once the permanent governing body is formed, they will be discussed here in that context.

Exhibit 9-1 Major board responsibilities.

1. Researching legal requirements which apply to the organization and taking necessary actions to comply and to maintain compliance.
2. Completing the organizational process begun by the planning committee; carrying out ongoing assessment of the board structure and reorganizing as needed to meet future change and growth.
3. Establishing and maintaining all necessary documents and records required by the formal organization. Depending upon the sponsoring agency or owner, these documents may include Articles of Incorporation; by-laws; organizational chart; board manual; job descriptions for committees and individual members; tax-exempt status, if applicable; and procuring of any required licenses or registrations.
4. Hiring the program director; replacing the director if circumstances require such action.
5. In cooperation with the director, determining program goals and objectives.
6. Establishing written policies and procedures for program operation.
7. Carrying out periodic review and evaluation of the program to ensure that the operation is consistent with service philosophy and is achieving program goals.
8. Establishing personnel policies and job descriptions for staff.
9. Formulating financial policies to ensure the financial health of the organization. These policies include developing a budget; planning for fund-raising; setting up a process for monitoring program expenditures; arranging for regular, independent audits of financial transactions; appraising and adjusting plans for funding when circumstances indicate a need for this.
10. Carrying out ongoing public relations efforts, which will entail interpreting work of the organization to the public, and helping to build visibility and credibility.
11. Participating in inter-organizational planning in the community, to secure for the program an integral role in the community services network.
12. Engaging in a continuous planning process, which includes setting both short- and long-term goals, evaluating progress, and revising plans to meet new or changed circumstances.
13. Planning and carrying out regular, internal self-assessment and evaluation of the work of the board and of its working relationship with the director and staff.

Nominating Committee.

Duties:

- To establish criteria for selection of members of the board, keeping in mind the unique and specific board functions and the talents needed by its members
- To conduct ongoing research in the community to locate able individuals to serve as board members
- To prepare and present to the board a slate of officers and board members

Criteria for Membership:

- Understanding of the organization and the qualities needed to achieve its purposes
- Contact with a well-established network of resources within the community which will serve as a source for potential board members
- Communication skills for "selling" potential members on the goals of the service and the contribution which the individual will make.

Budget and Finance Committee. Because a high degree of effort is required to raise funds for the adult day care program, it is advisable to have two arms of this committee: Finance and Fund-Raising. Close collaboration will be needed between the two; it is recommended that one or two individuals serve on both arms. The board treasurer should serve on the larger committee and perhaps on both arms.

Finance Duties:

- Work with the program director or other appropriate staff to project program costs by line item for the program budget
- Keep track of expenditures by use of regular financial reports and bookkeeping system
- Arrange for regular, at least annual, audits of financial transactions.

Fund-Raising Duties:

- Conduct ongoing research to locate potential sources of funds for operation of the program
- Based upon financial needs of the program, submit funding applications to funding sources; plan and carry out other methods of fund-raising to meet program costs. Plans should include procurement of funds for projections of future growth.

Criteria for Membership:

- Individuals who are skilled in money management and in fund raising.
- Individuals who have contacts within the power structure of the community and can open doors to gain the attention of those responsible for allocating funds to service organizations.

Personnel Committee.

Duties:

- Carry out recruitment and selection of a program director
- Establish written personnel policies and job descriptions
- Act in support of the director in hiring other program personnel
- Act in support of the director in resolving staff grievances
- Serve as a bridge between the director and the full board to aid in clarification of board and staff roles and duties
- Conduct a regular, periodic job assessment and performance review of the director's position.

Criteria for Membership:

- Understanding of personnel policies and management
- Understanding of the adult day care concept and needs of the population being served
- An ability to communicate well
- Good negotiation skills
- Understanding of board-staff relationships.

Public Relations Committee.

Duties:

- Develop a plan and carry out ongoing and comprehensive efforts to build public recognition, acceptance and support for the program within the community.

Criteria for Membership:

- Enthusiasm for the program
- Experience and expertise in planning and conducting public relations efforts.

Program Committee.

Duties:

- Work with the director to develop long- and short-term program goals
- Serve as a resource to the director in planning and providing program services
- Help to plan and conduct regular, internal program evaluations.

Criteria for Membership:

- Understanding of the population being served in the program and their needs
- Knowledge of effective methods of service provision.

Transportation Committee.

Duties:

- Provide assistance to the director in planning provision of transportation
- Assist with any vehicle purchase, lease, or contracts with transportation agencies
- Provide back-up services in emergency situations: helping with arrangements for transporting participants, arrangements for repairs, etc.

Criteria for Membership:

- Expertise in transportation methods
- Knowledge of transportation issues in the community: traffic patterns, distances, etc.

Facility Committee.

Duties:

- Develop plans for construction if a facility is to be built
- Plan and oversee any required renovations, alterations, adaptations, or expansion
- Assist the director with ongoing maintenance and repairs to the facility.

Criteria for Membership:

- Skills in building, architecture, real estate, engineering
- Understanding of facility needs for functionally impaired adults and how to adapt building design to meet needs.

Planning Committee.

Duties:

- Conduct ongoing research into the changing needs of the population being served by the adult day care program
- Based upon results of research, develop plans for any indicated growth, expansion and changes in direction for the program
- Develop a time line and outline action steps for achieving short- and long-range goals
- Work with the Finance Committee to devise methods for meeting costs of carrying out proposed plans.

Criteria for Membership:

- Ability to take the long view; skills for devising long-range goals
- Ability to project a time line and develop action plans
- Ability to communicate with other board members and motivate them to recognize future needs and work together to achieve growth.

Special or Ad Hoc Committees

Ad hoc committees are established to carry out any special assignment which does not fall into the job description of a standing committee. The committees are appointed by the board chair and disband when their purpose has been achieved.

For examples, an ad hoc committee might be appointed to carry out a special, one-time fund-raising event; to revise bylaws; to perform a preliminary investigation of the feasibility for a new project or a change of direction contemplated by the organization. Skills needed for ad hoc committee members will be dictated by the work to be done by the committee. The chair must understand requirements of the job to be done and select members accordingly.

Ad hoc committees carry out assignments which are within their job descriptions and as assigned by the board or by the chair. They meet as needed to achieve their purposes, conduct any indicated research, report upon actions, decisions, and recommendations to the full board. The board will act to approve or disapprove committee recommendations, and, based upon information provided by the committee, will decide upon further assignments.

Qualifications for Board Membership

After board duties and functions have been clarified, the next step in design of board structure is to decide upon qualifications needed by new members. A heavy emphasis should be placed upon formation of a board whose members possess a broad understanding of the adult day care service and the needs of individuals who will be participants. Further, they should know the community: its resources and needs.

For new organizations, it is strongly recommended that some board members be selected who have had prior experience in a well-organized and effective board. Such members will be useful in the preliminary organizational and developmental processes, helping to clarify responsibilities of board and staff and to get the board moving. When selecting these members, care must be taken to ensure that they possess the insight and sensitivity to recognize the differences between their prior situation and the adult day care board. Some adaptation of knowledge and method will be required if they are to work effectively as a part of the new board.

Each board member should be chosen to fill a special need. There should be an understanding of the role each member is expected to play in the work to be done. Some members will be selected because they possess a specific skill needed on a standing committee; others will be asked to serve for their understanding of board responsibilities; still others for an ability to command community recognition and support for the program. Careful assessment of potential members will allow selection of some individuals who will fill more than one role and offer multiple skills and talents.

The request to serve must be issued with a realistic acceptance of the amount of time which a member is willing to invest in the work of the board. Community leaders, such as a mayor, corporate leader, or pastor, may be unable to participate on a regular basis in the day-to-day work of the board; however, they are invaluable to the program if they are willing to lend their name and prestige to the board. They can be asked to provide assistance in special assignments, to help to open doors to the community power structure, and to gain community support.

The following specific abilities and personal characteristics are conducive to building an effective board.

business administration and
management
marketing
planning
money management
personnel management
legal expertise
leadership
intelligence
creativity
common sense
understanding of the community and its needs
familiarity with community resources
knowledge of the needs of impaired adults
experience with methods of service delivery
writing and speaking skills
a mixture of "thinkers" and "doers"

The major responsibility for leadership of the board rests with the president or chair. The nominating committee must exercise critical judgement when choosing the individual to serve in this capacity. The chair must be an individual whom the board can trust with decision making and who is comfortable with this role. It must also be an individual who is able to take necessary action when issues arise between board meetings and which are not covered by general policy of the board. There must be familiarity with the thinking of the board and ability to motivate the board to act. The chair must be accessible to and supportive of the program director.

Representative Membership

It is important that the adult day care board avoid the appearance of being controlled by a clique or of being an elitist group. An unreserved effort should be made to have membership reflect the population of the community being served. The board gains from the differing perspectives brought to the board by such representation. Furthermore, the board will profit from having established contact with all segments of the community, easing the task of gaining wide-based support for the program. In forming the board, planners should seek to balance community demographics in terms of social, economic, racial, ethnic, age, sex, and religious characteristics. In addition to these, the community service network and the care continuum should be represented.

It is especially important to include members who can represent the point of view of agencies and organizations providing services to the same or similar populations as will be served by the adult day care program. These members will serve as a source of referrals of participants and as resources for helping to understand and meet needs of participants.

Another and no less important group to be represented is the users of the service: participants and their families. They will supply a key perspective, helping the board to better understand and evaluate the service and methods of provision. If the functioning level of participants permits, having a participant serve as an ex officio member is one method of gaining such input. If this does not appear feasible, participants may be asked for their input in less formal ways: conversations with staff and board members; use of a suggestion box; holding group meetings of participants on a regular basis for the purpose of asking for their recommendations. Alternatively or additionally, positions on the board may be reserved for family members of participants.

Board Development

It cannot be overemphasized that an essential requirement for board members is a working knowledge of adult day care and an understanding of the population to be served. This is vital to the effectiveness of the program, but furthermore, members have the right and obligation to understand the purposes of the organization of which they are a part, to learn about its methods of providing service and about what is expected of them in their role as a member of the board. To accomplish this, an initial orientation should be provided for all new members as they come on the board and ongoing training made a part of the planning agenda.

Orientation

Orientation should be intensive; at least one or two days is recommended. This may be provided in whatever segments of time suits the convenience of the board. One may schedule one or two hours for several evenings or perhaps a weekend retreat.

At a minimum, the orientation should include a presentation by an individual who is well-qualified to speak about the service, an opportunity for members to ask questions, and a study of relevant materials, including state regulations applicable to the service. Study of the *Standards for Adult Day Care* (National Institute on Adult Daycare 1984) and reading of *Developing Adult Day Care for Older People* (Padula 1983) are recommended.

Once the program is in operation, board members should spend some time visiting, observing, and asking questions to further inform themselves about the service. Visits to other centers—especially those with a reputation for providing a high quality service—is another recommended learning method. Part of the board's orientation should be an opportunity to discuss board operating procedures and to make a study of the bylaws and board manual. Each member should have an opportunity to discuss specific roles and responsibilities of each position on the board.

Board Training

Ongoing training provided to the board should be on two tracks:

1. Continuation of the educational process about the service and the program.
2. Specialized training related to specific areas of board responsibility.

Topics for specialized training may include:

- Leadership training for the president or chair and others in positions of leadership
- Training in grant writing and fund-raising for those charged with responsibility for maintaining financial stability
- Personnel selection and management training for members of the personnel committee
- Marketing seminars for the full board
- Conflict resolution training for personnel committee members.

These are only a few from which the board could benefit. The possibilities are endless.

Board assessment should be continuous so as to determine specific training needs and to locate resources (listed below) which offer training to community organizations at little or no cost.

Community colleges and technical institutes

Voluntary action agencies

Junior League

United Way

Foundations

Adult day care state and national organizations

Red Cross

Banks

Local civic groups

Mental health or social service departments

Regularly checking the local newspapers, organizational newsletters, community bulletin boards, and the local library is suggested as a means of learning about any planned training events. A request to be placed on mailing lists of organizations which may be among the resources which offer training is also recommended.

Relationship Between Board and Director

All board members should have a clear understanding of the roles and duties of the program director and of the board. As the professional of the organization, the director should serve as an ex officio member of the board and its committees, providing the board with the benefit of the professional point of view, experience, and expertise. However, the board should not expect the director to carry out the work of the board. As stated earlier, the board should expect to function as a "working" board, acting cooperatively with the director to achieve goals and to carry out plans.

The following responsibilities belong to the board, with appropriate input from the director:

- Program, finance,and personnel policy setting
- Fund-raising: acting to maintain the financial health of the organization
- Maintenance of corporate documents and records
- Compliance with legal requirements
- Acting in support of the director
- Maintaining accessibility to the director.

The director will act to implement policies and plans as directed by the board; however, the board has a duty to be sure that these are clearly communicated. The director will not be able to function in a vacuum created by a lack of clear direction. All decisions requiring action by the director should be communicated primarily by one person, usually the board chair, and preferably in writing.

decisions requiring action by the director should be communicated primarily by one person, usually the board chair, and preferably in writing.

Open communication between the board and the director is essential to maintenance of a healthy working relationship. There must be freedom for professional disagreement, but once decisions are made, the full support of all involved is to be taken for granted. The support of the board is expected as long as the director is employed in the position. Any criticisms or recommendations for change should be communicated through proper channels as established in the organizational chart.

The board should never interfere in the day-to-day operation of the program; this is the jurisdiction of the director. Again, any recommendation for change should be made through proper channels. The board should feel satisfied that it has employed the most qualified person available for the director's position. Its role then is to provide direction and guidance, while allowing the director room to operate the program within the guidelines.

Size of the Board

The board should be large enough to accomplish its work without causing members to become overwhelmed with the magnitude of their responsibility. On the other hand, boards with too many members run the risk of losing their concentration; a tendency may develop to believe that someone else will take care of the work. If sufficient thought has been given to the design of the board and selection of its members, each member will be serving for a specific purpose and that purpose will be understood by both the individual and the larger board. This will ensure that there are no superfluous members.

It is also wise, if possible, to have members serve in more than one capacity, thus fully using their skills and abilities and helping to keep board size within desirable limits. This may not be possible for all members. An analysis of the tasks to be accomplished and of what can be reasonably assigned to one individual will be the determining factors in the decision about the size of the board.

Advisory Boards

In those situations where the program is owner-operated or is part of a larger organization with a board which oversees a number of programs, it is recommended that an advisory board or committee be formed.

A volunteer group with similar skills and abilities as those discussed for the board and with an interest in the adult day care program can carry out much of the role of the board which does not involve actual policy making or legal responsibility. This group can serve as a major support for the director. It can fill a vacuum which might otherwise exist when the director has no group or committee with the specific duty of encouraging and undergirding the adult day care program. Volunteers who are asked to serve in this capacity should understand the parameters of their role, and be willing to function within those boundaries.

Self-Assessment

Once a board is organized and operating, it becomes easy for it to continue to function in established patterns, losing sight of the need for change as circumstances change. To avoid this, the board may incorporate two mechanisms into their operating procedures. First, place a time limit upon the length of time which board members may serve before rotating off the board. By-laws may include a provision for this to ensure that there is a constant infusion of new talent with fresh perspectives and methods. Second, regular, periodic self-assessment and evaluation may be carried out.

Self-assessment will determine how well the board is carrying out responsibilities and how effective its work is toward accomplishment of stated goals. Self-assessment should include the points enumerated in Exhibit 9-2.

This self-assessment should reveal any weaknesses and indicate areas where improvement may be needed. Regular (at least yearly) participation in such an assessment is recommended. Findings of the assessment should be used to enable the board to maintain flexibility and responsiveness to current conditions and to continue a pattern of growth as required by program change and development.

Exhibit 9-2 Board of directors self-assessment.

- All legal requirements are met and the board and program are in compliance with any applicable laws or regulations.
- All necessary documents and records are being adequately maintained and are readily accessible for the board and program needs.
- The board is pleased with the way responsibilities of the director are being discharged, believing that the most effective person available is in that position.
- The board regularly examines written program policies to determine whether they continue to be fuctional and if not, to carry out indicated revisions.
- The board works with the director to carry out regular internal evaluations of the program to ensure that the service continues to be of high quality, that the appropriate population is being served with appropriate services, and that stated program goals are being achieved.
- Personnel policies and job descriptions are current and are working as needed.
- The organization is financially stable, and ongoing funding is adequate.
- Financial records are well-kept and readily accessible—the board receives regular and detailed reports on program expenditures and funds received.
- The program is well known in the community; it has achieved credibility and is looked upon as an asset in the care continuum.
- Ongoing public relations efforts continue to gain the needed support from the community in the form of referrals of potential participants, donations of materials and supplies, financial support, and volunteers.

Exhibit 9-2, continued..

- The organization has developed a place for itself as an integral component of the community services network and participates in inter-organizational planning.
- The board is actively involved in plan development, both for short- and long-range goals.
- Board members are active in the work of the organization: they participate in full board actions and serve on at least one standing committee; attendance at board meetings is high.
- Committees are functional, carrying out responsibilities within reasonable time limits, supplying appropriate, timely reports to the full board.
- All board members have participated in orientation and engage in available training as needed to improve their skills.
- The board continues to be representative of the community, and an active effort is made to maintain this status.
- Board leadership is effective. The chair is able to handle decision making, is able to motivate and lead board members to carry out action plans; chairs board meetings in a manner which expedites the business of the board; works well with the director; is accessible to the director and the board.
- The chair and the board are able to handle any crisis situations which may arise. Mechanisms are in place for calling emergency meetings and for polling members by telephone when necessary. In general, chair and board are able to respond effectively to unexpected developments.
- The board is organized so that logistics of routine tasks can be easily handled: signing checks, signing necessary documents, making needed purchases.

References

National Institute on Adult Daycare. 1984. *Standards for adult day care.* Washington, DC: National Council on the Aging, Inc.

Padula, H. 1983. *Developing adult day care for older people.* Washington, DC: National Council on the Aging, Inc.

10 The Director: Selection and Duties

Introduction

The director of an adult day care program occupies a pivotal position in the organization. This position provides linkage between the program and those bodies—governing body, funding resources, referral agencies, families, etc.—which relate to it. The position is also the bridge between the board and the staff, with the director reporting on the work of the staff to the board and interpreting policy as defined by the board to the staff.

The director must successfully unite a number of roles and be competent in numerous areas of responsibility. Because of the heavy demands placed upon this position, the search and selection process must be planned to locate an individual who possesses the needed qualifications of experience, training, and personal characteristics. Certain skills and knowledge will also be required.

Qualifications

Experience

There are now, in the 1980s, few individuals available who have had prior work experience in adult day care. Many state standards require that, in lieu of direct experience, the individuals have had some experience in provision of human services, preferably in service provision to functionally impaired adults.

Since the adult day care director must usually fulfill dual functions as an administrator as well as a program manager, it is important not to overlook the need for administrative experience. The individual who can best carry the varying roles and responsibilities of adult day care directorship is one who has had work experiences in jobs which combined administrative functions with human services content.

Training

Because methods of providing adult day care vary in their focus from the highly medical/rehabilitative to the social/preventive, individuals with a range of medical or social services professional training may be the best choice depending on the program's emphasis. No discipline has yet been established generally as the clear choice from which to select a director. Thus, those presently working in the field have come from diverse educational backgrounds.

Programs which provide skilled health care have often employed a director from the medical professions, usually an RN. Programs with less of a medical orientation have chosen social workers, home economists, recreational therapists, "generalists" (see discussion by Padula 1983), and from a number of other professions.

Deciding which professional training is best for a specific program should be based upon the functional level of participants who will be admitted to the program, the kinds and variety of services which will be provided, and the kinds of training other staff members will have.

Skills and Knowledge

Because the duties of the director are so diverse, the list of skills and knowledge needed is also diverse and somewhat formidable. Three qualities should be of highest priority:

- Understanding and acceptance of the precepts of adult day care
- Dedication to the philosophy of the service
- Familiarity with the needs of the population to be served.

Second in priority is the need for administrative skills:

Organization	Program implementation
Leadership	Budget management
Decision making	Problem solving
Planning	Human relations
Staff interview and selection	Conflict resolution
Staff training and development	Communication
Delegation	Social
Time management	

Effective discharge of position duties will require excellent communication skills, both written and oral. The job will require good communication with widely dissimilar groups and individuals: governing body, staff, participants, families, funding sources, referral agencies, volunteers, community organizations, the media, and the general public.

Personal Characteristics

Individuals who may possess the most laudable and desirable of qualifications in other areas may be unsuitable for working within the adult day care climate due to lack of certain indispensable personal traits or possession of others which will prove detrimental to leadership of the program.

First among needed personal qualities is an educated sensitivity to attitudes which constitute the prejudice of "ageism"; this must be coupled with a total absence of patronization toward the aging and toward any person with functional impairments. Secondly, there must be a clear understanding of what the adult day care program is meant to provide for participants: a place where they may receive support which enables them to experience growth and development, and to realize their fullest potential for independence.

Other desirable traits and attitudes include:

- A genuine concern and empathy for people
- An understanding of how the helping role should contribute to independence and autonomy for the recipient
- Acceptance of people; an absence of prejudiced or judgemental attitudes
- Patience, tact, and sensitivity
- Creativity, ability to be innovative
- Common sense and good judgement
- Friendliness, warmth of personality
- Being comfortable with self; accepting of self.

It is most unlikely that a search for an individual who possesses all the desired qualifications is likely to be successful. This manual has made an attempt to prioritize; the personnel committee who draws the job description and conducts the search and selection process will have to go farther, placing a higher priority upon those qualifications and traits which they consider essential to job performance within the specific program as it is planned.

Functions of the Director

As stated earlier, the adult day care director is responsible for dual functions, each of which entails multiple roles and varied duties. Effective discharge of all responsibilities will be governed by three key factors:

- The director must be well-qualified by training, experience, and personal characteristics to occupy the position.
- The job description for the position must clearly define all roles and responsibilities, must establish authority to carry out assigned duties, and must set up definitive boundaries between the duties and authority of the director and those of the governing body.
- The director must identify all roles to be carried out and be able to organize and manage the related duties and responsibilities.

The Director as Board Liaison

All administrative functions of the program can be delineated as functions of the board, functions of the director, or functions requiring collaboration. It is understood that while the director will be expected to provide input into most board decisions and actions, the director has the right to expect that roles are clearly defined, and that the board will discharge those responsibilities which rest with that body.

Ex Officio Member of the Board. The director will serve as an ex officio member of the board, and will discharge the following responsibilities in that role:

- Accounts to the board for all actions and decisions
- In conjunction with the board chair, prepares agendas for board meetings; takes charge of mailing agendas and other materials to board members
- Attends board meetings
- Provides and interprets information needed by the board for making policy decisions and for planning
- Presents regular reports to the board about all phases of program operation
- Makes recommendations to the board about the program regarding changes in direction, plans for future growth and expansion, etc.
- Provides linkage between board and staff
- Puts together information packets for new board members.

The director is also an ex officio member of board committees, with duties as follows:

Executive Committee	Responsibilities same as to full board.
Nominating Committee	Submits recommendations for individuals who are potential board members and officers.
Budget and Finance	Budget—provides assistance with preparation of the budget. Provides reports of expenditures. Oversees

	preparation of regular financial reports, audits, etc. Provides information about funding requirements.
	Finance—provides assistance in research of potential funding sources and helps with fund-raising efforts.
Personnel Committee	Provides assistance with the development of personnel policies. Recommends changes in policies, pay scale, and personnel structure. Works with the committee to clarify board and staff roles. Works with the committee to resolve grievances.
Public Relations	Provides assistance with planning and carrying out public relations efforts. Assists with development of internal publications such as brochures, flyers, and posters. Serves as liaison to other community organizations and agencies. Presents the program to the community. Speaks on behalf of the program to the media, groups, and individuals.
Program Committee	Provides assistance with the development of program goals. Recommends changes in goals. Works with the committee to carry out internal program evaluations.
Transportation Committee	Provides the committee with information concerning transportation needs of the program; makes recommendations concerning methods of transportation, purchase of vehicles, contractual arrangements, etc. Serves as liaison between the program and agencies who provide transportation.
Planning Committee	Provides information and makes recommendations for planning and development. Works with the committee to develop and carry out action plans for the organization.
Building Committee	Provides information and makes recommendations about the facility, including condition, safety, need for renovations, repairs, necessity for more space, etc.
Special Committees	Provides information, makes recommendations, and offers assistance as appropriate.

Board Developer. In addition to working with board committees, the director of the adult day care program must be willing to invest extra effort to cultivate a relationship with board members, sharing knowledge about the service, helping them to learn to serve more effectively, and contributing to board development. The result of this extra effort will be a more productive working relationship with the board. In this role, the director may plan and carry out some of the following activities.

- Provide assistance with planning and carrying out orientation and training of the board.
- Keep board members informed about the program.
- Provide new board members with informational materials about the organization and program: history, current status, purposes, goals, achievements.
- Extend invitations to new members to visit the center and meet the director.
- Hold periodic open house at the center for the board, offering members an opportunity to meet staff and participants and to see the program in operation.
- Provide assistance to the board in their self-assessment, helping to evaluate the board from the director's perspective, in such areas as:

  - Receptivity of the board to director's input into decision making process.
  - Familiarity of board members with goals of the program, and the needs of participants, and methods of service.
  - Availability of the board and its leadership to the director when needed.
  - Responsiveness of the board when program needs are called to their attention.
  - Understanding on the part of the board of the respective responsibilities of the director and the board, with effective discharge of those duties which are the province of the board.
  - Demonstration of confidence by the board in the ability of the director to implement policy; an absence of interference in the daily operation of the program.
  - Accordance of full respect due to the director for the professional contributions made to the program.
  - Clear delineation of lines of authority, with board and director fulfilling respective roles so that no vacuum of authority exists within the organization.
  - Support from the board for the director's involvement in community, state, and national activities which will contribute to the growth and development of adult day care.
  - Understanding by the board of the degree of competency required to be effective in the position of director and willingness to pay a fair and equitable wage.

Board Informant. The director must be responsible for keeping the board updated about all aspects of the program: successes, problems, needs. The board should also be kept informed about developments in the field, including new methods of service provision, changes in standards and licensure requirements, and legislative and financial developments. Information may be provided by either oral or written communication, or by both.

In using oral communication, whether in meetings or private conversations with individual board members, the director should follow basic guidelines.

- Stick to concrete data
- Be sure that data is accurate
- Use language which the board understands
- Be prepared for questions.

Guidelines for successful written communication include the following.

- Use to convey specific information
- Use an outline
- Have objectives firmly in mind
- Include all pertinent data
- Write from the frame of reference of the board. Keep in mind the distance of board members from the situation—what do they need to know?
- Write clearly and concisely
- Organize ideas.

Participant in Board Meetings. The director will assist the board chair to plan, prepare for, and carry out effective board meetings which achieve the purposes of reviewing and evaluating actions, planning, and setting policy.

Preparatory steps include agreeing upon an agenda for the meeting and making sure copies are mailed out to board members well in advance of the meeting, along with other background materials. Background materials include copies of minutes of the last meeting, committee reports, treasurer's report, and any other information board members will need to know prior to discussion of agenda items. The board chair and director should both be clear on details of agenda items before the meeting. Ideally, the director should arrive ahead of time and help to get the meeting set up. The director should be prepared to contribute to the board discussion.

Even though the board chair is the leader and facilitator of the board meeting, the director can be instrumental in helping to keep the meeting on track. This is accomplished by the director making the effort to act as a resource person, mediator, and coordinator.

Frequently it becomes the responsibility of the director to recommend specific actions to the board. In these instances, the recommended action should be offered as a solution to a problem, presented with information that includes available options. The information offered should define the problem, analyze the problem, offer possible solutions, give costs of solutions, in dollars or man hours. When the director wants to recommend one solution over others, options should be evaluated and reasons given as to why one is preferred. The director should also suggest a plan for implementing the recommended solution.

Board members should be provided with information prior to the meeting if they will be asked to make a decision on a major issue. The information may be relayed by written reports delivered in advance of the meeting or by the director or chair speaking personally with individual members. This preparation will allow board members to become familiar with background information and to think through ramifications of the problem without being pressured by restrictions of time allowed in the meeting. It also offers an opportunity to get any additional information requested, and is thus likely to result in better decisions being made.

The Director as Program Administrator

Fiscal Manager. The director will act with the board to ensure financial stability and sound fiscal management for the adult day care center. This may involve serving as an ex officio member of the board finance committee, providing assistance with budget preparation and with the treasurer, overseeing program accounting procedures to be sure that the accounting system complies with all legal and funding requirements. The fiscal manager will also be responsible for overseeing preparation of regular, detailed financial reports to the board. Finally, the director will carry out fiscal control practices to achieve financial accountability and maximum efficiency in use of program resources. These practices should include the following.

- Establish written procedures for purchase of supplies and equipment
- Require written authorization for those who handle funds or sign checks
- Require that all individuals who handle funds or financial records are bonded
- Establish written procedures for carrying out regular audits by an independent auditor
- Monitor expenditures on an ongoing basis to ensure that they remain within budgeted limits.

Personnel Manager. The role of personnel manager may include responsibility for:

- Working with the personnel committee of the board to develop personnel policies and job descriptions and to design the total staff structure for the program
- Providing linkage between the board and staff

- Recruiting, interviewing, and selecting staff members
- Conducting regular staff meetings
- Providing staff supervision
- Conducting periodic review and evaluation of staff job performance
- Making appropriate recommendations to the board for pay raises, promotions, or other indicated actions related to staff management
- Handling employee grievances according to personnel policies
- Acting to resolve staff conflict
- Maintaining awareness of staff needs and helping staff members to achieve personal work goals as a part of achieving goals of the program
- Planning and helping provide staff development and training
- Utilizing staff talents and abilities to the maximum for the greatest benefit to the program
- Delegating responsibilities to staff members as appropriate
- Discharging employees when necessary
- Organizing or supervising the volunteer program
    - Developing volunteer policies and job descriptions
    - Recruiting and training volunteers
    - Planning for use of volunteers
    - Supervising volunteers; carrying out evaluation and recognition activities
    - Planning and helping carry out volunteer orientation and training
    - Terminating volunteers, if necessary.

Public Relations Representative. The image of the program projected by the director, is, to a large degree, the image which shapes public perception of the program. For this reason, the position carries much of the responsibility for building public support for the program. The director should work with the public relations committee of the board to develop and carry out an ongoing public relations campaign. In addition, as the program representative, the director should help to build working relationships with other community service agencies and organizations. Also included should be an effort to educate the community about the need for and effectiveness of the service. This effort can include:

- Speaking to community groups
- Serving as a training resource for community workshops, seminars, etc.

- Serving on boards or advisory groups for other community service agencies
- Joining inter-agency professional organizations
- Offering the center as a training forum for students.

Center Manager. The director has responsibility for the day-to-day operation of the center, directing and overseeing the following activities and procedures.

- Meeting certification and licensure requirements
- Maintaining census levels
- Making decisions and instituting actions to solve problems and crises which arise at the center
- Providing information requested by funding bodies, public officials, service agencies, and others who are in need of such information
- Supervising and managing the center office to ensure that good office practices are instituted and maintained
    - All necessary records are current and updated as appropriate
    - Correspondence is kept current
    - Files are in order
    - Telephone inquiries are handled appropriately
    - Telephone messages are accurately recorded and promptly relayed to the proper person
- Supervising housekeeping to ensure that proper cleanliness is maintained
- Monitoring condition of the building to make sure that any necessary repairs are made as needed; planning for appropriate use of space; overseeing safety practices.

The Director as Program Manager

The program managerial function of the director requires overseeing and supervising all facets of service delivery.

Coordinator of the Admissions Team. With other appropriate staff or professional personnel, the director reviews individual information obtained from applicants and decides whether adult day care is the most appropriate method of care for the individual.

Coordinator of Service Planning. With other members of the care team, the director takes part in decisions concerning the service planning for individual participants.

Program Planner. The director is responsible for overseeing program planning and methods of carrying out program activities and service delivery.

Outreach Worker. As outreach worker, the director makes appropriate contact within the community to solicit referrals of potential participants for the program and conducts or supervises appropriate follow-up.

Counselor. Discharge of counselling duties involves acting as a mentor and advisor to staff and providing support to participants and to their families.

Work Load

The duties of an adult day care director, covering so many roles and responsibilities, may appear to be unmanageable. The foregoing discussion is a comprehensive listing of *all* responsibilities required for management of an adult day care program. Whether all duties described here will be carried out personally by the director is dependent upon a number of factors:

- The number of other staff employed in the program and the duties assigned to those positions.
- The structure of the organization: whether the board or advisory group works exclusively with the adult day care program and how much of the work load is carried by that body. If the board has responsibility for other programs and there is no advisory group solely responsible for working with the adult day care program, then the director will be expected to assume more responsibilities.
- Where the program is in its development: whether other staff positions are filled and the staff is functioning, or whether the director is the only staff person employed initially, making it necessary that responsibilities be assumed by the director which will later be assigned to other staff. These and other variables will affect the work load which the director will carry, as will the ability of the individual to effectively delegate tasks to others.

In almost all instances, however, the words of President Truman will be found to hold true for adult day care directors: "The buck stops here." Whether the actual work is done by the director or delegated to others, the ultimate responsibility for seeing that it is completed with the desired result will belong to the director. This should not be taken to mean that the director must attempt to carry a work load which is unreasonable and untenable. Every new director of an adult day care program should examine the job description and ascertain the expectations of the board or governing body for the position: If the work load appears to be such that one person cannot carry it out effectively—or if appears likely that early "burn-out" may result from attempting to fulfill expectations—he or she should negotiate for assistance.

Job Description

The job description for the position of director should be specific, while leaving room for obtaining needed assistance or for delegating tasks. (See Appendix A for a sample job description.)

Salary Range

The salary for the director should be set as high as is possible within the budget, commensurate with the qualifications required and the work load of the position. Low salaries will neither attract nor retain the highly qualified individual who is needed to successfully help with implementation and to operate the program.

Line of Authority

There should be a specific authority structure, specifying to whom the director is directly responsible: board chair, executive committee, full board, other? Paramaters of the position should be fully delineated, including power for decisions in the program operation; authority to hire, fire, and manage staff; representation of the program in the community; budget management; other.

Qualifications

Training and Experience. The director's background may include several possible combinations of education and work experience which will allow flexibility in selection. If the job description does not allow for flexibility, a highly desirable individual may have to be turned down for lack of one aspect of training or experience.

Skills and Knowledge. Qualifications may not be accurately reflected by training and work experience and should be listed separately and specifically: understanding of adult day care and its population; administrative skills; social, etc.

Personal Characteristics. Terminology must be carefully chosen in regard to personal characteristics; labor laws specify that only those personal qualities that can be demonstrated through an individual's work history can be named in a job description. Acceptable descriptive phrases include "creative," "emotionally stable," "highly motivated," and "self-starter."

Duties and Responsibilities

Administrative Duties. Administrative duties should be based upon administrative functions as outlined above. Use of words such as "supervise," "oversee," "manage," will allow room for the director to delegate or obtain needed assistance, while retaining final responsibility.

Program Duties. Program duties should be outlined as stated above. Again, wording should allow flexibility in discharge of duties.

Variables in the Job Description

Factors which must be considered when writing the job description are:

- Specific structure of the program
- Structure of the governing body (whether it is a working board or a board which acts only to set policy)
- Functional level of participants
- Services to be provided
- Financial status of the program
- Availability of community resources
- Other staff positions to be filled
- Any other relevant factors.

Summary

Perhaps no other decision made by the board or governing body of an adult day care program will have as much impact upon the program as the selection of the director. The search for the right person should take as long as needed to ascertain that the most qualified person available is selected. Many of the qualities needed in the position are hard to measure or objectify, making it necessary that the interviewers be skilled in interview techniques which will obtain the maximum amount of information. Discussions in the interviews should make clear the organization's expectations from the person selected, so that the people under consideration have an understanding of the responsibilities and will be able to make an informed judgements about whether their abilities are sufficient to meet expectations.

Adult day care directors wear many hats and function in a variety of situations, relating to a heterogeneous group of people. If this is not understood from the outset, the director may become overwhelmed by the tasks required to implement and manage the adult day care program. This may lead to a resignation with resulting loss of time and momentum. It is imperative that those who fill the position be completely conversant with the qualifications and characteristics needed to carry out the duties in an effective way.

Reference

Padula, H. 1983. *Developing adult day care for older people, a technical assistance monograph.* Washington, DC: National Council on the Aging, Inc.

11 The Director: Controlling Time and Responsibilities

Introduction

As discussed in Chapter 10, the director of an adult day care program has numerous duties, dissimilar in nature and requiring ability to organize and manage the work in ways which demonstrate leadership capability and support effective program operation. Chapter 11 is addressed *to* the director, with suggestions for fulfilling this broad role. Strategies and methods will be discussed which may be used by the director to control the responsibilities in ways which will enhance the capacity to provide effectual guidance for the program.

Organizing the Work Load

A first step in organization of work is recognizing the full extent of all tasks included in the role of director. Using the job description for the position and knowledge of the job, the director may compile a list of all work to be carried out by the director. The listing of work may be best done in two stages.

The Master List

First, a master list should be compiled of all work which is in any way the responsibility of the director. This will include work done in conjunction with the board or advisory committee, community agencies and other service providers, and staff, as well as those tasks which must be discharged by the director acting alone. The list should include all roles which are listed in the job description, with a complete breakdown of all functions encompassed within each role. It should be emphasized that all roles assigned to the director should be included within the job description. If, after the work listing is completed, there appears to be a marked discrepancy between the job description and the work necessary to program management, the job description must be revised to reflect the actual work load of the position.

After listing all functions, tasks may be further categorized as follows.

1. Tasks for which the director has full responsibility
2. Tasks which will be carried out in conjunction with the governing body or with a committee of that body
3. Tasks which will be carried out in conjunction with the full staff, with an individual member of the staff, with a program consultant, with volunteers, or with any others who may act in the role of program staff
4. Tasks which will entail working with another community agency or group
5. Tasks for which the director has the final responsibility, but which have some components delegated to others
6. Tasks which can be completely delegated.

This listing, in conjunction with the job description, will serve as a master work plan for the director and should be kept posted and easily accessible. The plan should be consulted each day to be sure that work is being carried out in conformity with the plan. This will help the director to feel comfortable that all required tasks are being discharged.

Review and revision should be carried out periodically to ensure that the plan remains an accurate statement of the work to be done. Such revision will be needed as the program grows and changes, altering the director's responsibilities.

The Specific Task List

A second listing that will prove helpful is a continuous task list, including all work currently in progress: all current assignments, commitments, ideas to be acted upon, phone calls to be made or returned, correspondence needing a response, etc. This list of specific tasks should cover all work which is the total or partial responsibility of the director: work being done alone; work which has been partially delegated; work completely delegated but requiring oversight, approval, or direction; as well as work for which results are to be reported upon.

This list should be maintained in a notebook or legal pad which will not be misplaced and which lends itself to daily updating. It should be kept with the daily calendar or schedule, so that it can be easily reached to record completion or progress on the work listed.

The list should be used as a tool to help plan the work of each day, with new tasks being added as they arise and others being deleted as they are completed. Tasks of high priority should be highlighted by underlining or starring, to help the director see at a glance those tasks which must be included in the work of each day.

In addition to serving as a tool for daily planning, the list helps the director to gain better control of the work load of the position.

Prioritizing Work

A further step in organizing and controlling the work load is that of developing a system for prioritizing tasks.

Given the number of duties to be discharged by the director, it is essential that a method be developed to assign a higher priority to some tasks than others; all work is not of equal importance to the program. Controlling the work load demands that the director be able to distinguish between those tasks requiring immediate or personal attention and those which can be deferred, delegated, or eliminated. Using the continuous task list and with knowledge of the program, the director may rank each task by use of the following criteria.

Highest priority should be assigned to those tasks which are critical, or which must be done today. *Examples:* Funding reports which are due immediately, or so soon as to require that work must begin immediately; reports to other agencies with service contracts or which provide services or funds and which have a deadline for completion; billing reports; scheduled meetings with funders; paperwork for emergency discharge of a participant.

Second in priority are those tasks which must be finalized. *Examples:* Decision about admission of a participant; selection of a new employee from among applicants; final arrangement for a staff development or fund-raising event.

Third in priority are those tasks which must have some components completed today, but can have other components deferred to a later date. *Examples:* Beginning work on a budget report or report to the board; necessary paperwork for admission of a participant; placing an advertisement for filling a staff position.

Last in priority are those tasks which are routine. *Examples:* Correspondence; daily reports; making or returning phone calls which are not urgent; information gathering, etc.

After tasks are ranked in this manner, further prioritization may be needed, and this may be facilitated by breaking each task scheduled for the day into manageable components; rescheduling any components not requiring immediate attention or action; eliminating any tasks which are extraneous to effective program operation; and delegating or referring to others all tasks which can or should be handled by others.

Scrutinizing the work of each day in this way will enable the director to make informed decisions about what must be included in the schedule for the work of that day.

Delegation of Tasks

The director must recognize that the work load of the position will be unmanageable without an ability to delegate some portion of the work to others. It is imperative that skills for delegation be developed.

Inability to delegate effectively can be caused by several weaknesses: lack of confidence in self or in ability to give orders; lack of organizational skills; a refusal to allow mistakes; feelings that the job can't be completed correctly by others; or a disinclination to develop the ability of the staff. The director must realize that time spent carrying out tasks which can and should be done by others will be more productive for

Exhibit 11-1 Tasks the director should delegate.

The director *should* delegate:

1. Tasks which are included within the job description of other staff members. For example, the director should not perform secretarial tasks if there is a secretary on staff. Routine correspondence, filing, and screening of phone calls and visitors should be assigned to the secretarial position.
2. Tasks within the capability of other staff members whose job responsibilities allow time for carrying out of additional duties. For example, many staff members are capable of keeping participant files updated, tracking admission procedures, updating the activity calendar, etc.
3. Tasks which are routine and can be handled by a staff member whose time is not as expensive as that of the director. For example, routine reports, telephone calls, and shopping.
4. Components of complex tasks requiring the work of more than one person. For example, planning and carrying out craft sales or other fund-raisers; planning staff development events; and carrying out admission procedures.

---

the program if instead it is used to fulfill the duties which *must* be done by the director, including planning, supervising, coaching and training, and developing the team concept among the staff. Decisions about what should be delegated and to whom should be made following the structure of the organization. The organizational chart should be used to learn lines of designated communication and accountability. Exhibit 11-1 discusses delegation in greater detail.

Effective delegation is dependent upon many factors.

- The appropriate person must be chosen, i.e., the individual whose job description includes such responsibility and who is able to carry out the assignment.
- The exact parameters of the assignment must be clearly delineated. The person to whom the assignment is made must be clear about what is to be done, the time line for reporting progress or task completion, and what results are expected.
- The individual carrying out the assignment should be offered any needed backup and support. This may be provided by either the director or by someone acting for the director.
- The individual chosen must be allowed to complete the task in an individual fashion unless the proposed methods will in some way be damaging to the program. The task is assigned in order to get designated results, not to demonstrate use of specific methods.

- Accountability must be required. A time table should be set for discussing progress or problems and regular conferences held to devise any needed changes in strategies or schedule. The schedule must be reasonable and within the capability of the person doing the work. The director may save time by requesting that reports be summarized rather than presented in full at each discussion or conference. Again, the assignment is for getting results.
- Accomplishment should be recognized and given full credit. This should be done both privately and publicly.

When delegation of tasks is well planned and carried out, the director and the program reap many rewards. First, the director's time is freed for other more complex or demanding tasks. The program operates more easily and efficiently. Leadership potential, knowledge, and competence are developed among the staff, making it possible for the director to delegate more tasks and more complex responsibilities. This becomes increasingly important as the program grows. Finally, there is a lessening of stress for the director, allowing more effective discharge of other duties.

There are basically two kinds of delegation. The director can assign to a subordinate total responsibility for a job or component of a job. In this instance the director will ask only that the staff member carry out the job and report when the task is completed. Expected results must be clearly stated and understood by both the director and the person receiving the assignment. Or, the director may use partial delegation. In this case, only the task is delegated, with no responsibility or authority for making decisions. Rather, the director will expect to be kept informed and will retain the right to make any necessary decision. Examples of partial delegation include gathering information, exploring available alternatives and preparing a report outlining these, completing paperwork for a participant admission, etc.

The director is responsible for making sure that the person receiving the assignment understands exactly what is being delegated. The parameters of the assignment should be stated or written in a memo. The person assigned the work may be asked to repeat the terms of the assignment or to sign the memo to indicate an understanding of what is expected.

Scheduling Work

It is critical that adult day care directors schedule and carry out the work of each day without getting bogged down in the minutiae which arise during each day in the day care center. To achieve this focus, the director should spend some time each day planning the work to be done that day. By consulting the task list and using the criteria outlined for prioritizing, the director can transfer the tasks to be included in the day's schedule to a daily work sheet. In addition to tasks from the task list, all appointments, new assignments, errands, or other commitments from the daily appointment calendar must be included. Additional tasks which may not have been written down, but which the director is aware of, also may have to be included. If these tasks do not meet the criteria for inclusion, they should be added to the master list. Exhibit 11-2 lists some helpful rules for planning the workday.

Managing Interruptions

Few days in the work life of an adult day care director go by without unscheduled or unexpected events occurring. Some of these events demand immediate attention; others can be prevented by use of forethought in planning, still others can be delegated for necessary action or be deferred to a later time. The director must arrive at a method for judging which category each interruption fits into and devise a system for keeping those which demand immediate attention at a minimum. To do otherwise will have the effect of leaving each day unplanned, with the director spending a large percentage of time reacting to such events, rather than exercising control over responsibilities.

The decision about which category unexpected events fit into will vary from program to program and with each director, depending upon the size of the program, number of staff, and the personal management style of the director. Among methods which may be used to forestall interruptions are the following.

- Schedule blocks of time to be available to staff for questions, advice, and conferences. Staff members should be familiar with this policy and know when time will be available so that they can make it a part of their schedule.
- Train staff to make a habit of requesting appointments to discuss issues of concern which cannot fit into or will not wait until the regularly scheduled time.
- Train staff to understand the director's definition of an emergency or crisis which justifies an interruption, and to recognize which situations can be dealt with by others and which can be deferred for later action. These definitions can only be decided upon by the director and must be clearly communicated to the staff.
- Ensure that the secretary and other staff feel comfortable handling routine calls or visitors during times when the director has scheduled uninterrupted time. The director must make clear what types of calls or visitors justify interruptions.
- Encourage leadership potential among staff, helping them to develop skills for handling crisis situations. The director will not always be present in the center and must be able to trust staff members to act if a crisis occurs during an absence. One person should be designated to be in charge in the director's absence so that there is no confusion about who will make necessary decisions.

Exhibit 11-2 Rules for planning the work day.

Rules for planning work day:

1. Do not overschedule. Experience will teach how much can be accomplished during a day. Attempting to do more than can be reasonably expected may result in work being poorly done, a high level of stress, or both.
2. Mark or star tasks of highest priority or urgency and work to accomplish those first.
3. Allow some time each day which is not structured or scheduled. This is flexible time to be used to handle interruptions or unexpected events.
4. Classify tasks as either "demanding" or "routine." Block out uninterrupted time to complete tasks requiring a high level of concentration; Schedule these tasks for a time when mental energy is at its highest level.
5. Group like tasks. Set aside a block of time for phone calls, report preparation (information needed for one report is often that which will be needed for others), or meetings with individual staff members. Changes in pace and concentration consume time, and using this strategy prevents having to make changes too frequently.
6. Try to schedule tasks to be done outside the center (meetings, errands, etc.) for consecutive blocks of time, so that one trip will take care of several obligations.
7. Analyze tasks which must be done in conjunction with others so that the appropriate amount of time can be scheduled for these. Remember to learn the schedule of others who are involved so that the time scheduled will fit into their time schedule.
8. Try to plan each day's schedule to include a mix of high and low priority items.
9. Break each scheduled task into its smallest components and work on one component at a time.
10. If meetings are on the schedule, be sure that adequate preparation is made and all needed materials or information are available. This will preclude having to hold subsequent meetings to take care of business which could have been handled at the first.
11. Meetings being chaired by the director should have all preparations made prior to meeting time: the agenda set; information needed by those attending the meeting sent out ahead of time; any information relevant to discussion readily available. Meetings should start and end on time; the chair should control the meeting to be sure that the agenda is followed and that discussions stick to the point. If meetings are frequent and time consuming, an analysis is in order to determine if some meetings may be grouped.
12. If too much work is scheduled for the day, the director should scrutinize the list again to decide which tasks or components of tasks can be deferred, rescheduled or, delegated.

The staff must recognize, however, that final responsibility for the program rests with the director and learn to be perceptive about not making decisions or taking responsibilities which are the province of the director. They should also be conscientious about reporting fully on any actions which are taken in the absence of the director.

Controlling Tasks

It is easy for the director to lose sight of long-range goals and plans during the hectic pace of each day. However, if the day has been well-planned and if interruptions are skillfully handled, the director should be able to retain control of the majority of the working time and be able to achieve goals set for the day.

The director should stress to staff that all messages and other information relayed to the director should be accurate and contain all pertinent information. The secretary and other staff members should learn to gather all information needed for the director if they expect action on any materials passed on by them. The director must be firm about interruptions, setting time limits upon conversations and deferring any problems or questions which can be dealt with later, thus helping staff learn to respect the time and schedule of the director.

The director should delegate all possible work to others, including information gathering, passing on routine messages, greeting unexpected visitors, etc. An aid in delegation is to develop form letters and reports which can be used for routine inquiries or in response to routine correspondence. These should be updated as needed.

The director should never make the same decision more than twice. If the same problem arises more than twice, a policy should be set for handling it in the future.

The telephone should be used as a tool to save time; the director should be careful not to allow it to control the schedule. Rather, a time for accepting calls should be set aside, and the phone should be used to eliminate meetings or errands, to gather information, etc.

Overlapping on tasks whenever possible will save time. Routine mail can be read and notes can be made on the letter, giving the secretary instructions for answering while making phone calls; work on similar reports simultaneously; brief all staff at the same time rather than individually, etc.

Most importantly, start on a task and stay with it until it is completed or until a natural stopping point has been reached.

Developing a Productive Work Style

The work and leadership style of each director is different. It is essential to good management that each director analyze working habits and strive to develop a style which is effective and productive, eliminating those practices and attitudes which detract from optimum functioning. Exhibit 11-3 details non-productive work practices, and Exhibit 11-4 discusses the kinds of habits and attitudes that should be avoided as non-productive.

Exhibit 11-3 Non-productive work practices.

Examples of non-productive work habits:

Failure to handle interruptions.

Failure to delegate appropriately.

Failure to organize and plan work. Directors need to recognize that planning time is not wasted, but is essential to avoid spending an inordinate amount of time "putting out fires," and *reacting* to situations rather than *acting* in ways which are orderly and systematic.

Failure to eliminate unnecessary work which is not rightfully that of the director. Each aspect of the work load should be analyzed to ensure that it is both necessary to management of the program and is indeed the responsibility of the director. Members of the governing body, staff, and others who should be assisting the director must be held responsible for those tasks which are a part of their duties. It is often left to the director to define parameters of the position, while also helping educate other members of the work team to recognize duties which constitute their role and responsibility.

Attempting to do too much. Most adult day care directors often cannot do all they feel they need to do and are expected to do. When this happens, they have a responsibility to analyze both the work load and their working methods to determine whether work can be further delegated and whether it can be better organized. If neither of these are possible, the director must ask for additional help.

In addition to non-productive work practices and attitudes, a lack of organization in the place of work may contribute to the inability to carry out work at top performance level. The office or work area should be examined for evidence of disorganization and for ways in which the space may be improved to enhance work ability. The desk area should be clear of everything except the project being worked on and any materials needed for information. When a project is completed it should be cleared away. *Filing* needs an efficient system. Files should be cleared periodically and obsolete or unnecessary materials discarded. Files should be reorganized so that they lend themselves to easy identification. Color coding is a helpful method. For example, red tabs can be used for participant files, brown for personnel, green for budget, etc. Equipment should be at hand and in good repair: typewriter, pencil sharpener, copier, calculator. Office furniture should be ample and comfortable: desk the right height and size; chair offering support and comfortable for long periods of sitting. The bookcase containing reference materials should be large enough and in a convenient location. Files should be within easy reach. *The environment* should also be examined. Is the area well lighted with non-glare lighting? Are acoustics such that the noise level is kept to a minimum? Is the work area pleasant, containing plants and pictures or other furnishings contributing to an agreeable atmosphere?

Exhibit 11-4 Non-productive work attitudes.

Examples of non-productive work attitudes:

Perfectionism. Perfectionists expect that desired results will be achieved 100 percent of the time and also that specific methods must be used to achieve those results. Indulging in such expectations is counter-productive. Leeway must be allowed for both the director and staff to make mistakes and to fail. Valuable lessons are often learned from mistakes; precautions in this area should be to avoid making mistakes which may have serious consequences for participants and staff and to avoid making the same mistake over and over.

Procrastination. Putting off necessary tasks until a crisis develops is fatal to good management of adult day care. Among techniques to use in helping overcome the tendency to procrastinate:

- Identify action steps of a task and make a start; begin with the easiest or most obvious step.
- Divide major projects into their smallest components and complete one component at a time.
- Set up a time schedule for completion of each component and for completion of the entire project. Constantly monitor progress toward these goals.
- Post reminders of the schedule on a bulletin board or other place where it will serve as a constant reminder.
- Once a job is started, stay with it until it is completed or a natural stopping place is reached.
- Make a start on the first task to be done the next morning before leaving work each day. Leave work on the desk where it will be seen on arrival.
- Allow some time for limited procrastination in stressful situations and if time permits. Take breaks when needed, or schedule some time for rest and relaxation. But set a definite time for beginning or resuming work.
- Create an environment which is conducive to working: quiet, restful, with music or whatever stimulates or helps to sustain good work habits.
- Change environments if necessary. The atmosphere in adult day care centers is often hectic and lends itself to procrastination. Work may be taken home or to a quieter location when this happens or when interruptions cannot be controlled long enough to complete tasks.

Indecision. Failure to make a decision is to make a decision. Adult day care directors will recognize that there is some risk involved in the position and that some decisions will require making hard choices. Making the best decision in the circumstances will have to be their goal. Decision-making can be facilitated by:

- Collecting as much information as is available
- Outlining the parameters of the problem
- Deciding upon the most desirable outcome

Exhibit 11-4, continued.

- Studying attainable alternatives
- Evaluating consequences of each alternative
- Selecting what appears to be the most attractive alternative
- Implementing the decision.

The director should allow ample time for making the decision, but once adequate information is available, there should be no further delay.

Rigidity or lack of flexibility. There are few human service programs which demand more flexibility on the part of the director than adult day care. Attempting to manage the program without the ability to adapt to changing situations and circumstances is likely to be unsuccessful. Overcoming a tendency to be rigid will require learning and accepting new methods of job performance, incorporating attitudes that are responsive to each situation which arises in the program.

Lack of concentration. Although daily events in most adult day care programs make it difficult to maintain concentration for an extended period, the director must find ways to work around this circumstance to be able to carry out responsibilities. Some techniques for doing so are the same as those for correcting habits of procrastination. Others which may prove helpful:

- Plan to do work requiring the greatest concentration during hours when there is least distraction, perhaps in early morning or late afternoon. Recognize what time of day mental energy is highest.
- Agree with the staff on a time of day when they will help keep distractions at a minimum by planning quiet activities or taking participants for field trips or outside activities.

Good management means first and foremost that directors learn to manage themselves, developing good work habits and attitudes which are productive and will result in effective programs. The first step in the learning process is an analysis of personal work styles to ascertain both strengths and weaknesses of present style. Keeping time logs for a certain interval (perhaps one to two weeks) to document how time is presently being spent (and with what results) is a way to get information needed for an analysis. During this period, normal time schedules should be followed so that information will be accurate and useful for the purpose. Analysis of the time logs should reveal:

- The present working styles
- Present working practices and attitudes which need improvement
- Strengths the director possesses to help overcome these
- How to develop the desired working style.

Exhibit 11-5 The management process.

1. Plan—set objectives, develop strategies, decide upon procedures.
2. Organize—establish structure in the work lead; prioritize.
3. Direct—delegate, motivate, coordinate, manage necessary changes
4. Control—require accountability, establish an effective reporting system, set performance standards, measure results, take any needed corrective action, reward satisfactory performance.

Source: McKenzie, A.R. 1972. *The time trap*. New York: AMACOM, a division of the American Management Association.

With this information, the directors are ready to set goals and work toward improvement. They should not attempt to work toward a total revision of any undesirable work habits all at once. Rather, it is best to effect improvements in one area before beginning work on improvement of another. Change and improvement are a gradual process.

Summary

Under the best of circumstances, leadership of a human services program such as adult day care is stressful for staff, requiring much physical, mental, and emotional energy. To work effectively in the position, directors must learn to recognize their personal limitations and to work at a pace and style which is comfortable and suitable for them. For example, one director may favor short bursts of intense effort, while another alternates hours of intense effort with work requiring minimum effort. Directors may intersperse work time with some relaxing activity, such as a visit to the program, or alternate periods of concentration with work of a more social nature: meeting with staff or visitors. Consciously deciding when to continue pushing to finish a project or when to stop working because tiredness develops, is part of a good working style. Recognizing the point when work becomes non-productive makes sense for the adult day care director. A rest or break allows replenishment of energy and will result in greater productivity in the long run.

Learning and using logical steps in the management process, as set forth in Exhibit 11-5, will help to simplify work.

Effective management also requires good communication. The director will need to make sure that the staff understands goals of management and the director's conceptualization of the adult day care program and that the staff is willing to work toward these goals.

The director must also provide rewards for achievements. Whatever allows feelings of reward should be indulged in periodically by the director and allowed for the staff. Rewards may be in the form of breaks, an occasional day off, or spending time socializing together. Any methods which achieve feelings of satisfaction and self-reward will pay off in terms of reduced stress and decreased likelihood of premature "burn-out" on the job.

Reference

McKenzie, A.R. 1972. *The time trap*. New York, NY: AMACOM, a division of the American Management Association.

12 Design of Effective Staff Structure

Introduction

Fundamental to successful adult day care is a carefully constructed design for staffing the program that facilitates making perceptive choices in selection of staff members. Many adult day care programs employ staff without having first worked out a plan for the total staff structure. The result may resemble a house constructed without benefit of a blueprint. By carefully considering how well the staff structure will "fit" other program components, planners can decide what positions are needed, what skills are needed for each position, and the most desirable combination of personnel categories—including paid staff, consultants, volunteers, and contractual services.

The position of director will probably need to be filled before the design is completed, since it is beneficial to have input from the director during the early planning stages and in making staffing decisions. However, the program's major focus and specific program goals should be decided upon before the director is employed.

Factors Influencing Staff Design

Among the obvious factors affecting staffing decisions are source of funding, budget constraints, availability of qualified staff, and program size.

Source of Funding

As discussed in Chapter 1, models of adult day care have often been developed in response to regulations governing sources of funds. For example, Title XIX regulations state that participants must require "active" health care services before they are eligible for adult day care paid for with these funds. Thus a large percentage of programs funded primarily by Title XIX have tended to emphasize health care professionals in the staff. Similarly, those programs funded primarily by Title XX have placed less emphasis upon medical health care provision and have given at least equal consideration to provision of social services. The result has been to have a large portion of the staff made up of professionals in the social services field.

In contrast, private funding sources such as foundations and the United Way may not require any specific care orientation, expecting only that the program will provide services as stipulated by terms of the grant, which is usually drawn up by the adult day care provider. Many foundations do, however, have areas of service priority and will fund only those programs whose applications demonstrate that the service will focus on areas within their priority list. This sometimes forces providers to structure their programs to fit a foundation's interest spectrum in order to qualify for funds from a specific foundation.

All contracts with funding sources must be scrutinized to determine any specific conditions of the funding which may affect how the program staff is to be structured so that staffing will be in conformity with terms of the agreement.

Budget Constraints

Although staff salaries are usually the largest item in an adult day care budget, most programs will still have to juggle the desired skill levels and number of staff members if they are to remain within budget limits. A common program goal is that of serving participants who are in greatest need of the service. These are often individuals who need highly concentrated care, and, consequently a higher staff-to-participant ratio and staff skill level. Planning the staff structure to stay within budgetary restrictions while carrying out this and other program goals and meeting high standards of quality will demand that planners keep program goals firmly fixed in mind. They will have to exercise flexibility and creativity in designing the structure, writing job descriptions, and selecting staff.

Availability of Staff

The number of qualified individuals available for employment will influence the structure of the adult day care staff. If there is a shortage locally of the trained professionals needed to plan and carry out services to meet program goals, and of the individuals qualified to work as staff assistants and aides, the adult day care program may experience difficulty attracting desirable staff. This will be especially true if salaries are not competitive.

To compensate when salaries are not competitive, and if staff is not readily available, the program must offer rewards other than monetary to attract staff members with the desired qualifications. A desirable working environment, opportunities for improving skills and for helping to improve quality of life for participants are features of working in an adult day care program which might interest potential staff members with the needed qualifications.

It is recommended, however, that salaries be set as high as the budget will allow. Individuals who are well-qualified are aware of their own worth and are likely to feel resentment when not adequately compensated for their abilities and efforts. Dissatisfaction leads to high staff turnover, since many staff members will leave if a more attractive opportunity arises. Almost nothing is as detrimental to program quality and success as a high turnover rate.

Program Size

Staff numbers should be sufficient to serve the number of participants enrolled and to meet staff-participant ratios required by state certification and licensure regulations and possibly by funding regulations. The National Institute on Adult Daycare (1984) recommends a minimum ratio of one staff member to eight participants, with a higher ratio if the program is to serve severely impaired participants.

It must be emphasized that a one-to-eight ratio is a minimum standard, adequate only when participants have relatively high functional capacity. A highly rehabilitative program may have an extremely low ratio of one professional staff person to 1-3 participants; other programs may barely meet the minimum standard. The very low ratio would not be recommended for most programs, since the cost would prevent them from operating.

If the staff ratio is to be the minimum, however, careful attention must be paid to admission of participants who will require extensive staff time, including help with ambulation, eating, toileting. Those who are disoriented or have a tendency to wander will also require greater staff attention.

For all programs, staffing decisions must take into account the amount of time spent on administrative duties as well as on clerical and bookkeeping responsibilities and program planning. When the program has a small staff, each member may have to assume multiple roles.

For safety and protection of staff and participants, however, it is strongly recommended that *all* programs, from the first day of service, have no less than two staff members present at the center at all times when participants are present.

Many programs expect that the director will be able to carry out all necessary staff duties when the program is new and/or the participant census is small. Adult day care is a complex service with many facets and requirements from the staff. No one individual is capable of performing all administrative and planning duties while also providing care for participants. When the director is the only staff member, some tasks will of necessity be left undone. An attempt to carry out all duties necessary to program operation may result in the director's becoming exhausted and leaving the program.

Admission Policies

Care must be taken that the staff structure includes persons with skills appropriate for meeting needs of the types of participants admitted to the program under admission policies. For example, if participants with severe physical disabilities are to be admitted, provision must be made for meeting their health care needs. Medical care professionals may be required. The amount and level of care provided will depend upon the exact parameters of the population to be admitted, including the severity of disabilities and the numbers admitted with very low functional levels.

By making a careful assessment of these parameters, centers may provide the needed care by a variety of methods. They may choose to employ staff who work on-site and have the necessary skills or else they can refer participants to other health care agencies for services beyond their staff's capability. In addition, contractual arrangements with consultants or other health care providers can be made, and part-time professional staff can be shared with other adult day care centers or service organizations.

Centers admitting participants with severe cognitive impairments must have staff available who are skilled in working with adults with these disabilities. The staff member providing this care may be a nurse, counselor, psychologist, social worker, or other professional or para-professional.

Much of the care for individuals with cognitive impairments must be furnished on-site, since the need for care is usually more constant than for those with physical impairments of the level typically present in adult day care programs.

Other special populations—developmentally disabled, orthopedically handicapped, those suffering from brain trauma—will require a staff structure capable of meeting their needs. They must not be admitted and left without the care needed to help them reach their highest functioning potential.

Admission policies must state the specific characteristics of the population to be served in the program. Those who are admitted have the right to expect that their needs will be cared for in a way which is most beneficial to them. Those in charge will want the program to be much more than a service which is only a "sitter" service.

Providing a program which supplies the appropriate care for each participant can only be accomplished when staff skills are carefully matched to the needs of those admitted so that services are available as needed.

Program Goals and Services

Goals for the adult day care program and plans for services and activities should be in agreement with design of the staff structure. When employment of the staff begins, each position should be filled with an understanding of the role to be carried out in support of program goals and the plans for services and activities to be offered. For example, to cover social services and case management, planners would seek some staff qualified in social work. Medical health care requires a physician (on-site, by arrangement, consultant, or other), RN, LPN, or other professional, depending upon the level required by the program plan. (See Appendix A for a sample job description for an RN.) Any specific therapies included in program plans must have staff qualified to provide the therapy—physical, occupational, speech, etc. For educational activities, the program needs staff with teaching or training skills. Program planners should obligate the program for only those services which can be provided, either on-site or by contractual arrangements.

All programs, however, must be staffed to offer those services which are intrinsic to adult day care (Chapter 19 of this manual discusses these fundamental services).

These and additional services needed by a majority of participants who enroll under terms of program admission policies should constitute the highest priority in program planning and implementation.

Staff Qualifications

Locating staff applicants will not usually present difficulty; locating and attracting applicants who are suited to work within the adult day care environment is likely to be more difficult. The qualifications of those who apply should be evaluated in three areas:

- Training and experience
- Skills and abilities
- Personal characteristics.

Training and Experience

It is unlikely that staff will be readily available with training or previous experience in provision of adult day care. Instead, most programs must accept staff with relevant or equivalent training and work experience. All staff should have had training and experience in the *type* of work they will be required to perform. The director should have administrative, program planning, and staff supervision experience; the activities coordinator, experience in planning and implementing group activities for impaired adults; the driver, experience in transporting impaired or handicapped adults, and so on.

Staff members in most adult day care programs must be capable of more than one role; versatility, with multiple interests and skills, is invaluable for those who work in the program. Programs may look for individuals whose major training and work experience has been in the area for which they will have primary responsibility, but who also possess broader interests and abilities.

Skills and Abilities

Certain abilities are essential for all persons who work in an adult day care program. They should be able to function as a team member, to set goals and make decisions, to handle emergencies, and to take appropriate action. Each staff member must be observant, noting behavior and appearance of participants and using the information to aid in planning appropriate care.

To a large extent, all staff must be self-starters, able to plan and carry out the work in their area of responsibility independently. They must be able to improvise and to adapt plans to meet changed circumstances.

Each staff member must be able to work with participants in groups and as individuals. Planners should select persons who are able to work with participants who exhibit problem behaviors and with those who possess some degree of mental, emotional, or physical impairments.

All staff must accept that the job requires commitment and hard work; each person must be willing to go beyond job requirements as stated in the job description and to assume responsibility for whatever tasks need doing. There are no hard and fast divisions of duties in adult day care programs.

As a team, the staff must possess a composite of skills and abilities in the areas of program planning and implementation, counseling, working with families, provision of personal care, creativity in utilizing program and community resources, teaching, and planning and carrying out craft and leisure-time activities. Within the team there must be some members who are skilled in pursuing public relations, writing reports, keeping records, performing clerical duties, and providing transportation.

Personal Characteristics and Attitudes

The importance of personal qualities cannot be over-emphasized. Many individuals who are well-qualified in other respects may unfortunately lack the personality traits and the attitudes which are indispensable for adult day care staff.

Acceptance of and respect for people, emotional maturity, and flexibility are of the highest priority. Also essential are a sense of humor, common sense, patience, energy, and enthusiasm. Other necessary attributes include an interest in and concern for the aged, sensitivity to needs of impaired adults, a desire to help people that is manifested in ways which contribute to independence and growth for the recipient.

All staff must be competent, ethical, and have respect for the confidentiality of any information concerning participants and their families.

All individuals who work in adult day care must understand and support the philosophy and goals of the service. Those who have had past experience and training in similar or related services must be able to adapt to the new service approach, and not remain wedded to methods learned and practiced in former work experience.

Provision of training for inexperienced personnel who are open to learning is preferable to attempting to re-train individuals who are insistent upon doing things in a certain way because that is the way they have been taught. This is especially true if these methods are in conflict with or do not support achievement of adult day care goals.

Undesirable Characteristics

It is critical that all staff members have those qualifications outlined above; it is just as critical that they do not possess attributes which will be detrimental to the program and the well-being of participants. Among those qualities which are most troublesome and difficult to correct or overcome are undesirable attitudes, such as paternalism and prejudice.

Paternalism and Patronism. Paternalistic individuals assume that they know what is best for participants and that they should make decisions for them, acting in the role of "parent." Such attitudes void the right of participants to self-determination and contribute to an increase in dependency. The participant thus affected may fail to work toward achievement of service goals and may become hostile and withdrawn.

These negative traits in the potential staff member may be such an inbred part of personality that they cannot become overcome, since the individual is often unable to recognize the problem. Those hiring staff should be alert to such attitudes and should not consider employing an applicant if it appears that the attitudes are so intrinsic to the personality that they cannot be eliminated by training.

Prejudice. Prejudice may surface against any population—ethnic group, religion, age group, sex, etc. The adult day care program is often a miniature "melting pot," serving and being staffed by individuals from a great variety of backgrounds. Each person in the program has the right to be accepted as a valued human being. It may only take one staff person failing to uphold this attitude to undermine the environment of acceptance.

As undesirable as poor attitudes in the staff candidate is a lack of dedication, energy, and team skills.

Lack of Motivation. Strong motivation is needed by all members of the adult day care staff if they are to function as team members and help motivate participants to function at their highest possible level. Working with impaired adults is often frustrating and emotionally draining. Only those staff members who are highly motivated will be able to maintain interest and enthusiasm.

Inability to Follow Through on Assignments. As mentioned, adult day care staff must be able to function independently much of the time. Those who require constant direction and supervision will not be as productive as is necessary.

Inability to Function as a Team Member. The reverse of inability to work independently is inability or refusal to work as a part of the team. Planning and carrying out program goals and working toward achievement of individual care plans will require the closest cooperation and collaboration among all staff. Those who plan and carry out responsibilities without consideration for how their actions fit into the overall program plan are likely to detract from the achievement of program goals.

Lack of Energy or Physical Stamina. The work in an adult day care program is physically demanding. Staff members must be able to stay on their feet for long periods and must sometimes help to lift participants or equipment. Some staff positions may require less stamina than others. If an applicant is deficient in this respect, but desirable in others, the level of physical strength or stamina required for the position may be analyzed to determine what is needed to carry out duties or whether duties can be adapted to abilities.

All applicants for jobs must be carefully screened to determine what qualifications and aptitude they possess for working in adult day care. All training and past experience as well as all references should be checked in light of both general program responsibilities and those specific to the position for which they are being considered.

Staff Positions

Before the program opens, a nucleus of staff should have been employed and have completed orientation. Decisions about which positions will be needed in the beginning will depend upon what skills are needed to supplement those of the director as well as upon the factors already discussed. The start-up staff must possess a combination of skills required to plan and implement program services and activities, to work with participants and families, and to perform clerical and bookkeeping chores. If transportation is to be provided, a driver must also be available. This core staff will be functioning in addition to the director, whose time will be needed for other duties, such as carrying out public relations in the community, recruiting and admitting participants, and establishing the adult day care center as a part of the care continuum.

Until the participant census grows, planners will understandably want to keep the staff as small as is consistent with providing quality service and enabling the program to grow. Deciding upon which positions to fill for the start-up staff will therefore require thoughtful planning.

Exhibit 12-1 lists staff roles which are carried out within most adult day care programs when they are at full capacity. Planners will understand that not all necessary roles have to be filled by paid staff who work on-site. Instead, the team concept may be developed by using a combination of paid staff, referrals to other community providers, contractual arrangements, and consultants and volunteers. The plan for staffing should include start-up with basic positions filled from the above combination of sources, and with other positions to be added as the program grows and as the budget allows.

Staff Responsibilities

Members of the staff must work together, establishing a team which translates the program philosophy into action, carries out the purposes for which the program was created, and achieves the goals of individual service plans. There are two primary areas of responsibility for each staff member: first to the program as a whole and second to each participant as an individual.

Program Responsibilities

Staff members should have a clear understanding of their roles as members of the program team and of their specific responsibilities. To accomplish this, the staff should have a well-developed plan of assigned duties covering all aspects of program provision. The assignments should be consistent with job descriptions and should utilize the talents, abilities, and interests of each individual so that the maximum contribution can be made to the program.

Exhibit 12-1 Staff positions in a full-capacity program.

- Director
- Administrative assistant
- Program aides
- Social worker
- Nurse/health care professional
- Activities director
- Therapists (PT, OT, speech, hearing, recreation)
- Driver
- Secretary/clerk
- Bookkeeper
- Nutritionist
- Custodian
- Housekeeper
- Public relations specialist
- Fund-raising specialist

Responsibilities to Individual Participants

Staff members will be able to function more effectively as members of the team if they are involved in program planning and developing the plan of care for each participant. Through this involvement, they gain understanding of the rationale for service goals, how services and activities relate to the plan for care, and how their role helps participants to achieve goals.

Staff members act in many roles to carry out their responsibilities. They serve as motivators, supplying challenges to participants. They will share the challenges and work in partnership, offering the participants encouragement to overcome existing barriers in order to improve functional capacity and self-sufficiency.

Staff members also serve as information seekers and givers, helping participants understand what options are available. They should strive to create an environment within which participants are free to select the option which is most attractive to them. They should provide whatever assistance is needed to utilize resources and carry out actions which support the choice. To this end, staff should work to keep the program flexible, with activities and schedules adapted to suit the needs of participants and with opportunities provided for their growth and development.

All staff members must be able to accept assignments and carry them out in a reliable and positive manner. They must behave in ways which demonstrate to participants that the staff works as a team and as individuals to provide whatever support is needed by participants to achieve desired goals.

Staff Development

Individual staff members may not automatically blend into a team which works together as required to achieve the greatest good for the program and for individual participants. The director is responsible for emphasizing this concept during staff orientation and for providing continuous reinforcement during all staff development and training.

In addition, staff meetings and daily discussions should constantly re-affirm the need to strengthen team ability and effectiveness.

Use of Outside Resources

Even those programs with a high staff-participant ratio are not likely to have paid staff which possesses all the administrative and programmatic skills and abilities needed. To supplement the staff and expand program capability, sources external to the program, such as consultants and referrals may be considered (see Exhibit 12-2). It will be up to planners to decide which staff roles may be carried out by these resources. The decision should be based upon two factors:

1. What services *must* be provided on-site to satisfy funding requirements.
2. How use of outside resources will affect quality of care.

Staffing Decisions

As was stated earlier, adult day care planners must exercise creativity and flexibility when making decisions about staffing the program. Asking the following questions will be helpful in the decision-making process:

1. Is it possible to provide some services by contract or other outside resources at a lesser cost and without affecting program quality?
2. Can some staff fill dual roles, e.g., can an occupational therapist, nurse, or social worker serve as director? Bus driver as program aide? Program aide as part-time secretary?
3. Can some staff be employed for only part of the day, to cover the hours when most of the participants are present?
4. Can some positions be shared: e.g., having a nurse for two days per week and a social worker or occupational therapist for three, etc.?

Exhibit 12-2 Use of external resources to fill staff roles.

Roles which may be filled by consultants:

- Therapists
- Mental health professionals
- Social worker
- Nutritionist
- Staff developer/trainer
- Legal advisers
- Fund-raising
- Management consultants
- Conductors of evaluations
- Adult day care consultants
- Marketing/public relations professionals

Services which may be provided by referral or by contracts:

- Professional health care: physician, nursing service, therapies, clinics
- Nutrition: hospital cafeterias, school cafeterias, restaurants, Title V nutrition site
- Social services: department of social services, consultants
- Building custodian/housekeeping: private cleaning/custodial services
- Fund-raising/marketing: private fund-raising/public relations firms
- Staff development/training: adult day care consultants, other trainers, community colleges
- Transportation: bus companies, mass transit, taxis, school, special transportation providers.

Roles for volunteers:

- Transportation provider
- Counselor
- Fund-raising/public relations
- Educator
- Clerical help
- Program assistant/aides
- Staff training
- Building repair

5. Are there other programs in the community with which staff could be shared: nurse, social worker, therapists, activity coordinator, etc.?
6. What community resources are available at little or no cost to the program: community colleges, students working on a practicum, Title V aides, etc.?

Planners will undoubtedly come up with other innovative ideas to help stretch program resources, at the same time making sure that the service remains of high quality, serving participants in ways which carry out the adult day care philosophy.

Reference

National Institute on Adult Daycare. 1984. *Standards for adult day care.* Washington, DC: National Council on the Aging, Inc.

13 Personnel Recruitment, Interviewing, and Selection

Introduction

Since the central role in adult day care provision is played by the staff, attracting and hiring individuals who possess suitable skills and the appropriate temperament for working in the adult day care environment is a key challenge for the director. The abilities and attitudes of staff will to a great extent determine both the quality of programming and the degree to which it can benefit participants. Before beginning the recruitment and hiring process, the director (or others responsible for hiring staff), must thoroughly understand the needs of participants and the functions and qualifications for each staff position as stated in the job description. (See Appendix A for sample job descriptions.)

Recruitment

If not carefully planned, procedures for recruiting and hiring staff may occupy an inordinate amount of the director's time. The recruitment process should be planned to 1) aim at recruiting well-qualified individuals with the least possible expenditure of time and effort, and 2) weed out unqualified applicants as early as possible in the recruitment process. Each step in the process will be planned and carried out with these objectives in mind.

Steps in Recruitment

Write the Job Advertisement or Job Listing. The advertisement should be a description of the individual being sought. Key words or phrases from the job description should be used. The following topics commonly need to be addressed.

Educational Background and Training. Be specific about what is required. State whether any degree or certification is needed and in what field, such as "a Master's degree in Social Work," "Two years post-secondary education in a health-related field," or "certification in advanced First Aid/CPR."

Work Experience. State both the field in which experience is needed and in what capacity:

> "Two years work experience with functionally impaired adults in a supervisory capacity. Must have supervised staff in program planning and implementation."
>
> "Two years experience in planning and carrying out recreational and leisure time activities for functionally impaired adults."

A combination of work and education requirements may be specified:

> "A combination of 5 years training and work experience with functionally impaired adults in a service provision setting."

Abilities. Mention those abilities which are basic to working in an adult day care program and to the position being filled:

Leadership ability

Ability to work independently

Ability to set up and manage a budget

Ability to work creatively with impaired adults

Ability to manage a one-person office

Ability to work as a team member

Ability to plan activities for impaired adults.

Personal Characteristics. Again, requirements should be specific to the adult day care program and to the position:

Emotional stability

Physical strength

Outgoing personality

Flexibility

Patience

Acceptance of people.

For each position, choose two or three characteristics which are of highest priority.

The advertisement should include words to attract applicants who will be desirable to the program. The organization and position should be described in terms that put the program in a good light. Use positive expressions to emphasize what the program can offer the applicant:

"Opportunities for using initiative"; "opportunity to be self-directed"

"Opportunities for learning"

"Growth opportunities"

"Good working atmosphere"

"Rewarding work for those who enjoy working with people."

The information in the advertisement should be accurate and adequate to inform applicants about program job working conditions. Details like the following may be included.

"Mon-Fri., 9-5, occasional evenings or weekends"

"Salary range: $12,000-15,000"

"Employee benefits: health/life insurance, paid vacations, holidays, etc."

Information needed for the reader to apply should be included:

How to respond—letter, phone, in person

Where to respond—P.O. box, street address, phone number, other

Deadline for responding

Name of person to be addressed, if any.

Advertise the Position. The decision about which methods to use in advertising the job will depend upon the level of the position being filled; the amount of time available for accepting inquiries; and how quickly the position must be filled. Methods which usually get fast response but which may be more time consuming because of the numbers of inquiries usually received are advertising in the newspaper and local newsletters; and listing with the Employment Security Commission and private employment agencies.

Other methods, which will yield a narrower but more select pool include reviewing applications already on file; asking for referrals from present employees, board members, and others; and contacting local schools and colleges.

Accept Inquiries and Conduct Preliminary Screening. As inquiries are being received, a preliminary screening is recommended to save time. The screening serves to determine if applicants possess basic necessary qualifications; discourage those who are unqualified; and inform eligible applicants of the interviewing process and set up appointments.

Preliminary screening will focus upon the following areas.

General Qualifications. These are qualifications basic to the position being filled and to the adult day care program.

Training and Work Experience. In regard to training and experience, the individual conducting the screening should seek answers to three key questions.

1. Does the applicant's training and experience match that specified; is it relevant to the position and the program?
2. Has the applicant demonstrated stability in work history?
3. Is the applicant over-qualified? Are the applicant's qualifications so much above those required as to indicate that no challenge will be found in the job?

Salary Requirements. The screener should be sure that the salary expected by the applicant is commensurate with what is being offered.

Those applicants who appear to possess basic qualifications and fit the other criteria should be asked to come for an interview. Those who do not meet requirements should be told (or notified) that their qualifications for the position are not as suitable as those of other applicants. They should be thanked for their interest and, if applications are kept on file, assured that they will be considered if a position for which they are eligible becomes available.

Interviewing

When the director is satisfied that a sufficient number of qualified applicants has been screened, the process of selecting the most qualified may begin. Methods of interview and selection may vary but the goal remains the same: to gain enough information about each candidate so that those responsible for selection will be able to choose the individual who has most to contribute to the adult day care program.

A recommended method is to have the director interview applicants who have met preliminary screening criteria, selecting several (perhaps three to five) of the most qualified. A personnel committee can then participate in a final interview. The varying perspectives and interviewing techniques of committee members is invaluable in eliciting full information from applicants.

After this interview, if the committee feels the need for more information or if two candidates appear to be equally qualified, the committee may ask them to come for still another interview. There should be no hesitancy about conducting second or third interviews if needed. Information is frequently gained in later interviews which did not become apparent during earlier ones.

Preliminary Interviews

Through the preliminary screening, the director will have selected applicants for an initial interview who appear to be most qualified from among those applying. This interview will focus upon a general assessment of the candidate.

- A visual screening of appearance, physical condition, and apparent energy level
- Determining mental ability; evidence of common sense and problem solving ability
- Quality of communication skills: ability to express ideas and to listen perceptively
- Evidence of good humor, patience, and flexibility
- Degree of interest in adult day care and grasp of the concept, as evidenced by both response to questions and by the questions asked.

Check References

Based upon information collected to this point, the director will select top candidates from among those interviewed and conduct a reference check.

Use of a prepared questionnaire when conducting a check by telephone is recommended; this will ensure that information is consistent for each applicant and that all critical points are covered. Open the conversation by giving your name and the reason for the call: to verify information given by the job applicant and to help determine appropriateness of the applicant for the position.

In checking a work experience reference, cover the following points.

1. Name of person giving information
2. Position and working relationship with the applicant
3. Job responsibilities of applicant in prior position
4. How well responsibilities were carried out
5. Strengths and weaknesses in the job
6. Attendance record
7. How long the position was held
8. General attitude toward responsibilities
9. Reason for leaving
10. Duties of the position which may be relevant to work in adult day care
11. Whether the applicant would be re-hired; if not, why not?

In checking a personal reference, cover the following.

1. Name of person providing information
2. Relationship to applicant

3. How long relationship has existed
4. What adjectives would be used to describe applicant: "Self-directed?" "Highly motivated?" "People oriented?" "Concerned for people?" "Patient?" "Flexible?" Other?
5. What abilities does the applicant have which would be of value to the work in adult day care: Ability to plan? To work well with others as a team member? Musical ability? Creative abilities? Other?
6. Any other information relevant to consideration of the applicant for the position.

As important as answers in reference checks are any noted omissions. The questioner should listen for a lack of enthusiasm in answers to questions; and an absence of positive or spontaneous comments or of praise for the applicant. If hesitancy or lack of enthusiasm is noted, attempt to determine whether the informant is being guarded in comments, or whether the informant appears to be holding back information.

After all references have been checked, compare the information from this source with that already learned from the application and resume, preliminary screening, and initial interview to get a comprehensive picture of the individual's qualifications for the position.

The Interview

After screening and reference checks have been completed, the director will evaluate all available information about each candidate and decide upon good choices for the second interview with the director or with the personnel committee. The interviewers goals are both to acquire complete and relevant information about each candidate and to analyze and interpret information in light of program and position requirements.

For a successful interview, the questioners should try to do the following.

- Put applicants at ease, helping them to talk spontaneously about themselves
- Carry out interviews so that the maximum amount of desired information is elicited
- Adjust the interview process to the applicant
- Listen perceptively and analyze content of conversation in terms of body English, voice inflection, and other clues to personality and abilities
- Correctly interpret all data received.

The interview should be conducted in a warm and friendly atmosphere. Applicants should be greeted by name and introduced to all members of the interview committee.

Start with a short period of small talk on a topic upon which the applicant is able to speak knowledgeably. A good topic to choose can be learned from the application or from the initial interview. This tactic serves to help the applicant relax and begin talking spontaneously. Care should be taken to phrase an opening question which cannot be answered with just a "yes" or "no," but rather requires a lengthier response.

A member of the committee will then lead into the body of the interview by giving a brief outline of the agenda for the meeting, which should include a discussion of position requirements and of how well the applicant will fit the position. Srongly emphasize the need to fill the position with an individual who can best of utilize abilities to benefit the program. In order to accomplish this, the interviewers will need the applicant's help in getting enough information to make an informed decision.

Major topics to cover during the interview include the educational background of the applicant; past work experience; any special skills and abilities; and the nature and extent of the applicant's interest in adult day care. All questions should be open-ended, giving the applicant the responsibility for providing complete information. For example, say, "Tell us about your educational background and how you believe it has prepared you for this position in adult day care."

Ongoing encouragement should be provided to keep the applicant talking until the committee feels that all relevant issues for each topic have been covered. Comments by interviewers should be brief, indicating interest without interrupting the flow of information: "I see," "Could you elaborate?" or "Yes, I can understand that", a nod of the head can be sufficient. To obtain more data on a given topic, questions such as, "Tell us more about your work experience with impaired adults," may be used. Encourage the applicant to be open and willing to give both favorable and unfavorable information on each topic. Leading questions such as, "What aspects of the work caused frustration for you?" coupled with a non-judgemental attitude, will help to accomplish this.

When it appears that a topic has been covered adequately, the committee should provide a natural progression to the next: "Now, can you tell us why you are interested in the position in the adult day care program?" Interviewers have the responsibility for keeping the conversation on track, while allowing ample time to cover each topic. Comments like "Yes, that is interesting, but I would like to hear more about your last work experience," will prevent the applicant from rambling or spending more time on a topic than the interviewers feel is needed. The interviewers should exercise caution, however, to be sure that each committee member feels satisfied that the topic has been thoroughly covered before moving to the next.

Concluding the Interview

As a prelude to concluding the interview, the interviewer may summarize each topic which has been discussed. At this point, ask questions to fill any gaps which became apparent during the review, as well as offer the applicant an opportunity to correct errors or misperceptions. Applicants may also wish at this time to provide additional information. The statement of review should cover why the job is desirable, what assets the committee believes the applicant has to offer, what weaknesses in qualifications may have been observed, and ways in which weaknesses may be compensated for or remedied.

The interviewer will then bring the interview to a close by asking the applicant whether there is anything further to add or any other questions to ask about the job or the program. Members of the committee should express their appreciation to applicants for their interest in the program and for their time spent in the interview.

Even if all candidates have not been interviewed and no decision can be made at this point, the interviewers should be experienced enough at selecting staff for the program to enable them to know whether the qualifications of the applicant merit further consideration. In fairness to the individual, closing remarks should give some indication of the candidate's standing. For unqualified candidates one might say something like, "Although you possess many of the qualifications needed in the position, we are hoping to find someone with more work experience with older adults," or "While you do possess many of the qualifications needed, there are one or two applicants who have somewhat better qualifications for the position." For applicants whose qualifications lead interviewers to believe that the position would not present them with a challenge, an appropriate statement might be, "We appreciate your interest in working with us, but believe that the position will not use your abilities to the fullest extent." For those whose qualifications appear to place them among the finalists, say, "Your qualifications certainly look impressive. We will be concluding our interviews by [give date] and will be in touch as soon as possible."

All applicants should be told in general terms what the decision making and notification process is to be. Unsuccessful applicants should be notified of the decision either by mail or phone within a day or two.

Recording Interview Results

Most interviewers will make brief notations of important information during the interview (making sure not to distract the applicant from the conversation), but more complete information should be recorded after the applicant leaves and while details are still fresh. If this is done systematically, perhaps using the system by which applicants are evaluated and rated, the task of comparing applicants and arriving at a final decision will be simplified.

Rating Applicants

Upon completion of the interviews, credentials of all applicants should be reviewed and evaluated to decide which applicant comes closest to possessing qualifications needed in the position. To help interviewers in this process and to be sure that all applicants are ranked in an uniform manner, the committee should make use of a rating system.

One ranking method is that of listing areas to be evaluated and assigning each applicant a numerical rating from 1 to 5 in each area:

1 = superior

2 = excellent

3 = average

4 = below average

5 = unacceptable.

Rating requires looking at the assets and shortcomings of each applicant in each area of evaluation, using information gained from all sources of the employment process: application and resume, preliminary interviews, references, interview with committee, observation and inferences drawn from interviews.

Applicants should be evaluated in the key areas outlined in Exhibit 13-1 (along with any others from the job description).

Making a Decision

The process of deciding among applicants involves weighing each candidate's assets against liabilities and then weighing each candidate against the others to choose the most qualified. No applicant will possess all qualifications listed in the job description; all will possess liabilities. The interviewers must decide how close each candidate comes to satisfying major requirements for the job and to what degree liabilities are likely to impede job performance. They should ask: Are assets desirable enough to overcome liabilities? Are liabilities such that training or work experience may help to eliminate them or at least to reduce their impact?

There are certain liabilities which may automatically disqualify an applicant, unless there are extenuating circumstances which are acceptable to the interviewers. These include evidence of dishonesty, lack of sincere interest in working with impaired adults, prejudice toward groups of people, lack of motivation, and inability to accept direction or to work well as a team member.

The interviewers should carefully consider each candidate in turn, assigning a rating in each category of evaluation and deciding upon a final, over-all rating for the candidate. The rating should reflect the interviewer's estimate of how well the individual can perform responsibilities in the position being filled.

The suggested ratings can be defined as follows:

1 = Superior. The applicant possesses nearly all qualifications needed for the position; liabilities in the specific area are insignificant. In the opinion of the interviewer, job performance is expected to be of high quality.

2 = Excellent. Assets far outweigh liabilities. Job performance is expected to be considerably above average.

Exhibit 13-1 Assessing applicants for staff positions.

Areas to be considered in staff selection:

Education and Training

- Are qualifications in these areas adequate and appropriate for work in the adult day care program? For the specific position?
- Does educational background indicate that services such as adult day care have been of interest to the applicant? If not, what have been priorities? Do these have any relevance or potential for adaptation for working in the program?

Work Experience

- What jobs have been held? Does past working history indicate a long-standing interest in services such as adult day care?
- What have been the most successful work experiences? The least successful? Does the work history demonstrate stability?
- What has been the responsibility level in previous positions? How well do these match the position being filled?
- What strengths have been demonstrated in past work? What weaknesses?
- What assets have been gained which will be useful in the program?
- Does past work history demonstrate that the applicant is moving toward positions with more or less responsibility?
- What motives does the applicant have for wanting the position? How does the work fit into career goals?

Physical Health and Stamina

- Does the applicant have any outstanding health problems which may interfere with work? Does past attendance in prior jobs indiate any chronic health problems?
- Does the energy level of the applicant appear to be adequate for discharge of job responsibilities? If physical strength and/or dexterity are needed for the position, does the applicant appear to be well qualified in this respect?

Emotional Health and Stability

- Does the applicant indicate acceptance of responsibility for any past failures or mistakes as well as for successes?
- Do past experiences show evidence of emotional stability? Of an ability to formulate appropriate goals and to work toward achievement of these, even if it means delay of present satisfaction?

Exhibit 13-1, continued.

- Does the applicant appear to have a level of maturity consistent with others in the same age group? Did interview behavior demonstrate self-confidence and an ability to meet people easily?
- Did the applicant appear to be accepting of self and others? To be non-judgemental? Non-prejudicial?
- Has the applicant worked successfully as a member of a team? Does the applicant appear to give a fair share of credit to others where this is appropriate?
- Does the applicant demonstrate flexibility? An ability to handle unexpected crises or changes in plans?

Leadership Ability

- Has the applicant demonstrated an ability to function without having constant supervision? Does the applicant seem to welcome responsibility and to handle it well?
- Does the applicant appear able to make appropriate decisions in unstructured situations? To accept consequences of decisions?
- Does the applicant appear to be poised and confident? And give indications of possessing a realistic appraisal of assets and deficiencies?
- Does the applicant show evidence of leadership in group activities? Show initiative in seeking answers to problems or in getting things done?
- Has the past work record indicated evidence of follow-through and perseverance? Are there clues to show that the applicant has skills in time management? Skills in planning?

If the position to be filled includes supervision of others, the committee will want to evaluate the applicant in areas which demonstrate supervisory capability.

- Has past work or other experience placed the applicant in the position of supervising others? Does the record indicate abilities in this area: To motivate others? To delegate successfully? To require accountability? To help others utilize their full potential? To attract and retain employees?

Personal Characteristics

- Do observation and references support an assumption of good morals and ethical standards? Of honesty? Sincerity? Loyalty? Willingness to give or share credit with others?
- Does the applicant appear to be unaffected and natural, not presenting a facade? Is there evidence of warmth in the applicant's personality? An ability to reach out to others?

Exhibit 13-1, continued.

- In conversations about the population being served in adult day care, does the applicant demonstrate empathy without giving evidence of paternalistic or patronizing attitudes?
- Does the applicant demonstrate creativity and productivity? Show evidence of being hard-working and highly motivated to perform well on the job?

Communication Skills

- Does the applicant demonstrate good verbal and writing skills? Are ideas expressed clearly and in understandable terms? Is the applicant able to listen perceptively and respond appropriately? Are differences of opinion expressed tactfully and with consideration of the other person's point of view?

Leisure Time Interests and Hobbies

- How does the applicant spend leisure time? Is there participation in volunteer activities? In hobbies which can be shared with adult day care participants?
- Does the applicant show strong social orientation? To spend time with others? To help others?

---

3 = Average. Qualifications are average and liabilities are about on a par with assets. Job performance is likely to be respectable and unexceptionable.

4 = Below Average. Liabilities outweigh assets, or liabilities are of a nature that warrants serious concern about job performance in an adult day care setting. Work is likely to be unsatisfactory.

5 = Unacceptable. Liabilities are such as to prevent serious consideration of the candidate for employment in an adult day care program.

If one candidate rates as superior in most or all categories, and all others are average or below, the decision to hire will not be difficult. If, however, as is likely to be the case at this point of selection (since less desirable candidates will have been eliminated), one or two candidates are approximately equal in assets and liabilities, interviewers have a more difficult task. To make a final decision, two further ratings may be made.

1. *Prioritizing of assets.* A value will be assigned to assets in order of their importance to the program. Each candidate will then be scrutinized more closely in these areas.
2. *Capacity for further growth and development.* Those individuals who appear to have developed to their maximum potential will not be as satisfactory over the long term as those who are anxious to expand knowledge and improve skills and recognize opportunities for this in the position.

This final ranking should enable interviewers to select the candidate who will be most valuable to the program and for whom the position will present both a challenge and opportunities for expanding their abilities.

Summary

Selection of adult day care staff is a time-consuming task and one requiring skill on the part of those who have this responsibility. Because having a capable and committed staff is important, however, there should be no attempt made to shorten the process in ways which may impede recruitment and selection of the most desirable person who can be found to fill each position. The time and effort spent will pay off in program quality and in service to participants.

14 Personnel Orientation, Training, and Management

Introduction

An adult day care director is responsible for providing the direction, training, and management needed to develop staff skills and abilities to their fullest potential, enabling staff members to make their maximum contribution. This type of direction is particularly important because adult day care staff have usually come to the field from varied backgrounds and professions, and rarely will have had education or training in the field of gerontology. Even more rarely will staff have had experience with provision of adult day care itself. Adult day care directors and planners must provide intensive orientation to staff members as they begin work, furnish on-the-job training, and carry out regular in-service events designed to focus on specific training needs of the staff.

All new staff—and especially those who are new to the field—should be reassured that ample training will be provided or arranged for. In addition to more formal training activities, the director and other experienced staff should make themselves available as a training resource for those new to the staff. The staff as a whole and as individuals should engage in opportunities to increase and sharpen skills in areas which are applicable to their specific job responsibilities. The director, in particular, has a duty to work with each staff member to discover their training needs and to help locate resources which will meet the needs.

Responsible management practices include both helping staff to develop abilities for the benefit of the program and working to blend the staff into a team which functions cooperatively and effectively.

Orientation and Training

Orientation

The orientation phase of staff training may be the individual's first exposure to the service of adult day care. It should prepare the new staff member to begin developing a personal work philosophy consistent with the program philosophy and goals. Exhibit 14-1 outlines the areas to cover in the orientation sessions.

Exhibit 14-1 New staff orientation.

To be included in staff orientation:
Phase I

1. An introduction to and grounding in the philosophy and definition of the service of adult day care.
2. Training in methods of service provision within the program; exposure to goals which the program is expected to accomplish.
3. Learning state certification and licensure requirements for the program; understanding the role of the staff member in meeting requirements and helping to remain in compliance.
4. A study of national adult day care standards; learning the rationale for the service as well as the service "state of the art" in the state and the country.
5. Learning about the organization: chain of command, program and personnel policies, admission and discharge policies and procedures, program operating policies.
6. Methods of program planning; how individual plans of care are developed.
7. Availability of community resources and how they are used to supplement and enhance program ability to deliver services.
8. Training in First Aid and cardiopulmonary resuscitation (CPR). This training is required by standards of most states and must be renewed annually. (The Red Cross offers training in First Aid and CPR periodically in many locations; the program may choose to have staff participate in training when it is offered by this agency. In some programs, arrangements have been made to have training provided at the center. Some have arranged to have staff and participants take the training together as a part of program activities.)

Phase II

9. A week (or more) spent working under close observation. This will offer an opportunity to discover how well the individuals translate their knowledge into practice. It also affords opportunities for conversations about issues which may be new to the new staff person.

On-the-Job Training

On-the-job training will probably be the most effective provided, since it is constant during working hours, can be extended for as long as needed, and is always relevant to the job. It deals with problems as they arise and allows the trainee to see a practical application of training.

Personnel new to the program should be considered as "trainees" for a period of perhaps three to six months. This may be planned to coincide with a probationary period which should be standard for all new employees. During this period, the employee will not work without supervision (unless equipped to do so by prior training or unless in a situation not requiring training) and will have access to an experienced staff member at all times. The supervisor should be knowledgeable about the program and the service, and able to help with problems and discuss any issues which may arise. New staff members should be provided with frequent feedback about their work methods, skills, and attitudes. It is much easier to correct poor or undesirable work habits during the period of probation than after they have become well-established.

All staff receive on-the-job training, whether it is planned or not. They learn by observation of other staff members. It is wise, therefore, to use this opportunity to develop desirable work methods and attitudes and to reinforce good work performance patterns.

In-Service Training

In addition to orientation and on-the-job training, training needs may be met by developing a well-planned training program for all staff. The training may take place on-site and/or may take advantage of training opportunities through outside resources.

In collaboration with the staff, the director will establish training objectives for the staff as a team and as individuals. The team objectives will be based upon conferences with the personnel committee, discussions with the staff, and the director's observations of the staff at work. Goals for training should also be influenced by records kept of questions asked, issues arising in staff meetings, and the director's recognition of problems indicating gaps in staff knowledge and skills. Using these methods to develop the plan means that training can be directed toward specific needs as revealed by the staff. This ensures that the plan is tailored to remedy deficiencies and improve staff skills.

In addition to on-site training provided by staff members or resource persons from the community, plans for staff development should include using training opportunities from other sources. Most communities frequently hold training events from which adult day care staff can benefit. These events are offered by a variety of sources: community colleges, community service agencies, state and national conferences on aging in general or on an aspect of service to aging or impaired adults. Workshops and seminars are sponsored by miscellaneous organizations. Information about these events should be scrutinized to see whether content is germane to adult day care staff.

Staff meetings may also be used to provide training. Staff should be asked to keep notes of questions for which they need answers and bring them to the meeting. Questions and answer sessions and discussions about issues which arise in the program are good ways to take advantage of the time when staff is together. Sharing new information in the form of printed materials, video, or movies is another.

Scheduling time for training is a problem for most programs. Efforts must be made to schedule staff meetings and training events for times when staff members can be together without disrupting the program. A variety of plans have been used by adult day care programs.

1. Scheduling a work day once each month during which the center is closed to participants. This may not be possible for all programs, since some participants are dependent upon the program to provide them with a safe environment during the day and may be left without care if the center is closed. If families are consulted about the need for staff to continue to develop skills, however, they may be able to make arrangements for one day.
2. Scheduling meetings for early morning before participants arrive or for afternoons after they leave. Often the first and last hours of the day have few participants present. In this situation, volunteers may be recruited to care for those who are present while the staff engages in training.
3. Scheduling a training event for a Saturday. Many programs are reluctant to require staff to participate in training on weekends. However, if this appears to be the best option, staff may agree to the plan and be allowed compensatory time during the week. An advantage of this plan is that intensive training is provided for a full day, with disruptions and distractions at a minimum.
4. Scheduling a meeting for the breakfast or dinner hour. Again, staff may be reluctant to use time off for training, but may agree in the interest of obtaining training and if compensatory time is provided.
5. Scheduling training or staff meetings during the lunch period, with volunteers recruited to work with participants. Caution must be exercised that volunteers are trained to work with impaired adults and are aware of any significant conditions of participants which may call for close attention and assistance. The staff should be close enough to be reached if the need arose.

Training Goals

All staff training can be categorized as directed toward one or more of three primary goals: attitudinal development or correction; expansion of knowledge; and skill improvement.

Attitudinal Development or Correction

Attitudinal Development may be the most important area of training for adult day care personnel, since attitudes affect every aspect of service provision. The effect of improper attitudes upon participants and their feelings of self-worth and self-esteem may sabotage all efforts to help them regain or develop skills of independent functioning.

Individuals who work in helping professions often feel themselves to be free of prejudices or biases toward aging and impaired adults. Because of this, they sometimes fail to recognize the subtlety of attitudes intrinsic to their personality, which affect their work with participants. The commonest of these negative attitudes can be defined as follows.

1. *Paternalism.* Feelings on the part of staff that they know what is best for participants, that they must take charge and decide upon appropriate goals and actions to be taken to achieve goals. This denies the participant the right to be self-directed and diminishes the ability to become more independent.
2. *Patronism.* An assumption of superiority. This attitude, prevalent among many people toward the aging and impaired, assumes that these individuals are somehow inferior, and that they are somehow responsible for their own problems.
3. *Pity.* Feelings of pity may also be symptomatic of feelings of patronism; they symbolize a sense of superiority. There is a fine shade of difference between "empathy"—identifying with and entering into the feelings of the other person, and "pity"—"feeling sorry for" the individual, and this difference is most important in the adult day care setting. Participants, as most people, resent demonstrations of pity and can react with anger.
4. *Anxiety and aversion.* An aversion to the aging and impaired caused by anxiety about their condition. In other words, feeling that what has happened to the other may happen to the self and by avoiding the afflicted person, the problem can also be avoided. Again, participants are aware of this reaction and will not respond well to staff members who hold these feelings.

Whenever these attitudes—or the potential for their development— are detected among the staff, aggressive action must be taken. Staff must be made aware of the attitude and of the likely result of failure to eradicate it. They must clearly understand the effect which such attitudes have upon the program and skills of the staff members themselves.

Training should always be planned to include topics which address these attitudinal issues.

- Sensitivity to all issues involving the aging
- Learning to develop skills of empathy
- Effective communication skills
- Acceptance of own aging process
- Development of positive attitudes toward the aged: learning that they have knowledge to share, are of value as friends, etc.

Varied methods can be used to correct improper attitudes and to help the individual replace them with more positive ones, including role playing, role reversal, assigned readings, and group discussions.

Expansion of Knowledge

Adult day care staff often have little prior information about the population in need of the service or about the goals and methods of service provision. Because of the uniqueness of the service, it is important that all staff members be evaluated to determine whether gaps in their knowledge of the service exist and to help plan training. The staff is likely to need training in the following topics.

- Adult day care philosophy and goals
- Adult day care as a part of the long-term care continuum
- Biological changes of the aging process
- Psychology of aging
- Social dimensions of aging
- Aging and society
- Role losses of aging
- Pharmakinetics
- Availability and use of community resources
- Developmental processes of aging
- Value of the life review process
- Techniques for working with functionally impaired adults.

The list of topics in this area is long; evaluation of the staff will give indications of specific training needs. Training should be planned to provide knowledge, overcome preconceived, erroneous ideas and teach appropriate methods of relating to the participants in the program. Knowledgeable resource persons can be used to provide this instruction, as well as individual study, courses offered in community colleges or other educational facilities, films and videos, workshops with other providers, and demonstration sessions. Staff can also be encouraged to attend symposia and conferences on the local, state, and national levels.

Skill Improvement

Numerous skills are needed in provision of adult day care, some of which may be new to staff. All skills will not necessarily be needed by all staff members, but the staff as a whole should have skills in the following areas.

- Recognizing characteristics common among the adult day care target population
- Evaluating strengths and abilities of participants
- Assessing participants' needs
- Developing individual care plans for participants
- Utilizing community resources
- Planning programs to achieve goals of care plans
- Conflict resolution
- Techniques for transferring participants who are not ambulatory
- Involving participants in helping to plan the program
- Counseling
- Therapies
- Art, music, drama, etc., as used in programs for aging and impaired adults.

The director should attempt to employ staff members who possess a combination of skills. Training should be provided to increase both the number and quality of each individual's skills. Investigation of sources for learning specific skills should reveal numerous community resources which will offer the necessary training such as community colleges, professional groups or individuals, libraries, periodicals, seminars and workshops, and training conferences.

Benefits of Staff Development

Although provision of staff training and development is a time consuming task, benefits to the program are profound. Participants, and staff members also directly benefit:

1. *Benefits to the Program*
   - High quality service delivery
   - Good public relations
   - Achievement of program goals and objectives
   - Staff support of the service concept and philosophy
   - Reduction in staff turnover
2. *Benefits to Participants*
   - Improved quality of care
   - Care meets needs for improvement in capacity for independence and reinforcement and self-esteem
   - Stability and consistency of care
   - Security of environment
3. *Benefits to Staff*
   - Increase in knowledge and skills
   - Development of positive attitudes
   - Feelings of satisfaction in doing the job well
   - Personal growth and development
   - Improved morale
   - Increased interest in the service of adult day care
   - Feelings of job security.

Staff Management

Successful management of the staff is central to provision of the service of adult day care if it is to produce the desired results. To be an effective manager, the director must recognize the roles encompassed within the office of staff manager and be proficient in carrying them out. These roles include those of Staff Leader, Staff Trainer, Delegator, Staff Coach, Counselor, Motivator, Staff Evaluator, and Staff Disciplinarian.

Staff Leader

A successful leader encourages each staff member to make the maximum contribution to the program. Melding individual staff members into a unit within which each is provided opportunities to best use abilities is among the greatest challenges the adult day care director will face.

A chief strategy for success is to lead by example. Attitudes of the staff are largely determined by the example of the director. Positive, helpful attitudes, creation of a supportive environment, establishment of a cooperative spirit among the staff—all of these will become a natural part of the program if demonstrated by the director in relationships with those in the program. The director's serving as a model for these attitudes demonstrates their importance to achievement of program goals.

The director should work with each staff member as an individual, observing skill and knowledge levels in order to understand personal goals and ambitions and to help each member achieve work and personal objectives. Progress toward personal goals and toward program goals should be synchronous if the staff has been well chosen and receives appropriate training.

The director should make the effort to involve staff in the decision-making process. Holding open staff discussions about problems and opportunities of the program and providing each member with a chance to contribute suggestions will help with problem solving and with forming the staff into a team.

The staff should be encouraged to recognize problems. All staff members working together to recognize and solve problems as they arise will result in quicker and easier resolutions. This type of collaboration helps forge the staff into a creative team.

The director should involve the staff in program planning. All staff should be included: professionals, para-professionals, aides, drivers, and volunteers can contribute a great deal to all phases of service planning. Areas for staff contribution can include participant assessment, development of individual plans of care, methods of service delivery, evaluation of the program, and planning to remedy deficiencies.

Finally, the director must treat all staff with equal fairness and with respect.

Staff Trainer

The need for providing ongoing staff training and the goals of such training—have been discussed above. While planning or providing training, the director comes to know the employees, their skills and abilities and any gaps in knowledge levels. Any need for attitudinal change is detected. This information enables the director to provide the types of training that will raise staff abilities to the desired level. In addition to active observation of staff members at work, the director should question individual staff members to get their assessment of training needs. The director should engage the full staff in deciding upon realistic goals for staff proficiency and in developing a plan for obtaining the training needed to achieve the goals.

Delegator

The director's need to delegate has been discussed in detail above (see Chapter 11). In relation to staff management, delegation is an area in which many adult day care directors share a difficulty. Feeling responsible for the program, they tend to believe that they must personally carry out all duties of administering and overseeing the program.

However, effective staff management and team development will depend to a large extent upon how well the director learns to delegate, including what can be delegated to whom, as well as how to require accountability. As with other components of staff management, successful delegation will demand that the director possess a thorough knowledge of the staff: the skills, abilities, strengths, and weaknesses of each member.

Staff Coach

Coaching the staff is a never-ending responsibility of the director. This should be looked upon as a form of—or extension of—training. It requires both ongoing observation of the staff at work and private meetings with individual staff members when there is a need to correct performance or when a need for skill improvement has been identified.

Coaching also involves provision of supportive feed-back: praise for a job well done and for contributions to the success of the program. Individuals as well as the staff as a whole should be recognized in this way. Commendation of staff during staff meetings should be a part of each meeting and is a method of making sure that praise which is deserved is not overlooked.

Counselor

The director must be sensitive to the status of morale among the staff. Symptoms that morale may be low include change in work habits or attitudes, argumentativeness, hostility, lack of attention to work, and tasks left uncompleted. The director must respond immediately to such symptoms.

An attempt must be made to learn reasons for the behavior by talking to employees in private. The problem may be an individual one or stemming from one person. If it appears to be prevalent among the majority of staff, a group meeting may be indicated in which all members are encouraged to make suggestions for alleviation of the problem. If counseling is indicated, the following outline for the discussion will be helpful.

- Put the employee at ease
- Bring up the problem
- Offer an opportunity to discuss reasons for problem behavior
- Listen to the employee
- Offer support for problems or stress being experienced
- Discuss possible solutions to the problem
- Outline options available to the employee
- Decide upon course of action to be taken
- Set a time to discuss progress.

Exhibit 14-2 Motivational strategies.

- Provide challenging opportunities within the job
- Arrange job assignments which offer a high chance for success
- Provide needed encouragement: strokes, praise, and recognition
- Help toward achieving personal work goals
- Provide training needed to achieve growth in job capability
- Make each member feel a valued part of the team
- Express confidence in ability to do a good job
- Demonstrate respect
- Keep staff informed about the program: plans for changes, new developments, successes, failures
- Give credit for successful completion of assignments.

Motivator

All directors are "motivators" of their staff; the only question is whether the motivation is to be toward progress and achievement or whether it is toward poor attitudes and work performance.

A goal of adult day care directors must be to help staff members to become excited about their work and the contribution they can make to the program. To be successful in this, the director must learn what will motivate staff members and help them to realize what is expected of them. Most staff members have a desire to be successful in their job; it is the director's responsibility to help achieve this goal. Motivational strategies are listed in Exhibit 14-2.

Staff Evaluator

Adult day care directors are responsible for conducting regular, periodic job performance evaluations for each staff member and for discussing the results with the individual. Only by understanding how well their job performances stack up against expectations can members know whether work performances are satisfactory. The evaluations should include:

1. The employee's own assessment of job performance
2. The director's assessment
3. What improvements are needed

4. What actions can be taken to bring about any needed improvement, including what the staff member can do, how the director can help, and how to use any other sources of help
5. What strengths the employee has exhibited
6. The contributions made to the program.

Staff Disciplinarian

There will be instances in all programs when all efforts to help an employee improve job performance have failed. In these situations, the director must issue a warning that the employee is not meeting expectations. This should be carried out in a way which allows the employee to maintain self-respect. Disciplinary action should be conducted in a private meeting, where the director can

1. Discuss the problem(s)
2. Ask for employee's input concerning causes and possible remedial actions
3. State parameters of expected performance in clear terms
4. Decide upon what remedial actions to take and the time limit allowed for improvement
5. Set a time for a follow-up discussion
6. Record the meeting and ask the employee to sign the record.

If, after reasonable opportunities have been given to meet performance goals, the employee still fails to meet these standards, the director has no choice but to terminate the employee. This is always a difficult decision to make and to carry out. However, to retain employees who do not make the needed contribution to the program is to shirk a responsibility which is the highest priority of the adult day care director: that of ensuring the well-being of the program and provision of high quality care for participants. Keeping an employee who does not carry out assigned duties also places an extra burden upon other staff members, since they must help to fill the void created by poor performance.

Reasons for termination include the following.

- Gross insubordination
- Work habits which are detrimental to the program
- Work habits which are potentially harmful to participants
- Work habits which create stress and tension among staff
- Repeated and/or unexplained absenteeism
- Extreme conflict with the director.

When termination is indicated, the director should be careful to complete the following procedures.

- Document insubordination or other reasons why termination is being considered
- Document all meetings held with the employee to discuss work improvement
- Document all warnings which have been given to the employee, including the time limits which were set and any notice given
- Document reasoning leading to the decision to terminate; time and method of termination; note whether an employee is to be given a two-week notice or is to be paid in lieu of notice.
- Carry out all actions in conformity with employment policies, including allowing the employee opportunities for filing a grievance claim.

Summary

Having staff members who are committed to the service, are willing to go beyond requirements of their job description, are willing to be a part of the team effort, and who spend of themselves to provide quality care and service, is the heart and soul of an adult day care program which operates in accordance with established goals of the service. Development of such a staff is dependent upon the director's possessing skills needed to attract and select appropriate personnel, to recognize training needs and provide training which will enable staff to function at their optimum level, to know each staff member and the tasks and contributions they are capable of, to conduct regular evaluations of each employee, to provide praise when earned and discipline when justified, and to make the hard decision to terminate an employee when indicated for the good of the program. Most important of all is that the director successfully create an atmosphere and working environment which allow staff members to make their best contribution. This can only be done by example: the director must demonstrate those attitudes and work methods needed to provide high quality service in the adult day care program.

15 Supplementary Staff and Services

Introduction

Adult day care programs with a limited budget, or those serving populations with a wide variety of needs, may experience difficulty in obtaining staff with sufficient skills to provide all services needed by the participants. To remedy this, the director may supplement the staff with volunteers, consultants, and use of off-site contractual services. Extending the staff in this way increases the program's ability to meet a wide range of needs, and allows the program to offer more services and activities than staff ability might otherwise permit. Thus supplemental staff often strengthens program quality and effectiveness. Furthermore, costs may be reduced by providing services (which may be needed by only a few participants and for only part of the time) on-site. Savings may also be realized because equipment (which is provided by contractual arrangements) need not be purchased.

The staff structure should be reviewed and decisions made about which services to provide by use of outside resources. The decision will be based upon the characteristics of the participants being served; the range and degree of their impairments and specific needs must be considered. The combination of staff members and supplemental services decided upon should form a team capable of offering comprehensive services as needed by participants.

Use of Volunteers

A well-trained, committed cadre of volunteers can be among the most valuable assets of an adult day care program. They bring a variety of talents and interests which can supplement staff skills and add new dimensions to the program. To be effective, the volunteer program will require careful planning and managing. It is a good idea to have one person act in the role of volunteer coordinator. This can be a member of the staff or a volunteer who is willing to serve in this capacity.

Before beginning recruitment of volunteers, the provider should develop a plan for their use, including a recognition of specific program needs they can fill and the skills and abilities needed for these. Creative thinking will produce a myriad of possible uses for volunteers; some common uses are discussed below.

Program Aides

Using volunteers as aides is the most likely starting point for planning their use in the program. Those who work in this capacity will function much as do paid program aides, helping to set up activities, providing one-to-one assistance to participants who need this, helping with meals and snacks, offering assistance with walking, eating, and other functions.

Volunteers who work closely with participants must possess attributes needed in this role: acceptance of people; and lack of prejudice, paternalism, and other harmful attitudes. They must be able to offer help without creating or increasing dependence.

Planning and Execution of Special Events

Many volunteers prefer to contribute time to a specific project, rather than volunteering on an ongoing basis. There are many individuals within a community with talents to offer for this type of assistance.

Volunteers can plan and carry out parties on holidays and birthdays; help with craft sales or other fund-raising events; put together a slide or video presentation to be used in public relations; write public service announcements for TV and radio; and produce program publications such as brochures, posters, or the volunteer handbook.

Administrative Assistance

Some individuals would like to make a contribution to the program, but have reservations about their ability to work effectively with participants. The volunteer coordinator may have reservations about the likelihood of the volunteer's ability to work effectively with participants. Such volunteers can be used to help with office tasks (typing, filing, answering the phone, greeting visitors), produce the program newsletter, help with correspondence, shop for supplies, run errands, etc. Such individuals may also be willing to help with maintenance chores or yard work if that is needed.

Participant Education

Retired teachers, social workers, doctors, and nurses, among others, may make a valuable contribution to the program by using their skills to carry out educational programs for participants. The possibilities for topics are endless and can be geared to specific needs and interests of participants.

Assistance with Special Interests

Volunteers can be of great help to the staff by sharing a talent with a participant who has an interest about which staff members are not knowledgeable. Often the schedule allows no time for even knowledgeable staff members to offer help with the interest.

Among such interests may be gardening, woodwork, quilting, sewing, knitting, cooking, music, bridge, checkers, history, or other special studies.

Volunteers may also wish to share a special interest or talent of theirs with participants. Requests to individuals who possess skills which can be shared with participants will usually be met with willingness to do so. Adult day care staff should be alert to find these individuals. Examples include baking, flower arranging, drawing or painting, music, making holiday decorations, furniture refinishing or repair, embroidery, pottery, tatting, and quilting.

Community Agency

Volunteers who represent a community agency are often willing to visit the center to inform participants about work of the agency. Among those which might be of interest to participants are nature science centers, animal shelters, home and farm demonstration agencies, recreation programs, little theater, music clubs, Red Cross, agencies for prevention of substance abuse, civic organizations (Lions Club, Civitan, garden clubs), senior citizen's organizations and agencies. Research into what is available will yield a great variety of agencies whose representatives will be glad to visit and speak with participants about the work of their organization.

Special Services Offered by Community Groups

Volunteer groups will often help with a program or with filling a specific program need. There are organizations within each community whose objectives include provision of assistance to programs such as adult day care.

For example, the Telephone Pioneers of America may be willing to help with the purchase of special equipment or provide funds to meet a special need of a participant; Lions Clubs may help with equipment or programming for participants who are blind; the Mayor's Committee for the handicapped may provide educational programs or help with funds for equipment for a handicapped participant; the Easter Seal Society may help with special equipment for impaired participants, transportation for medical appointments, and summer camp for handicapped individuals; the Heart Association will provide education and training for participants with cardiovascular problems.

Staff Development

The use of volunteers to provide staff training can add greatly to staff capability. Individuals who possess knowledge which can be shared with adult day care staff are numerous in every community and should be utilized by the program. Topics that can be covered in this way include working with special populations such as the blind or deaf; meeting nutritional needs; working with emotionally impaired participants; and planning activities for physically impaired. The possibilities for increasing staff capability by this method are limitless.

Exhibit 15-1 Documents for volunteer recruitment.

Documents to do with volunteers include:

1. *Volunteer job descriptions.* Each job responsibility to be assigned to a volunteer should have a job description outlining the major tasks to be carried out, qualifications needed by the volunteer to discharge tasks, orientation and training required, time and place where work is to be carried out, length of time job will last, and lines of supervision.
2. *Volunteer handbook.* In order for a volunteer program to function well, volunteers need to understand the goals and objectives of the program. The handbook should provide background information about the agency and a description of the population being served, including special needs, functional limitations, and specific do's and don'ts to be observed while working with participants. All program policies applying to or affecting the volunteer should be stated in the handbook. A statement of the rights of participants should also be included.
3. Participant *confidentiality form.* Each volunteer should be aware that information learned about participants during their work in the program is confidential and not to be discussed with or divulged to persons who have no authorized reason for knowing the information.
4. *Volunteer application form.* Volunteers should be viewed as job applicants for a position with the adult day care program, even if it is not a paid position. The application form should be designed to obtain information needed to make a decision about the appropriateness of the individual for the position in which they are to work. Volunteers should also be given some idea of whether the position is appropriate for them. This form should include:
   - Volunteer's name, address, phone number
   - Special skills or talents which will be valuable in the program

Each center will have unique needs which can be filled by volunteers. A careful assessment of program and participant needs, analyzed in light of staff capability and skills, will reveal the extent of the requirement for volunteers and the specific responsibilities that can be assigned to them. This will have to be an ongoing process as program and participant needs change.

Planning for Volunteers

Once the extent of the need for volunteers is established and before recruitment begins, preliminary planning must take place. Certain documents should be in place within the program so that both the volunteer and the program have an understanding of terms of the agreement between them. These documents are outlined in Exhibit 15-1.

Exhibit 15-1, continued.

- Any past work experience which will be helpful
- Any work for which they *do not* want to be considered
- What work is preferred
- Days and hours of availability; length of time they expect to continue to volunteer, if there is a limit.

5. *Interview summary sheet.* It is helpful to record impressions of the interview with an individual applying to be a volunteer. This information will be useful when deciding whether the person is qualified to be a volunteer in the adult day care program. This record should include:

    - Volunteer's name
    - Interviewer's impression of the applicant's atittude, either negative or positive
    - Special aptitudes which will be advantageous in the adult day care setting: skills, talents, knowledge, past work experience, interests
    - Any limitations upon working as a volunteer: time constraints, health, transportation, attitudes, motivation
    - Action decided upon: acceptance; acceptance for specific jobs only; referral to another agency; decision by volunteer to withdraw application.

6. *Record keeping system.* This should include a time sheet for each volunteer to sign in and out, with the time and date. Also included in the records should be a statement of duties assigned and carried out, with notations of any special difficulties or accomplishments.

In addition to these necessary documents, the program should have a well-developed plan for carrying out orientation, training, and recognition of volunteers. Much of the same information included in staff orientation can be used in orientation of volunteers, although probably not in the same depth as that designed for the staff.

Volunteer orientation should include:

- Explanation of program goals and objectives
- Description of adult day care population
- Introduction to staff and participants
- Guided tour of the facility, including storage arrangements, bathrooms, where to keep personal belongings, etc.

- Explanation of safety rules and practices, including emergency procedures
- Discussion of volunteer responsibilities and duties
- Lines of supervision
- Discussion of program policies, participants' rights, do's and don'ts as outlined in volunteer handbook
- Description of a typical day in the center
- A welcome to the program and an invitation to ask questions and make suggestions.

Volunteer training may not be the same for all volunteers. Depending upon the tasks to be performed, the amount of time to be spent in the program, and the depth of knowledge needed to carry out assignments, the amount and content of training will be planned and adjusted to meet needs of the individual or group of volunteers.

Training needs should be assessed and analyzed at the time of the screening interview and on an ongoing basis, with volunteers being invited to participate in any training which will increase their ability to work with participants and carry out their work. Volunteers may be able to benefit from some training offered to staff, or may need to have training planned especially for them. Training may be conducted by staff or by outside resources, or the volunteer may attend training events held in the community by other agencies.

Volunteers will benefit from knowing how well they are meeting the program's expectations of them; a regular evaluation of their job performance will help them to understand their strengths and weaknesses. The evaluation should include assessments of the volunteer's dependability; their fulfillment of the job description; their ability to work in accordance with volunteer policies; their observance of do's and don'ts; the effectiveness of their interaction with participants (for those working in this area); and their ability to work well as a part of the team.

The volunteers should participate in the evaluation and may be asked to evaluate the program from the volunteer perspective. They could be asked to address questions like the following.

- Are program expectations of the volunteer in line with job description?
- Is the volunteer treated with respect and courtesy and made to feel a part of the team? Are their contributions valued?
- Are orientation and training adequate?
- Is supervision adequate?
- Is assistance from staff and supervisor available when needed?
- Are relationships with staff, participants, director, and other volunteers cordial and cooperative?
- Are adequate recognition and support offered?

Recognition of volunteer services should be included in plans for using volunteers in the program. Informal recognition should be offered each time the volunteer is in attendance at the center. A thank-you for time and effort expended and for the contribution made should be voiced by the volunteer coordinator or supervisor. Providing time for volunteers to discuss any problems or ask questions is also a way of recognizing their contribution and making them feel part of the team. Anniversaries of the time they began working in the program should also be commemorated.

More formal recognition events should be planned and carried out on a regular, periodic basis. This may take the form of a dinner, banquet, reception, or other appropriate event planned to focus on volunteers and their donation to the program. Awarding of certificates or other tangible form of recognition is recommended.

Another method of showing appreciation is that of recommending outstanding volunteers for awards given in the community by other agencies or organizations, such as the Red Cross or Voluntary Action Center. Offering ample recognition and appreciation is vital for helping to keep volunteers motivated and interested in remaining with the program.

Volunteer Recruitment

Volunteers are where you find them and they may be found almost everywhere. A well-planned recruitment effort will cover all areas of community life and will use varying methods. Recruitment should be directed toward both individuals and groups. Organizations which may have individuals within their membership who are potential volunteers or which may volunteer as a group include senior citizens' clubs and organizations; youth groups; church groups and organizations; civic organizations; and professional organizations.

A requirement for a volunteer with special ability or training or for someone who can plan and carry out a specific event may best be met by assessing the ability needed and approaching an organization with a known interest or knowledge in the area of need. Many such organizations prefer to volunteer for short-term or one-time activities, rather than making a commitment for a long term. Sources for such volunteers include:

families of participants

families and friends of staff and board members

Council on Aging

Voluntary Action Center

Red Cross

schools and colleges

civic and professional clubs

court systems which require offenders to render community volunteer service: DWI, juvenile court, etc.

business

service agencies

churches

Recruitment methods used should have the objective of getting the need known to as much of the community as possible. A number of strategies can be used for this kind of broad appeal:

- Requests on TV and radio, using public service announcements (if the program is nonprofit)
- Announcements in newspaper columns which announce such needs
- Announcements in the center newsletter
- Posting the need in places frequented by potential volunteers, such as shopping centers, beauty and barber shops, banks, churches, businesses, schools
- Listing job descriptions with Voluntary Action Center and other volunteer recruitment agencies; college and school clubs; church groups; senior citizens' clubs, etc.
- Contact with student advisors of schools and colleges, church secretaries, etc.
- Contact with college professors in the fields of psychology, sociology, nursing, gerontology, etc. whose students might be given credit for volunteering in the program.
- Personal appeals to community agencies and groups
- Word-of-mouth by staff, participants, board members, and present volunteers.

Program supervisors should keep in mind that some persons who may express an interest in volunteering in the program will not possess qualifications needed. A careful screening process should be carried out, beginning with the initial conversation with a prospective volunteer. If this results in a favorable impression, the individual should be invited to visit the program and fill out an application.

An in-depth interview during the visit is the next step. The volunteer coordinator should review with the applicant the application, job description, and volunteer policies. Often, at this point, unsuitable volunteers eliminate themselves. If this does not occur, the coordinator will have to discourage those who are unsuitable in a gentle manner, perhaps recommending that they consider volunteering in another agency or service for which they appear better suited.

Matching the individual's qualifications with the needs of the job is also an important part of the interviewing process. While some individuals may not appear to be suitable for the adult day care climate, they may be able to contribute by performing office or outside chores. Some individuals may lack necessary skills or knowledge, but adequate training may remedy this to the degree that they can become a valuable volunteer. No individuals should be turned down if creative thinking and action will alleviate barriers to their becoming volunteers.

Use of Contractual Services

While reviewing the staff structure to determine what gaps may exist in staff capability for delivering services, an assessment may be made about whether such gaps may be filled by use of contractual services. Services not needed by all participants and those needed only intermittently may often be provided at lower cost—and more effectively—by contracting with an agency who can provide the service. Such services may include those discussed below.

Meals

The equipment and staff needed for preparation of meals each day can demand an inordinate portion of the program budget. A contractual arrangement with a hospital cafeteria, Title V meal site, school or other agency will usually be more cost effective. Arrangements with such suppliers have a further advantage in that therapeutic diets may be obtained for participants who need them.

A possible problem with contractual meal service is that of transporting the meals. Containers and utensils that meet health and safety codes and will keep food at the correct temperature while in transit must be used. Research into what is available and conferences with possible suppliers and with the health department will be needed to decide upon a solution to this problem.

Transportation

Many factors will influence the choice of an outside agency for transportation. These considerations include the number of miles to be covered each day; the impairment level of participants; the number needing to be transported with impairments requiring a lift or other such device; the number of vehicles which can be purchased by the program; and the number of staff whose time would be taken up in providing transportation. Community transportation projects, Mass Transit, or other organizations in the business of transportation may make the service available at a lower cost than it can be done in-house.

Some disadvantages can attend hiring an outside service. There will be no control over staff who do the transporting, and this may cause conflict if there are complaints or problems with the service. The program also loses benefits of having transportation vehicles available to use for other purposes, such as field trips, medical appointments, shopping, etc.

Therapies

Since most therapies for adult day care participants are likely to be needed by only a part of the group, arranging to have these provided by an outside therapist or in a therapy center will possibly be more cost effective. Provision of such services within the program to all participants when they are needed by only a few increases cost of care across the board, causing some participants to pay for an expensive service they do not need.

Medical Services

If the community has facilities for providing medical care needed by participants, it makes financial sense to use community facilities insofar as they meet needs, rather than duplicating a service already available. Using clinics, public nursing services, etc., can cover a wide range of participant needs. Factors which will influence this decision are impairment level of participants, constancy of need for medical care, setting of the program (programs located within a hospital or other medical facility will be likely to have access to services from the facility), funding requirements, and program goals and objectives.

A compromise may be the best course. A full-time or part-time nurse on staff can monitor the health status of participants, provide some care on-site, and make referrals to other sources for more intensive health care needs.

Mental Health Care

As with physical care, arrangements may be made with mental health clinics, therapists, or other mental health professionals to supply mental health care for participants in need of such care. Costs will be lower, and use of such facilities may provide greater access to the service than is possible for the program to provide.

Consideration must be given, however, to the number of participants with mental health impairments and also to the degree of impairment. Some such individuals will require constant attention by a staff member skilled in working with people with mental health impairments.

Housekeeping and Building Maintenance

Housekeeping and maintenance services are usually contracted for. The organization providing the services should have a clear understanding of the cleanliness and safety codes which the program must meet: floors may have to be mopped more often that is usual; floors may not be waxed; mopping cannot be done while participants are in the center (at least in areas in use by participants); storage of cleaning materials must be done so as to be safe for confused participants; cleanliness must meet public health codes.

In general, when making decisions about what services may be provided by contractual arrangements, consider the number of participants likely to need the service, how often it must be provided, and what method is likely to offer the highest quality at the least cost to the program.

All contracts should be made with goals and philosophy of the program in mind. Providers of the contracted services must understand that everything done for participants is directed toward helping them to maintain or improve their capacity for independence and that everyone involved with the program must cooperate to help achieve this goal.

Contracts entered into should be explicit, spelling out terms of the agreement, including what each party is expected to do, under what circumstances, for what period of time and at what cost. Terms of agreements should also include the quality of care, product, or service to be provided, what action is to be taken to correct any shortcomings, and the degree of control which can be exercised by the program over outside personnel working with participants. It is recommended that the program retain the right to request that staff be replaced if they are not providing care or service consistent with adult day care philosophy and goals.

Use of Consultants

The same criteria for deciding whether or not to use contractual services may be used to determine whether consultants should be used. Most commonly, the use of a consultant for a service which may not be needed by all participants or is needed only sporadically should be considered.

In addition to providing direct services to participants, consultants may be used to perform other tasks for the agency. Direct services would include:

therapies

mental health care

social services

nursing and medical care

nutritional planning

education or training.

Indirect services may include:

fund-raising

public relations

management evaluation and restructuring

program evaluation

staff development and training

marketing

legal services.

Using consultants has the advantage of obtaining highly qualified personnel and paying for their expertise only while it is needed. A further advantage is that of being able to supplement staff abilities with a broad array of skills, greatly increasing program quality and capability.

Contracts with consultants should be made with the same concerns as for other contractual arrangements. Care provided must be designed to carry out program and individual service goals. Contracts with consultants may be with a group or with an individual. The contract may be for a one-time service or for open-ended service which allows the use of a specific number of hours at the convenience of the program, for a set price.

Summary

Adult day care is a complex service, which requires a great number of professional skills and a wide range of knowledge in both administrative and programmatic issues. It will not be possible for most programs to employ staff to supply all the expertise needed to carry out the program as planned and to meet all needs of participants. The use of volunteers, contractual arrangements, and consultants allows the program to command unlimited knowledge and skills, expanding program capability and enhancing program quality.

Careful thought should be given to which program purposes can best be met by providing services on-site and thus retaining complete control, and which can best be met by use of outside resources, with the program retaining some elements of control.

Use of contractual resources requires care that terms are explicit and cover all issues having to do with quality as well as with cost.

16 Defining the Adult Day Care Population

Introduction

Admission policies of adult day care are among the most important of program policies, since they establish parameters of the population which will be served in the program. The policies should describe in detail criteria for admission to the program. Those drawing up the policies must thoroughly understand the characteristics and parameters of the general population for whom adult day care is the most appropriate method of care. Further, they must be clear about the specific population they intend to serve based upon the program goals, capabilities, and limitations.

Defining the Adult Day Care Population

A number of descriptions of the population considered to be in need of adult day care have been formulated.

In a speech to the membership of the National Institute on Adult Daycare (April 1982), Padula presented the point of view that the population to be served is essentially the homebound.

Trapiano (1978,[1]) states that adult day care is needed for elderly persons whose disabilities do not require full time care in traditional environments, but who are not capable of total independent living and require a protected environment during the day.

Weiler and Rathbone-McCaun (1978, 7-8) define the population in three ways. First, there are those who live alone and cannot care for themselves completely. Second, there are those who live with others who need relief from total responsibility for the care. Third are those recently discharged from an institutional setting.

The National Institute on Adult Daycare (1984, 22-23) identifies the target population as follows:

> The population served will vary according to the identified needs of the community and the capability of the organization offering the services. The target population includes one or more of the following groups:

1. Adults with physical, emotional or mental impairments who require assistance and supervision.
2. Adults who need restorative and rehabilitative services in order to achieve the optimum level of functioning.

These varying definitions indicate that all adult day care programs will not serve exactly the same population. In practice, however, individuals in need of adult day care can generally be distinguished from those who are able to function in a more independent setting, or who, conversely, need more care and supervision than can be provided within the adult day care setting. Adult day care should be recognized as an integral, but distinct, point of care within the system of supportive services needed by the functionally impaired adult. This system should be designed so as to direct individuals into the least restrictive form of care possible for them, consistent with their abilities and needs.

In general terms, then, the population which may be said to need the service consists of adults who are essentially homebound, and who, because of one or more impairments, cannot live at home without supportive services, but who do not require 24-hour institutional care. The impairments may be physical, mental, or emotional, or a combination of these. Frequently, economic or social impairments will have contributed to the development or worsening of the condition.

Appropriate candidates for adult day care are persons who can be helped to maintain or improve their ability to manage at home and those whose families need relief from full time physical and emotional responsibility for the dependent member. They may require care on a short-term basis for the purpose of stabilizing or correcting an acute problem (with the expectation of improving functional capacity) or on a long-term basis to prevent premature or inappropriate institutionalization.

Adult day care providers must exercise vigilance to ensure that participants being served in their programs are getting the care which is most appropriate for them. If the participant has been misplaced, or if a change in status occurs so that day care is no longer appropriate, providers must offer assistance in helping to re-locate the participant into the level of care which is needed.

Assessing Program Capacity

Admission policies of each program must be formulated in light of what level of care the program is capable of providing. Before the question "who shall we serve?" can be answered, there must be an answer to the question "who can we serve?" This question is answered by reviewing the program facility, staff structure and abilities, and other resources available to the program.

Facility

If the program is considering serving participants with visual, motor, or cognitive impairments, the facility must be evaluated in terms of their needs.

Visual Impairments. The facility must be lighted in a manner suitable for those with poor eyesight; these must be ample, non-glare lighting. Obstacles which may present a hazard for these participants must be eliminated. The facility should have open passages, level floors, doors which open easily and do not swing back when opened, and furniture which stays in place and is not easily tipped over. Planners must be sure that in both facility and furnishings there are no obstacles and impediments that would prevent participants who are blind or have poor vision from attending the program with assurance of safety and the ability to function at a maximum level of independence.

Mobility Impairments. For participants who have limited or no ability to be mobile, the facility must have open passages wide enough to accommodate wheelchairs, walkers, and canes. Furniture must be suitable for use by these participants. The facility should have chairs which will provide some assistance (lift) in rising and tables and other furniture without sharp corners (round tables are preferred). All furniture must be sturdy and not easily tipped over.

Cognitive Impairments. Participants with Alzheimer's disease or other mental impairments resulting in mental confusion, memory loss, or other symptoms preventing normal functioning will need space in which to pace, both indoors and out. Additionally, there must be a means of securing the program space so that wanderers are not able to leave the facility unobserved.

Furniture must be covered with washable or easily cleaned materials, in case of accidents with spills or with incontinence.

There must be some means of locking up medications and potentially harmful cleaning materials; all program equipment and tools which may be used as weapons by mentally impaired participants should also be securely locked up.

Bathroom doorways and other program areas should be marked so that they are easily identifiable by those who are confused.

There must be space where individuals who may become agitated can be taken to separate them from the group until they are able to control their behavior and rejoin the group.

Impairments Requiring ADL Assistance. If participants are to be admitted who require assistance and/or training with activities of daily living, the program space must be planned to accommodate this: space and equipment for bathing and personal care, facilities for clothing care, meal preparation, etc.

Impairments Requiring Bed Rest. If participants are admitted who will require regular and frequent bed rest, the facility must be planned and equipped to meet this need. There must be a room set aside for this purpose with enough beds for the number of participants who will be admitted having this need.

Staff Capability

As discussed in Chapter 12, the numbers and skills of adult day care staff must be carefully matched to the needs of participants admitted to the program under the admission policies. Persons requesting admittance who will need more intense or more specialized treatment or care than the staff can provide should be referred to another facility or level of care. Below are discussed examples of impairments which require special staff skills in the adult day care setting.

Participants Needing Daily Nursing Care. Included among those who need this care are persons who use special equipment for elimination, persons who must have daily injections, persons with problems subject to needing emergency treatment (seizures, diabetic coma, etc.), individuals subject to cardiac arrest, persons who must have help changing bandages (those with cancer, accident victims, etc.), participants who must have blood pressure monitored each day.

Participants Who Need Therapies. Individuals needing physical, occupational, speech, or other types of therapy may receive it from a staff member or be referred to another source. Planners should be clear about the method to be used so that participants are admitted with an understanding of what the arrangement is to be.

Participants with Severe Psychiatric or Psychological Problems. The need for psychiatric treatment or professional counseling is often more constant than the need for treatment of physical impairments. It is important, therefore, that planners give careful attention to whether such applicants will be admitted, what degree of mental impairment can be handled by the staff as it is structured, and the numbers which can be admitted and have proper attention paid to their needs. For individuals who have these impairments but whose need for treatment is less intense, arrangements may be made to treat them through an outside source. Again, planners must be clear about what the arrangements are to be and design admission policies to reflect this.

When decisions have been reached concerning the levels of care which the staff has capability to offer and for which the facility is equipped and adequate, consideration must be given to how many participants to admit with specific conditions requiring staff attention on a one-to-one basis for much of the time. Caution must be taken that the staff is not overwhelmed by the number of participants who have a high level of dependency necessitating intense care. A balance must be maintained between these participants and those who have a functional level that will require less attention. Admission of each individual must therefore be considered in light of the participant configuration at time of application. This policy must be stated in the admission policies.

The following types of participants may require one-to-one treatment for much of the time and thus may need to be admitted in limited numbers.

Participants Who are Blind. Blind participants usually need assistance to move about the facility and with toileting or eating. These participants may also need much assistance with carrying out program activities. Admitting them will probably necessitate planning much of the program with their needs in mind or being able to adapt it to their abilities.

Participants with Limited Mobility. Participants who must have help to move about may use a wheelchair, walker, or cane, or may be dependent upon the assistance of another person. Those using wheelchairs will sometimes be unable to propel the chair without help or will need to be assisted with transferring to a car or other vehicle.

Participants with Confusion. Cognitive impairments may be present in varying degrees, and all participants who are confused will require some special attention. They may need full-time attention to prevent them wandering away from the center, help with eating to prevent choking (including reminders to swallow), or reminders and assistance with using the bathroom. They must also have concentrated attention and assistance from the staff in order to engage in program activities, which must usually be planned to suit their functional level.

Participants Who are Deaf or Who have Speech Impairments. These participants will need staff assistance to be kept aware of what is taking place in the program, either by use of sign language, written notes, or other means of special communication.

Participants Who Exhibit Deviant Behaviors. Those who have emotional or other psychological problems will demand large blocks of staff time and attention if they are to be successfully assimilated into the program. Deviant behaviors include extreme anger or hostility, acting out, withdrawal, inappropriate sexual behaviors, paranoia, anxiety, loss of emotional control, or catastrophobic reactions.

Participants Who are Subject to Seizures or Comas. Individuals with illnesses which include a tendency to seizure or coma will require close attention from the staff to help prevent such episodes occurring and also to provide treatment in the event of an occurrence.

Participants Who are Incontinent. Incontinence requires assistance with toileting as well as training to learn more self-sufficiency in this respect. When accidents occur, participants will need help with clothing changes. More effort will also be needed to keep the building clean and odor-free.

Participants with Substance Abuse Problems. Those addicted to alcohol or drugs or who may be recovering from such addiction may require intensive help and attention from the staff to stay in control of the addiction.

The foregoing is not meant to be an exhaustive list of participant impairments which will require additional staff time and special attention from staff, nor is it meant to discourage providers from admitting individuals with these specific impairments. These are common problems among the population defined as needing the service; to exclude them would be to lose sight of the purpose of adult day care. Rather, the list is meant to stimulate thought on the part of those deciding who will be served in the program. Such participant impairments are among the key factors which must be considered when designing admission policies for the adult day care program. Policies must be designed so that only those participants whose needs can be met will be admitted, and in numbers which will not compromise quality of service.

Admission Policies

In addition to the way in which impairment level affects program capacity (as discussed above), there are additional factors—such as age, geographic boundaries, ability to pay, etc.—to consider when deciding parameters of the population to be served by a specific program.

Age

Some funding sources impose specific age limits for admission to an adult day care program funded by them. (Example: Older Americans Act funds.) There may be other reasons unique to a program which cause limiting the population to a particular age range. In general, however, excluding individuals from the program for reasons of chronological age should *not* be considered a valid reason. Many physiological, mental, and emotional problems recognize no age barrier. Adult day care may be the best and most appropriate method of care available to either young or old persons with impairments requiring that they be cared for during the day.

Functional Level

The ways in which functional impairments impinge on admission policies have been discussed in detail above. It should be reiterated that functional capacity must be considered among the most important elements in design of admission policies.

Geographic Boundaries

Some limits may have to be imposed upon the geographic area to be served if transportation is to be provided or if large numbers of persons needing the service reside within the area. This is likely to be true if the region is unusually large or heavily populated. Drawing boundaries will provide the program with the means of controlling time and effort spent in transporting participants and of limiting numbers of applications if this is needed.

Matching of Need with Level of Service

If an individual is able to function in a setting which is less structured or one which provides a lower level of care, adult day care services are inappropriate and this should be stated in the policies. Individuals to be admitted should also have need for care which is consistent with the particular services to be offered by the specific program. If, for example, nursing service is not available, individuals in need of this should not be admitted.

Ability to Pay Fees

Ideally, no person would be denied admission because of inability to pay for the service. If the program has ample resources from funding bodies, or can obtain them by raising funds for scholarships, financial barriers to admission can be disregarded. If, however, the program is dependent upon payment of fees to continue operation, or there are other limitations upon available funds, policies will have to state program requirements for fee payment.

Amount of Space

The number of participants enrolled at a given time must be consistent with the number allowed by regulations for the available space. State standards and licensure regulations should be checked to learn what is required. The national standards state that at least 40 square feet of program space should be allowed for each participant.

If the population to be served is very frail and will be likely to have a high absentee rate, enrollment for each day may exceed the number allowed by the number of expected absences. This adjustment may be precluded, however, by state or funding regulations. Care must be taken to learn whether it is permissible. If the program is going to follow this policy, records should be kept for a period of time to learn what the absentee rate is likely to be.

Comfort Levels

Numbers admitted should not exceed ability of the program to provide comfort, which is defined as having sufficient furniture, adequate number of bathroom facilities, adequate storage; space for rest, quiet, and to withdraw from the group; and adequate space for carrying out appropriate program services and activities. Even though the number of bathrooms meets regulation requirements, admission of very frail individuals, or those needing assistance with toileting, may necessitate a larger number.

Included in the admission policies must be guidelines for deciding when the adult day care program is no longer the most appropriate method of care for an individual and under what circumstances discharge will take place. This policy should be included as a part of those defining the population to be served in the program. Policies should include guidelines for carrying out both emergency and planned discharges.

Emergency discharge may be required in the following cases.

- Communicable disease requiring isolation or presenting a danger to other participants and staff
- Uncontrollable violent or abusive behaviors posing danger or harm to self or others
- Intentional or continuous disruptive behavior
- Uncontrollable wandering
- Uncontrolled incontinence (if the program is not equipped to handle this)
- Addiction to alcohol or drugs resulting in unmanageable behavior.

Planned or routine discharges may result when:

- Functional abilities improve to the degree that the individual is able to move into a more independent setting
- Need for care increases to the degree that adult day care can no longer meet outstanding needs.

Discharge policies should state the reasons which will prompt both kinds of discharge and the process to be followed in both: notification method, length of notice (if any), and adjustment and assistance to be provided by program staff. The policy should also include circumstances under which readmission will be considered.

Summary

Deciding to include policies which will deny admission to the adult day care program or which will require discharge is difficult for providers. It must, however, be recognized that making an attempt to serve everyone who applies for service may result in a failure to serve anyone adequately. Each program must decide upon the specific population toward which its major effort is to be directed and refuse to lose sight of this purpose.

The uniqueness and strength of adult day care lies in its ability to plan and provide services designed to meet specific needs of each individual admitted to the program. Therefore, each applicant must be considered in light of how safe the program will be for that individual and how well their perceived needs can be met. Admission and discharge policies must be based upon a realistic assessment of program resources and liabilities. With these in mind, providers must clearly delineate parameters of the particular population to be served by their program from within the larger population to be served by adult day care.

Outlining parameters of this group should not mean that no flexibility is allowed in admission decisions; flexibility is a benchmark of the service of adult day care. Therefore, policies governing admission decisions should be used to examine needs of each applicant so that an informed decision can be made as to whether the program possesses or can obtain resources to meet those needs. It should be kept in mind that one need not be limited to on-site resources, but should also consider what might be available through contractual arrangements, use of volunteers, consultants, or other service providers or resources in the community.

No individuals should be denied admission if adult day care appears to be most appropriate for them and if creative thinking and planning by the staff can devise a means of providing needed care without overtaxing or disrupting the program.

References

National Institute on Adult Daycare. 1984. *Standards for adult day care.* Washington, DC: National Council on the Aging, Inc.

Padula, H. April 1982. Unpublished speech delivered to the National Institute on Adult Daycare.

Trapiano, F.M. 1978. *Initial planning considerations for developing an adult day care center.* Denton, TX: Center for Studies in Aging, North Texas University.

Weiler, P.G. and E. Rathbone-McCuan. 1978 or 1981. *Adult day care: Community work with the elderly.* New York: Springer Publishing Company.

17 Admission and Discharge

Introduction

Locating and recruiting participants in need of the care and services porvided by adult day care and who are able to function as required by program admission policies often proves to be an ongoing task for providers. The decision of whether each applicant can fit into the program and benefit from enrollment is done in conformity with admission policies, using information obtained by carrying out specific steps: enrollment procedures. Similarly, discharges will be carried out according to specific procedures of the program, using the information gained during the admission process in conjunction with what has been learned about the participant during the period of attendance in the program. (Sample enrollment and discharge forms can be found in Appendix C.)

Identifying Participants

The lower an individual's functional level who needs adult day care, the greater the need for the service; yet such a person will usually be the last to learn of its availability. Even those who learn of the service may lack the energy, motivation, or ability to find out more about the program and how to avail themselves of its services. Providers must develop strategies for both locating potential participants and be prepared to use persuasive techniques to motivate them to become interested in applying (Exhibit 17-1).

In addition to the strategies outlined in Exhibit 17-1, ongoing efforts should be carried out to educate the community about the program and to gain support from the community.

Recruiting Participants

Identification of potential participants is only the first and least difficult step in the enrollment process. Individuals in greatest need of the service will often resist enrollment for the same reasons which prevent them from learning about the program. In addition, frail adults who have been isolated or home bound for a long period may feel threatened by new experiences. Other barriers to enrollment include impairments so that the individual does not recognize the need for care. Also, the family or potential participant may be unfamiliar with the concept of adult day care and unaware of its

Exhibit 17-1 Locating adult day care participants.

Methods and sources for potential adult day care participants:

1. Contact community agencies which serve populations likely to include persons needing such a service. *Examples:* Department of Social Services, Departments of Mental and Public Health, police and fire departments, Council of Older Adults, Area Agency on Aging, senior citizens' centers and clubs, nursing homes, hospitals, clinics, outreach departments of libraries.
2. Contact civic groups and organizations which include older adults and/or their families among their membership. *Examples:* garden clubs, women's clubs, Junior League, Lions Club, AARP, NRTA.
3. Contact agencies which recruit volunteers and may number potential participants among recipients of their services. *Examples:* Red Cross, Voluntary Action Agency, Retired Senior Volunteer Program (RSVP), hospitals.
4. Place listings of the program in telephone directories and with local information and referral services.
5. Place listings in community directories of human services.
6. Advertise in local newsletters of churches, medical society, nursing association, etc.
7. Notify professional associations of the service: nursing, medical, physical therapists, respiratory and speech therapists, etc.
8. Place posters and brochures where potential participants and/or their families visit or congregate. *Examples:* Shopping areas, cafeterias, restaurants, banks, beauty and barber shops, places of employment, churches, doctors' offices, clinics, places of recreation (parks, bowling alleys, etc.).
9. Hold open house, inviting representatives from the groups and organizations listed above as well as public officials and representatives of funding sources.

participant may be unfamiliar with the concept of adult day care and unaware of its benefits. They may not be convinced of its value, or may simply prefer another method of care. Lack of funds or lack of available transportation may also contribute to hesitancy about joining the program.

When confronted with such barriers, adult day care staff may have to assume the role of counselor, helping individuals and family members identify their problems and needs and to learn what options are available to them. The staff can offer assistance in determining which option will come closest to providing services needed to resolve the problem. If, in the professional judgement of the adult day care staff, the program appears to be the service most likely to meet the need, and if individuals are eligible for enrollment under program admission policies, education about the service and encouragement to use it should be offered to these individuals and their families.

In situations where resistance is offered, the staff is confronted with a dilemma. Applying pressure on the participant to enroll may have overtones of paternalism, or be seen as attempts to take from the individual the right to make decisions. On the other hand, failure to persuade the individual to enroll, at least on a trial basis, means leaving that person without the help which may increase the quality of life. In this situation the staff experiences feelings of defeat; the program itself may fail if it occurs often enough.

Ethics involved are difficult to resolve; however, it appears in the best interest of both the individual and the program to use persuasive methods to encourage at least a trial visit or a temporary enrollment of at least one week. This often results in a fading of resistance as benefits of attendance becomes apparent.

Although a trial enrollment will eliminate resistance for many, others who may be disoriented or who do not adapt quickly to a new environment, may need a longer adjustment period to feel comfortable in the program. It may take longer for them to feel a degree of improvement which will convince them of their need to remain in the program. Faced with this type of need the staff must again decide how much persuasion to use. Judgements must be made as to whether the individual may adjust if given more time, or whether the program appears unlikely to be the most appropriate form of care. Adult day care is not the answer to everyone's problems, and attempts to make it so may result in the spending of excessive energy with reluctant individuals, to a degree that deprives other participants of needed attention. It may also result in enrollment of an individual who may be better served by another service. When the staff believes this to be true, attempts should be made to help the person find a more appropriate method of care.

Several persuasive strategies can be recommended to help convince individuals to give the program a try while ensuring a good match between participant and program. A current participant can be taken along when making a home visit to a prospective enrollee. Candidates will often respond more readily to a person whom they perceive to be a peer than to a staff member. The participant who goes on the visit should possess good communication skills, be empathetic, and must be able to convey positive feelings about the program with sincerity.

During the initial visit to the center, the new participant should be placed under the wing of someone who has been enrolled in the program for some time and who can offer assistance in learning the program routine and facility layout. The guide can help the new participant become acquainted in the program and begin to develop relationships within the group.

Staff should spend whatever time is necessary to provide sufficient information to the family and participant to help them to make an informed decision. Information offered should include philosophy and purposes of the program, how services are planned and carried out, admission policies and procedures, withdrawal and discharge policies and procedures, and a general statement of expected benefits for the participant and the family/caregiver. Questions should be encouraged and answered in detail and to the satisfaction of the person making the inquiry.

Enrollment procedures should be carried out with sensitivity for the family and participant and with understanding that this is a new and potentially threatening situation for them. Evidence of concern for their needs should be shown throughout the process. Staff members should take the approach of helping to educate the participant and family about the service and how it will benefit them. Throughout the process, the staff should take advantage of the opportunities offered to learn about the participant's needs so that the information can be applied in developing the plan of care.

The strategies outlined above are applicable to already established centers. New programs may have to use additional tactics to enroll participants and fill the center.

One recommendation is to offer one day of free attendance for those who display interest in the program. (This may also be used by established programs who may be experiencing difficulty in keeping their center filled.)

Holding open house early soon after opening the program—inviting only those persons who have made inquiry about the program but have not made a decision to enroll—is a good way to introduce a new program to the community. The open house should last at least several hours, with a program planned which is typical of a day in the program. Activities should be carried out for a period of time ample to demonstrate the program, at least half a day. The visit should be free and should be followed by a home visit or other measure to answer any questions the attendees may have and to further explain the program.

Admission Procedures

The actions outlined above are considered preliminary steps in the admission process. The total process will entail seven steps which are discussed in detail below:

1. Intitial Contact
2. Functional Assessment
3. Home Visit
4. Visit to the Center
5. Enrollment Decision
6. Completion of Enrollment Procedures
7. Integration Process.

Initial Contact

The first contact with a potential participant is frequently by phone, less frequently by personal contact. The program should use this original contact to obtain basic information about the prospective participant.

Basic Information:

- Name of individual
- Age
- Address and phone number
- Problems and/or needs prompting inquiry: diagnosed physical and/or mental health problems; others
- Living arrangments
- Information candidate needs about the service and the program
- Follow-up action desired from the program (any promise must be carried out promptly and efficiently).

This initial contact should also be used to impart information about the program:

- Program purposes
- Admission policies
- A brief sketch of services and activities provided, and how they can be used to meet needs as revealed in the conversation
- Outline of staff structure
- Enrollment procedures.

Program information need not be related in detail at this time, but only to the extent that the person making the inquiry appears ready for the information. More complete information can be given at the time of next contact.

Functional Assessment

Information obtained by use of a multi-dimensional functional assessment is usually the most complete from any source. The assessment should cover:

- Physical and mental/emotional condition
- Functional ability
- Living arrangements
- Financial and social information
- Strengths and needs of the applicant.

(The assessment will be discussed in detail in Chapter 18; Appendix D comprises a sample Functional Assessment form.)

Home Visit

A visit to the home of a potential participant can reveal a lot of vital information about the applicant which may be difficult to obtain by other methods. During a home visit living arrangements, family relationships, safety of environment, how well the applicant functions within the home, and adaptations made in the home to accommodate functional impairments may be assessed. The visit also offers an opportunity to begin building a trust relationship with the applicant, especially important in situations where there is some reluctance to visit the program. Another advantage of making the visit is that it provides applicants with a familiar face during their first visit to the program, helping them to feel more at home.

Visit to the Center

Having applicants visit the center serves a number of purposes. It allows the staff to observe how well they adjust to a new environment and how well they are able to relate to the other participants. Functional levels at home versus in the center may be compared. The visit also offers the applicants an opportunity to change pre-conceived or negative ideas about the program. It allows them to begin the process of adjusting to the program and to the group and to get answers to questions which may arise after seeing the program in operation.

A second visit is recommended. This should be longer than the first and the applicant should join in group activities. The extent of participation must be based upon an assessment of how ready the individual is for this. Family members should be requested to leave the applicant at the center for this visit, returning at a time decided upon. A visit of least one-half day is suggested; however, this will depend upon the individual's ability to cope with the new situation.

Enrollment Decision

When the foregoing procedures have been completed, staff members who have responsibility for deciding upon admission applications should review all available information to decide whether adult day care appears to be the most appropriate service for the applicant.

The decision will be based upon three criteria: 1) Whether functional abilities are within the parameters outlined in program admission policies; 2) whether the program has the capacity to meet outstanding needs of the individual; and 3) whether the individual can adjust to the group situation and will not be excessively disruptive of the group process.

Completion of Enrollment Procedures

When the decision is taken to accept an applicant and the individual has decided to enroll, the enrollment process may be completed with the submission of a formal application (this may have been done earlier in the process, along with completion of the functional assessment). At this time the medical form should be completed, financial and transportation arrangements finalized, and the individual plan of care developed. (A sample admission form is included in Appendix C.)

Integration Process

The process of integrating a new participant into the adult day care program should be planned and carried out with sensitivity and with the functional level of the individual in mind. Each adult day care program should have well-developed strategies for helping individuals make the adjustment to the program, offering them whatever assistance is needed to become involved in interaction with the group to the extent that they are able. The new participant should be extended a warm welcome and helped to feel at home in the program environment.

Methods to help accomplish this include the following:

Home Visits by a Staff Member. An initial home visit will probably have been made during the application process. More than one visit may have been indicated by the response of the applicant. In any event, the fact that the new participant is now acquainted with one staff member, and there is a familiar face to offer greetings at the center, is helpful in beginning the adjustment process.

Preliminary Visits to the Center. Earlier visits, including an introduction to a friend who helped to "look after" the applicant during the initial visit will have already begun the applicant's assimilation into the group. A continuation of this arrangement for at least a few days—until the new participant begins to form other relationships—is recommended. Care must be taken that the participant providing the assistance does not become overwhelmed by the situation and the responsibility. Staff members should keep a watchful eye upon both individuals and step in at any point where this seems to be happening.

Welcome by a Staff Member. Upon arrival at the program and for the first few days of attendance, the new participant should be greeted by a staff member. It shoud be the same one each day, if possible, and preferably the same person who made visits to the home. This person will help the newcomer to become settled, provide an introduction to the participant who will serve as helper, offer assistance in becoming involved in an activity or in joining a conversation. (The extent of immediate involvement depends upon the individual; some may not be ready for much at first.) The point is to make the newcomers feel at home and feel that at the center they will find helpful friends. Assistance should be offered to participants to help them learn their way about the center, how and where to obtain supplies for activities, and where to keep personal belongings, and helped to begin learning the routine of the day.

Some prior exploration should have provided information to the staff concerning what activities will be of interest to the new participants. The staff should have made preparations to involve newcomers in an activity in which they had previously shown an interest. In this way the starting activity will have elements of familiarity and will utilize past skills and experience. A familiar activity—such as quilting, knitting, gardening, woodwork, or games such as checkers and cards—will be less threatening than something completely new.

Introduction to the Group. Introduction to the group as a whole or to selected individuals should be carried out at a rate and in a manner comfortable for the individual, with help provided to find common ground with some of the other participants. Again, this must be carried out based upon the ability of the participant to handle the new experience; some individuals will be unable to handle being involved in a group at all in the beginning. Some current participants could be alerted beforehand to provide a welcome and to offer assistance. If this is to be done, they should be provided with information about the new person which will help them to facilitate conversation.

Transportation Procedures. If the individual is to be transported to the program by a staff driver, the driver must be included in planning the integration process. It is important that the new participant and the family or caregiver have been introduced to the driver and that the driver be alert to any special need for assistance or unusual appearance or behavioral characteristics of the participant.

The driver must be provided with clear directions to the home and with instructions on how to handle emergencies which may occur en route; where to take the person if any unmanageable behavior is exhibited or a need arises for emergency treatment. The driver should also be provided with a telephone number where a family member or other responsible person can be reached, if needed.

Conflict Resolution. Even with the most detailed planning, there will be instances when a new participant does not fit easily into the group or the program. Some newcomers will exhibit problem behavior. Knowledge of the individual gained from documents used in the admission process, prior visits, etc., should have alerted staff to the potential for such problems, so that they are prepared to handle the situation.

Types of behavior and methods of coping are varied and will require understanding and skill on the part of the staff. With most participants, such behavior will improve after a few days at the center; however, some will always have the potential for creating problems within the group. The latter situation necessitates careful attention and planning on the part of the staff, if the participant is to be kept in the program. Some extreme or agressive behaviors may not be manageable within the adult day care setting. The individual may have to be discharged from the program, possibly to be referred to another level of care. This may take place during or after the trial enrollment period. A month is suggested as a trial enrollment, although some situations may warrant dismissal under emergency discharge policies before the end of the period. In most cases, a month will allow time for the person to become assimilated or to discover that adult day care is not appropriate.

Before dismissing a new participant (except in extreme situations), all avenues should be explored to determine whether the behavior can be altered by treatment. The staff should be sure that an accurate diagnosis has been made of the underlying cause and that all possible treatments have been tried.

Enlisting Families and Caregivers. While the primary recipient of adult day care services is the participant, those who are responsible for their care in the home are also beneficiaries. Padula (1981) accurately observes that the measure of success with adult day care participants is not how well they function in the center, but how well they function in the home. Adult day care is most effective when participant, family, and program staff form a team, working together to help the participant achieve more independent functioning, thereby lessening responsibility and stress for the family. Family involvement and participation should be encouraged and expected from time of initial inquiry, throughout the admission process and while enrollment in the program continues.

While the staff has responsibility for establishing communication and a working relationship with the family, family members also have some responsibilities to the program. Since they know the participant best, they must help with deciding upon realistic service goals. If the plan of care is to be successful, family members must continue it in the home.

Special events to which families are invited, invitations to stop by for visits using family members as program volunteers, are all methods for helping the family to feel a part of the program and for keeping them informed. Other methods include putting them on the mailing list for the center newsletter and including them in a family support group. The newsletter lets the family know the program schedule and keeps them updated about happenings in the center.

The family support group can yield multiple benefits. Families gain support from other families who are experiencing problems similar to theirs and benefit from the opportunity to engage in learning skills for coping with problems. The center benefits from increased family involvement, resulting in more effective support for the participant. The support group also functions as a communication forum between the family and the program. Benefits are probably greatest for the participant, whose care is improved as a result of the working relationship and of receiving consistent reinforcement in both the home and the program.

A part of the center's responsibility is counseling and support for the family which is handling the stress of caring for a dependent member. Families frequently need help to understand what options are available to them and to learn how to use resources. Counseling should begin during the admission process, with the assistance provided in helping the family decide whether adult day care is the most appropriate method of care for its dependent member. It should continue throughout the period of enrollment and during discharge. The support offered during the discharge process will be that of working with the family and the participant to decide whether discharge is indicated and what the plan of care is to be after discharge.

The staff should offer support for the duration of the working relationship with the family. (The term "counseling" as used in this context is not meant to be synonymous with formal counseling expected from a mental health professional. Rather, it is used to describe a *helping* relationship, within which the staff acts to support and sustain the family in their efforts to care for the dependent member.)

Some families will display initial resistance to becoming involved in the program and the family support group. However, if they can be persuaded to do so, the rewards—lessening of stress, support for handling problems, and improvement of the participant—may provide the incentive needed to overcome resistance.

Discharge Policies

Adult day care policies for discharge of participants are nearly as important as admission policies, since keeping participants in the program after it has ceased to meet their needs may be as harmful as admitting individuals whose needs cannot be met. Careful attention must be paid to formation of discharge policies.

As discussed earlier (see Chapter 6), there are three kinds of discharge, emergency, planned, and voluntary.

Emergency

An emergency takes place when the participant's condition or extreme behavior makes it dangerous to the individual or to others to keep this person in the program.

Such conditions or behaviors include:

- Communicable disease requiring isolation
- Violent or abusive behavior with potential for inflicting injury on self or others
- Intentional or continuous behaviors which are so disruptive that the program cannot operate normally
- Extreme behavior which is upsetting to other participants
- Persistent wandering, uncontrollable by staff and/or dangerous to the participant
- Uncontrolled incontinence in programs not staffed or equipped to deal with this condition.

Emergency discharges may be rescinded if, in the opinion of the director, treatment has brought the problem under control. If such improvement appears likely, the director may decide to suspend rather than discharge the individual pending expected improvement from treatment.

Planned

Each individual plan of care should include a plan for discharge of the participant if optimum conditions occur. In addition, discharge may have to be planned for reasons which are negative: for example, if participants fail to respond to treatment, their health deteriorates, or they die. As a part of the periodic review of the plan of care, the question of whether adult day care continues to be the most appropriate method of care for the individual should be considered. Discharge may be recommended if:

- Functional abilities have improved to the degree that the individual is able to function in a more independent setting.
- The need for care has increased to a degree which adult day care can no longer meet.
- It has become obvious that the individual is not responding to care within the adult day care environment and another level of care is indicated.

Voluntary

Participants will voluntarily leave the program for a variety of reasons:

- They move to another location.
- They or their families prefer another method of care.
- They feel well enough to continue to function without care (this event should have been foreseen by staff and discharge recommended).
- They lack transportation or funds to pay fees.

A survey of discharges from Vintage, Inc. (Rhodes 1982), an adult day care program in Pittsburgh, Pennsylvania, during a 12-month period shows that 22 participants exited the program. Follow-up interviews were completed on 16. Reasons given for leaving included:

- Need for care exceeded that which the program and family resources could provide
- Hospitalization and subsequent placement in a nursing home
- Participant was negative to adult day care
- Participant exhibited abusive physical or verbal behavior
- Participant enrolled in another adult day care center
- Death.

The study does not indicate which discharges were recommended and which were a decision of the participant in cases where the participant moved to another level of care. The group moving to another level of care constituted the largest segment exiting the program: 37% moved to a more intensive level of care, and 2% to a lesser or comparable method (one to a boarding home, one to another adult day care center). This pattern is indicative of discharge patterns for many programs, given the fact that the population served is usually severely impaired.

Discharge policies as formulated by the program should speak to each of the three kinds of discharge and specify the reasons which will prompt emergency discharge and which will indicate planned discharge. Written policies should also include program rules regarding voluntary withdrawal. It is customary for programs to require written notification of expected withdrawal, with at least two weeks notice being given. If no notice is given, the program may reserve the right to require payment of fees in lieu of the notice.

Discharge Procedures

Discharge planning from adult day care should follow four major guidelines.

1. Since discharges are a regular event, programs should have a well-developed plan for carrying them out. (See Appendix C for a sample discharge form.)
2. Discharge policies and procedures should be included in written program policies.
3. Procedures for provision of counseling during the transitory period after discharge has been decided upon should also be a part of program planning.
4. Ways of handling the death of a participant should be established.

Counseling is a form of support that will be needed for both those who move into a more independent setting and those who move to more intensive care. The adult day care program has become a large part of the lives of those who have been enrolled for any period of time, and leaving friends and familiar surroundings is likely to be a traumatic experience for them.

If discussions for planned discharge in the event of improvement have been a regular part of service planning, and if "graduation" has been viewed as a desirable goal toward which the participant is working, the move can be viewed as a positive step.

Those who are being discharged because the program no longer meets outstanding needs and they require more intensive care may need more support. The adult day care staff should work with the family and participant to ease the adjustment required by leave-taking. Discharge plans should not make departures abrupt, but, whenever possible, allow some time for transition. During the transitional period, the participant could perhaps spend some time in the new setting while still attending day care, making the discharge process a gradual one.

Even if the move is to a more independent setting such as a senior center, or to staying home except for daily visits to a nutrition site or to other arrangement, this may be a good plan. The participant in every case should have opportunities to verbalize and work through feelings of sadness and perhaps of rejection, with reassurance and support provided by the staff and family. Some participants will also experience grief at the leaving of a person who is their friend. Support should be offered to them and opportunities to express their feelings.

Some formal leave-taking event may be planned in situations where this seems feasible, if the individual leaving is able to participate in such an event and this person's attendance at the center has been meaningful to other participants. A "going-away" party, with cards and gifts made at the program, may be beneficial to both the person leaving and those who are staying. The participant should be invited to return for visits and be helped to maintain contact with friends in the program for as long as a need for this exists. Participants should also be offered reassurance that if the new situation does not work out, or if they need to return to the program, they will be considered for re-admission, receiving priority status.

Former participants who leave the program should have the right to have their names placed at the top of a waiting list, if one is in existence.

Death of a participant is a traumatic experience for both participants and staff. Some observance of the death should be held to allow for expression of grief and loss. A memorial service, attendance at the funeral or mass, or visit to the home are among methods which can be used to allow a sharing of grief and to offer opportunities to remember and talk about the meaning of the life of the person who has died. The staff should not attempt to gloss over the loss or any formal recognition given to the death. To do so would indicate to those who are left that their deaths would be treated summarily as well, implying that their presence was of little or no importance to the people in the program.

Summary

Careful planning and sensitive handling of both admitting and discharging of participants in adult day care are of key importance. Both events must take place under clearly defined and stated policies of the program and in accordance with well-developed procedures. Both call for close attention and participation by the staff, who must offer tactful and empathetic support to participants and to families to ease the adjustment and transition periods.

References

Padula, H. 1981. Toward a useful definition of adult day care. *Hospital Progress*. March.

Rhodes, L.M. 1982. *A Weissert profile and functional task analysis of Vintage, Inc*. Pittsburgh, PA: Vintage, Inc.

U.S. Federal Council on the Aging. 1978. *Assessment and plan of care: Public policy and the frail elderly*. Washington, DC: Government Printing Office.

18 Individual Service Plans

Introduction

The individual plan of care for each participant is the hub of all program planning in adult day care. The service has evolved as one which utilizes information from a comprehensive assessment of each participant's needs, interests, resources, and strengths in order to establish goals of care and to provide services and activities in support of those goals.

Steps in Developing the Plan of Care

The process of developing the individual plan of care should be systematic and follow four major specific steps: 1) Identify the participant; 2) Carry out intake procedures; 3) Review available information; and 4) Design the care plan.

Identify the Participant

Referral of an individual to an adult day care program is an indication of unmet needs or an impending crisis. Acceptance into the program based upon admission criteria and procedures (as outlined in Chapter 17), signifies a belief on the part of the provider that adult day care is the most appropriate form of care for the individual and that the program has the capability to work with the individual toward meeting needs and resolving problems.

Carry Out Intake Procedures

Intake procedures should be geared toward getting complete information so that care can be planned to meet the unique needs of the individual. An holistic view of the participant is needed; participants should never be regarded just in terms of their problems, but also in terms of their strengths and resources.

Application. Information to be provided on the application will include

1. Demographic data: name, date of birth, address, phone number, name and phone number of nearest relative or other responsible person, name and phone number of physician or other provider of medical care

2. Source of referral and reasons for referral
3. Attendance schedule and transportation arrangements (if these are known)
4. Financial arrangements
5. Any special information on conditions or arrangements
6. Any other information needed by the program.

Some states have standard application forms and will provide samples of these. Providers may wish to develop their own form so as to have one specific to the program; approval for this must usually be given by the state monitoring agency. (Appendix A includes a sample application form.)

Medical Report. The medical report should provide information about the participant's current health status; past medical history; current medications (with instructions for their use); prescription for therapeutic diets, if needed; limitations upon activity; instructions for special exercises or for therapies; notations of conditions requiring special care or attention (e.g., wandering tendencies, incontinence, violent or abusive behavior patterns, drug or alcohol addictions, etc.).

Comprehensive Functional Assessment. This assessment is perhaps the single most important component in the intake process. It should provide information about the functional capacity of the individual, including ability to cope with and adapt to changed circumstances. Problems, needs, strengths, and resources should be identified in six areas: social, physical health, emotional and mental health, economic, activities of daily living, and the living environment.

Information obtained from the assessment will be the primary basis for deciding upon goals of care; planning services and activities for the individual; and monitoring changes. Because the instrument used for assessment is so important in planning effective care, it should be carefully selected. Several models should be studied to choose one which comes closest to serving program purposes. If no available model proves adequate the program may elect to develop its own in order to cover all areas in which information is needed. A number of existing assessment tools and instruments have been used by adult day care programs, but at this time none has been selected by consensus as being ideal for adult day care purposes. (Appendix D comprises a sample Functional Assessment.) In a study undertaken by the Department of Health, Education, and Welfare, Office of the Assistant Secretary of Planning and Evaluation (Jacobs 1981)17 instruments were identified as the source of origin of other instruments being used for in-depth assessment of frail older adults. From these, the United States Federal Council on the Aging selected two which in their view, came closest to providing the multi-dimensional focus which they advocate for assessing care needs of the frail elderly (1978).

The two instruments selected were *The Philadelphia Geriatric Morale Scale* (developed by M. Powell Lawton and Elaine Brody of the Philadelphia Geriatric Center) and the *OARS Multidimensional Functional Assessment* (Older American Resource and Service Program, Duke Center for the Study of Aging and Human Development, Durham, NC).

Interview and Observation. During the admission process, the adult day care staff will be afforded several opportunities to observe the potential participant.

A home visit should be included as a part of the process if possible; and one or two visits to the center by the participant are also recommended. At least one visit should be planned when the participant can be involved in program activities for an extended period (i.e., several hours or a full day, depending upon the individual).

Such visits enable the staff to carry out skilled observation of the participants' living environment, functional ability in the home, and relationships with family members. In the center the staff can observe how the individual reacts to new situations and how well adaptation to the group proceeds.

Consultation with Family and Caregivers. The plan of care cannot be intelligently formed without information from those who are responsible for care of the individual, both at home and in professional capacities: family members, physicians, chore workers, therapists, social workers, etc. These individuals, having been in contact with the participant over an extended period of time, will be able to provide a dimension of knowledge not available from other sources.

Review Available Information

Data collected from the intake process should be sufficient to make the following determinations.

- Identify problems and unmet needs
- Allow classification of problems as short-term, long-term, or chronic
- Indicate whether problems require crisis intervention, immediate action, or planning for provision of long-term services
- Indicate how well individual is coping with problems and taking care of needs
- Identify resources which are being utilized
- Identify gaps in resources
- Identify strengths of the individual which can be used to work toward functional improvement
- Reveal ways in which enrollment in adult day care will be beneficial to the participant in working toward resolution of problems and meeting needs.

Design the Care Plan

When the staff is satisfied that the information it has is complete or the maximum obtainable, the development of the plan for provision of care can proceed.

The staff should work with the participant to develop a comprehensive plan. Input and participation in deciding upon care goals and methods must be invited from family and other caregivers. Staff, family, and caregivers together with the participant will constitute the care team, necessary to support the participant in working toward what will perhaps be difficult goals. (Appendix E comprises a sample Plan of Care.)

The broad care goal, which must be understood by all members of the care team, will be that of enabling the participant to maintain or improve functional status. Achieving this goal will involve deciding upon what objectives must be met, what the individual plan of care is to be, and how to overcome barriers to accomplishment.

Classify the Information. Break all information down into its component parts so that each problem and need can be addressed separately.

State Each Problem or Need. Write out each problem or need, describing what barriers exist to resolving the problem, and what strengths and resources the participant possesses to aid in overcoming barriers.

Determine What Options are Available. The staff should explore all options for resolution of each problem. These should be discussed with all members of the care team and with the participant. Options must be viewed realistically, with functional capacity of the participant and other existing barriers in mind.

Decide Which Option is Most Satisfactory. The participant should decide (if able to do so) upon the most satisfactory course of action. Staff and other members of the team must take care that they do not impose their choice of options upon the participant. If they are to be motivated to work toward goals, participants must be encouraged to decide upon the course of action which is within their capacity and which is desirable to them.

Decide Upon the Desired Resolution or Outcome. All actions taken should be planned to achieve an objective. This principle should be expressed in terms which are clear to the participant and other members of the care team. Everyone involved should be in agreement about the desired outcome.

Decide What Resources Will Be Utilized to Achieve Objectives. Resources will include the strengths and abilities of the participant, family members and other caregivers, resources of the adult day care program, and other resources and service providers in the community.

Decide Upon All Actions Which Must Be Taken to Achieve Objectives. This will include actions by the participant, program staff, family and caregivers and any others who will be involved in provision of care or who will be supplying resources.

Decide Who is to Be Responsible for Carrying Out Each Action. All members of the team should be clear about their specific areas of responsibility. Participants should be encouraged to assume as much responsibility as is consistent with their functional abilities. Motivation of an individual to accept this responsibility requires that a trusting relationship exist between the participant and other members of the team. This relationship will be achieved by placing the participant in the position of making the necessary decisions to the greatest extent possible, clearly outlining available options, and making sure that expectations are realistic and within the abilities of the individual.

A paternalistic attitude which assumes control and imposes decisions will result in increased dependency. This *must* be avoided.

Decide Upon the Expected Result of Each Action to Be Taken. Team members must understand what they are expected to accomplish and how their actions fit into achieving objectives and into the total plan of care. All actions should be coordinated to avoid duplication or gaps.

Decide Upon a Time Line for Carrying Out Each Action. Action plans should not be open-ended; each person should operate within a time line for carrying out assigned responsibility and reporting results. It is not expected that all actions will fit neatly into a time schedule. However, designing the plan with some objectives which are achievable within a limited time frame will help the participant to see that progress is being made and help to maintain motivation.

State How Monitoring Will Be Carried Out. Ongoing monitoring of all actions and their results is important to the care plan. Periodically, the plan should be measured against what is being accomplished in terms of services being delivered, amount and quality of services, results of service delivery, as well as evidence of progress on the part of the participant. Such periodic assessment should be a regular part of the monitoring process.

Decide How Results are to Be Evaluated. The measure of success for the plan lies in whether objectives are being accomplished as decided upon. The staff will confer with the participant and other team members to determine the degree of success. Their observations, along with documented changes in functioning status and attitudes and feelings of the participant constitute evidence of results. Favorable changes in functional abilities indicate that the plan was well conceived and carried out.

Lack of success, indicated by failure to improve or by regression, may result from a number of factors:

- Goals were unrealistic or beyond the capacity of the participant
- Participant was not motivated to achieve goals
- The care team failed to carry out its role effectively

- Needed resources were not available
- Participant experienced worsening health which was beyond control.

Decide Upon How Review and Revision of the Plan Will Be Carried Out. After results have been evaluated, the plan should be analyzed in light of those results. Success or failure should be examined to learn what factors contributed to either, so that successful measures can be replicated or remedial action taken in situations where goals were not achieved.

The review process should lead to indicated revisions of the care plan.

The steps in planning, as outlined above, are meant to be revolving, so that when the review process is completed, the team will begin again with the first step. The revision will utilize results of the evaluation and review to help decide what new decisions and actions are needed.

It cannot be overemphasized that goals must be kept within the ability of the participant to accomplish with the assistance of other team members and resources. An attempt to accomplish too much too quickly will result in the participant's becoming overwhelmed and losing motivation to continue. When problems and needs are numerous, prioritize goals, rather than attempting to work on them all at once.

Document All Components of the Care Plan. Complete and well-organized records should be kept of the total process, including goals decided upon, actions to be taken, responsibilities of team members, results of actions, results of evaluation and review, plans for revision, and any known reasons for success or failure.

A well-maintained record will have the following attributes.

- Allow easy access to information
- Provide for exchange of information among service providers
- Assure confidentiality of information relating to participant
- Record all decisions and plans
- Help to clarify plans
- Help to avoid duplication of effort
- Preserve continuity of action
- Be uniform.

The records should include the following sections.

- A statement of the participants functional status at beginning of care plan
- Participant's feelings and attitudes about problems and plans
- Documentation of the decision-making process

- Options discussed
- Options decided upon and reasons for choice
- All actions taken
- Assignment of responsibility for each action
- Results of each action
- Results of evaluation and review
- Plan revisions.

Records should be kept as brief as is consistent with completeness. Repetition should be avoided; each word should count. The recorder should keep in mind how the information will be used and who will use it. Information should be kept in chronological order. Some actions should be recorded in detail; other information can be summarized.

Planning for Discharge

An integral component of each plan of care is a plan for reviewing the participant's status in the program. At an appropriate interval, consideration should be made of whether the participant will continue to benefit from remaining in the adult day care program or whether some other care method will be more appropriate. The terminology "discharge planning" as used here may seem inappropriate, since many participants will be in the program for the long-term, but use of the term emphasizes that continued enrollment should never be taken as a matter of course.

While developing the plan of care, team members should decide what scenario is most likely to be true at the time of evaluation and review of the care plan.

1. The participant will most likely be the same.
2. The participant is expected to improve but will most likely need to remain in adult day care.
3. The participant is likely to improve to the degree that a lesser level of care will be recommended. Or,
4. The participant is likely to need a more intensive level of care. It may be desirable to discuss the last scenario out of the presence of the participant. To indicate that there is little hope for improvement may result in the participant's making little effort to improve. It must be remembered that even when indicators point to worsening of a condition, this cannot always be accurately predicted. Any discussions of expected regression must always be handled with sensitivity for feelings of both participant and the family.

Whatever scenario appears most likely should be included in the care plan and be analyzed at the time of review. If the likely scenario appears to have changed, a revised scenario should be a part of the revised plan. At time of review, the functional status of the participant must be examined to determine whether adult day care is presently providing the care which best meets existing needs, with neither under- nor over-provision of service.

In light of this review, a decision must be made. If the participant is maintaining functional level, but not experiencing hoped-for improvement, adult day care will still appear to be the most appropriate level of care. The participant may have improved functional status, but still needs the level of care provided by adult day care; the participant may have improved to the point that adult day care is no longer needed, and may be discharged to a lesser level of care or released from any structured care. Or, the participant may have regressed, but is still able to function in and benefit from enrollment in adult day care. In the last possible case, the participant's condition has worsened to the point that adult day care can no longer provide the care needed.

If the decision is made to refer the participant to another level of care, discharge must be carefully planned and implemented. Termination from the program should not be sudden (except when emergency discharge must take place), but should be carried out in a way which gives the participant time to recognize the need for change and to make the adjustment needed for the move. This period of time should be utilized by the staff and participant to evaluate what has been accomplished during the time spent in the adult day care program and to re-affirm goals or to set new ones. The participant can benefit from this time to assimilate the experiences and friendships of adult day care, while assessing the value of these to the quality of life.

The inclusion of a plan for discharge in the total plan of care makes the participant aware that there is an expectation that discharge will take place. This prevents feelings of shock and a need to make sudden adjustments when the need to leave becomes apparent.

Summary

Each adult day care participant is a unique individual with specific needs from the program. It is the task of the adult day care staff to help determine the extent and nature of those needs and to work with the participant in a structured way to meet the identified needs as fully as possible.

The services and activities required to meet needs of individual participants must be integrated into the total program plan for the center.

Throughout the process of planning and working to achieve goals, the autonomy of the individual must be preserved. Team members must recognize that their role is not that of taking charge and directing the participant into a course of action which they may view as suitable. It is rather to help isolate problems and needs, to research and clarify available options, to help identify strengths and resources of the participant, and to offer support and assistance to participants. A staff which successfully fulfills its role will motivate participants to make decisions and work toward goals which are desirable and appropriate for them.

References

Jacobs, B. 1981. Working *with the at-risk older person: A resource manual*. Washington, DC: National Council on the Aging, Inc.

United States Federal Council on the Aging. 1978. *Assessment and plan of care: Public policy and the frail elderly*. Washington, DC: Government Printing Office.

19 Planning the Program

Introduction

The term "program" in adult day care is broadly defined: it includes every service and activity provided for participants, and applies as well to the rationale for provision of program components and method of provision.

Planning the program is therefore a complex process. The point of departure for all planning is understanding three basic principles which underlie program design:

1. The program must be planned and carried out to achieve broad program goals and objectives; each program component serves to support the service philosophy and concept.
2. The program plan must include provision of certain basic services which are fundamental to the service of adult day care.
3. All program services and activities must be planned to carry out specific goals of individual care plans for participants; every facet of the program must be provided in support of these goals.

In short, the total program exists to encourage growth and independence for participants and to support families in their efforts to maintain the dependent member in the home. Use of these precepts as the foundation for the planning process will facilitate the work of creating an effective program.

Philosophy of Program Planning

Adult day care programs whose care provision fulfills the precepts outlined above do not "just happen." They are carefully planned with concern for the needs of each individual participant. Service is offered in an environment which encourages participants to function at the highest level possible for them. This positive atmosphere is reinforced by all elements contributing to care, permeating the total climate of the program and involving all those helping to provide the care.

Planning which produces a program of this kind does not begin at the point of deciding upon the calendar of services and activities for the month; it begins at the inception of the program with making and carrying out key organizational decisions:

1. Appointing a director who is aware of the need to achieve outlined goals of the service and the program.
2. Employing staff members who work to support the adult day care ideology.
3. Providing staff training and development which enhance staff ability to provide the desired care.
4. Designing admission policies which admit only those participants for whom the program can provide appropriate care.
5. Carrying out admission procedures which provide information needed to plan care suited to the needs of each participant.
6. Researching the community to locate resources required to meet needs of participants.

Basic Planning Principles

Exhibit 19-1 outlines certain basic principles which should be observed when planning programs for impaired populations such as those in adult day care programs.

Basic Services

There are certain services which are essential to provision of adult day care. The National Institute on Adult Daycare (1984) outlines eight which are to be provided to achieve goals of individual care plans for participants:

1. Personal care
2. Social, leisure, physical, and educational activities
3. Health monitoring
4. Nutrition
5. Transportation
6. Emergency services
7. Counseling
8. Community relationships (advocacy, information, and referral).

Basic services can be categorized as falling into four groups: social, health care, supportive and transportation.

Exhibit 19-1 Basic Principles for Planning an Adult Day Care Program.

1. Planners must understand the characteristics and needs of aging or impaired adults to be admitted to the program and methods of planning effective programs for them.
2. Planners must be familiar with characteristics of the specific population being served in the program, including life style, interests, habits, and functional level. Consideration must be given to community customs and ethnic and cultural backgrounds.
3. Programs should be designed to capitalize upon strengths, abilities, and coping skills of participants and to provide challenge, stimulation and opportunities for growth.
4. Planners must be aware of community resources and methods for using them to meet needs of participants. Services needed by adult day care participants are complex and varied, often beyond the capability of the program to provide without utilizing other community resources.
5. Planners and staff must be cognizant of the mental and physical levels of participants and be able to adapt activities in ways which will enhance their ability to participate and succeed.
6. Participants must be expected to function to the maximum that they are able, and the program must be planned to reinforce this expectation. Expectations must be kept realistic, however, with proper recognition of functional limitations.
7. Adult day care participants are adults; all activities must be planned on an adult level.
8. Every service and activity is planned and carried out to achieve a purpose; busywork is not a part of adult day care.
9. While there must be some structuring of the program, it should not be rigid. Participants should be granted the right to refuse to participate in any given activity.
10. Participants will, to the extent that they are able, be included in the planning process. They will also be involved in program evaluation.
11. Planning will be ongoing, with current programming always being based upon the present configuration of participants, their needs, interests, and functioning abilities.

Social Services

Social services in the adult day care program may be defined as those services which support the well-being of participants and which promote restoration of social skills which may have become impaired due to effects of illness, isolation, or loss of important roles.

Social Interaction. Both formal and informal activities should be planned to provide opportunities to re-activate or develop communication and interaction skills.

Examples include directed and informal conversations, group discussions, parties, drama, music, volunteer activities, and group and individual therapy.

Leisure Activities. Leisure activities are planned to offer fun and enjoyment, to stimulate and motivate participants, and to help develop the ability to fill leisure hours both in the center and at home. Arts and crafts of all kinds, games, music, reading or talking books, community outings, and sports events fall into this category. A careful assessment of participants' interests and skills should determine what activities are to be offered in this area.

Community Involvement. Community activities encourage participants to maintain and enlarge their involvement in the greater community. They should become more aware of the community and how they can participate and contribute.

Examples include community celebrations (holidays, special events, anniversaries, etc.); religious celebrations and events; political activities (voter registration, political rallies, voter education, speakers, voting); educational events (community college classes, seminars, etc.); volunteer activities (Red Cross First Aid training, envelope stuffing, Christmas toy shop, and collecting for United Way and other community fund drives).

Diversional. Diversional activities are those which result in a finished product and which foster feelings of accomplishment and self-worth. They should be planned to encourage learning, group interaction, creativity, and personal fulfillment.

Examples include chair caning, quilting, building bird houses, furniture refinishing, rug hooking, embroidery, cooking, and gardening. Activities in this category should include both group and individual projects.

Task-Oriented Activities. Task-oriented activities are planned to achieve an objective, through group or individual effort. They offer participants a sense of achievement and methods of problem solving. Participants should be helped to understand abilities and limitations as well as to develop new coping skills.

Examples include: individuals helping with snacks, planning and carrying out devotions, watering plants, washing dishes, sweeping and providing assistance to other participants and to staff. Groups of participants can plan a party or other event, write the program newsletter, make a quilt rug or other product requiring the cooperation of several people.

Health Care

Since adult day care is designed to focus upon wellness of participants rather than illness, health care in this setting is defined as "holistic" and includes all services which support good health, teach good health practices, and help to maintain or increase the capacity for self-care.

Physical Examination. Although the physical examination required for admittance to adult day care is not usually provided on-site at the center, the requirement for an initial examination and an annual check-up thereafter constitutes a first step toward creating awareness of health status. For many, this leads to learning to take better care of their health.

Health Supervision. Enrollment in an adult day care program provides participants with close and constant observation of their health status by staff members who are skilled in such monitoring by virtue of training and experience.

Any observed changes in functioning status—appetite, toileting habits, respiration, skin color or condition, walking gait, mental agility, behavior, attitudes—should result in one or more of the following actions: the participant (and/or responsible person) should be questioned to gain additional information; staff should compare notes and decide any actions to be taken; family or caregiver should be consulted or reported to; physician or other health care professional should be contacted; health care team should be conferred with; participant should be referred for treatment.

Actions taken and the sequence followed will be based upon what is deemed appropriate by the staff member(s) observing the change, and the participant and family or caregiver.

Nutrition. Poor nutrition is frequently the cause of poor health for older people; they often lack motivation or ability to prepare adequate meals and may lack transportation for shopping or funds to purchase food. They may be unaware of nutritional value of foods or of how their nutritional needs may have changed with age or health status.

The hot meal and daily snacks offered at the adult day care program are a vital component of the service, since the meal must supply at least one-third of the daily nutritional requirement for an adult. This ensures that participants have at least one balanced meal per day; if snacks are planned with good nutrition in mind, the combination of the meal and snacks offer an adequate diet to improve health problems caused by inadequate or inappropriate food intake.

It is important that provision be made for prescribed therapeutic diets, since those adults in need of the diet are often too impaired to be able to prepare these for themselves.

For those participants living alone, or unable to obtain meals when not attending the program, arrangements should be made for them to receive home-delivered meals.

The program should also offer nutritional counseling and training in habits of sound nutrition, skillful shopping (i.e., best nutritional value for the money), and planning of meals with consideration for chewing or absorption problems, energy levels, and family size. Obesity is a health hazard for many older adults who exist on diets with high carbohydrate concentration. Training and assistance with this problem should be a part of the program for those for whom this is needed and appropriate.

Assistance with Medications. Those persons who are unable to be responsible for keeping and taking their medications at the prescribed time and dosage should have this done for them. The medication should be brought to the center in the container in which it was dispensed by the pharmacy, clearly labeled with the full name of the participant, name and strength of medicine, dosage, and instructions for administering.

Careful and accurate documentation of any medications given by a staff member must be kept by that person. All medications must be kept in a locked, safe place.

For participants able to keep and take their own medications, appropriate training should be offered, including how to handle medications in a safe manner, and memory techniques for remembering to take medicines at the proper time, both at home and at the center.

A further service in this area is that of providing careful observation to detect any serious side effects which may occur from taking of medications. Many older people experience idiosyncratic reactions to medications; some physicians have not received adequate training in geriatric pharmacology and fail to recognize that aging bodies do not always react as younger or middle-aged persons do. Since the adult day care staff is in contact with participants for long periods of time, they are often in the best position to exercise vigilance to detect any such reactions and take appropriate action.

Caution must be exercised at all times in this particular service of the program, since the potential for creating or failing to eliminate a hazard is great.

Self-Care. Helping participants to learn or re-learn skills for their own self-care is of great importance in helping to improve functional capacity.

Training in this area should include activities of daily living, clothing care (laundry and mending), use of the telephone, learning to use public transportation when it is available and appropriate, personal hygiene and grooming, home safety, consumer skills, assistance with ambulation (as needed for blind persons, those using walkers, canes or other supportive devices), and any other self-care needs revealed by functional assessment or participant.

Physical Activities. Older people and other adults who are impaired will often slow their activity level to the point that they become sedentary. A session of physical exercise, planned and carried out with functional abilities of participants in mind, must be included in the daily routine of every adult day care center. Consultation with a physical therapist or other person experienced in planning physical activities for impaired adult populations is recommended to help design an exercise program which is effective in increasing physical ability and is fun for participants.

The exercise should be carried out under the leadership of a staff member possessing enthusiasm and motivational skills needed to encourage participants to engage in the activity.

Additional physical activities should be included as a regular part of the program: neighborhood walks, shuffleboard, ping-pong, pool, horse-shoes, and dancing are among suggestions. Planning must be based on interests of participants, and some activities may have to be adapted to suit participant abilities.

Supportive Services

While all services of adult day care can rightly be called supportive, for purposes of this discussion the term will be used to refer to those services which are somewhat less structured than those already described, but which are needed to support participants' efforts to maintain or improve independent functioning and to support family efforts to continue providing care for the individual within the home.

Coordination of Services. Adult day care participants are frequently experiencing multiple problems requiring help from a variety of resources. In these instances, adult day care serves as the portal of entry into the service delivery network of the community, with adult day care staff assuming responsibility for helping to organize and coordinate available services to meet identified needs of the participant. The staff makes contact with other service providers, provides any needed assistance to use the service, monitors the outcome, and periodically re-assesses the situation to determine how well needs are being met.

Examples of services which may be coordinated include medical or mental health clinics, social services, social security, visiting nurse service, home-delivered meals, library outreach, commission for the blind, transportation services, legal services, consumer counseling.

Education. Education as a supportive service of adult day care includes not only those activities which are traditionally defined as educational, but also those which have the objective of broadening awareness, understanding and skills of participants. The program can provide training to participants and families or caregivers to learn to better recognize needs and how to find and use available resources to meet those needs.

Areas that can be covered in this type of educational effort include sensitivity to health status and how to use the existing health care system; obtaining counseling to help with adjustment to losses and assuming new life roles; consumer counseling to improve money management skills; use of community agencies to learn drug safety and home safety; classes from community colleges to improve communication and other skills.

An additional goal for educational programming is that of providing opportunities for self-development. The list of possible subjects for this is endless, and, with some room for experimentation, the choice of subject matter should be based upon interests of participants. Topics include local history, literature, art or music appreciation, political process, Bible study, photography, and bird watching.

Counseling. Intrinsic to the service of adult day care is provision of counseling for participants and their families. Many are coping with substantial levels of stress caused by losses, required role adjustments and increasing dependence. Families also experience stress from the added responsibility of caring for a dependent member. Staff must be sensitive to these needs and provide opportunities within a supportive, non-judgemental environment for discussion of feelings and for working through problems.

Among strategies to use are informal and directed conversations, group therapy, individual counseling, and family support groups.

Staff should not attempt to work with mental or emotional problems which may require more in-depth therapy or treatment than staff members are trained to provide. Participants needing more intensive treatment must be referred to professionals with the required level of expertise. Staff training should be provided which will enable staff to recognize their limitations in this area and know when and where to refer participants if necessary.

Surrogate Family Relationships. While building relationships may not be defined as a service in the strictest sense of the word, the opportunity to form meaningful relationships in the program is among the greatest of benefits of attendance for many participants. Isolation and loneliness are among the most common problems for older and impaired adults, caused by loss of mobility, loss of meaningful others, and often worsened by low income and lack of available transportation.

Atchley (1977, 289) states that primary relationships will form within a group if members are in frequent and enduring interaction, if they are close to each other in space, if the membership is small, if there is basic equality among members and if membership remains stable. This general definition of group interaction accurately portrays the healthy adult day care environment. Formation of new and needed relationships are among valuable benefits of attendance. Enrollment provides participants with a place where they are cared about as an individual and are members of a surrogate family, an ongoing community. The staff should capitalize on the opportunity to enhance self-worth through the formation of social bonds; creative planning can enlarge upon the situation. Program planning should be designed to include frequent activities designed to encourage social interaction between participants.

The staff is responsible for creating a warm and caring environment, one that encourages participants to feel responsibility for each other and for the community within the center. Participants should be provided with opportunities to make contributions to each other.

Examples of such activities include use of a "buddy system" for new participants, asking a participant who is established in the program to help make a new participant feel at home; and "pairing" participants who have complementary abilities: e.g., asking those who can see to help those who cannot; asking those who are ambulatory to assist those who are not. Group conversations, with a leader skilled in helping people to share inner concerns within a non-judgemental environment, can help participants to voice feelings of loneliness and other problems and can facilitate their receiving group support. The group as a whole can be asked to express concern for participants absent because of illness by sending cards and flowers, or making visits or phone calls. The program should also provide opportunities to mourn the death of participants or other individuals who are a part of the center community. This may be done by attending the funeral, holding a memorial service at the center, or by other expressions which are meaningful to participants. In general, friendships can be encouraged through small group projects, remembrance of birthdays, and other special events in the lives of participants.

Family Respite and Support. Full time care for a dependent adult for an extended time creates an almost intolerable burden for the caregiver. Research indicates that most families want to continue caring for the dependent member, but become overwhelmed unless some respite and support are made available. Enrollment in adult day care for the dependent person is often the answer for families in this position. The relief offered is twofold. First, they receive relief from providing full time physical care. This allows the caregivers to have time for themselves, for participation in activities meaningful to them, or to become employed outside the home. Second, they receive relief from total emotional responsibility. Participants in adult day care have interests and relationships outside the home, thus relieving the family of the obligation to meet all emotional needs.

Additional support may be made available to caregivers in the form of counseling or group support. In this setting they may learn to help themselves by gaining a better understanding of needs of the dependent member and developing skills for coping with the altered relationship and increased responsibility. Support groups composed of participant caregivers may be formed if there appears to be a need for or interest in this. Such groups offer opportunities to members to discuss issues involved in care of a dependent member, to share concerns with others in this situation, and to gain support from the group. If a decision is made to sponsor such a group, time and place of meetings should be those most convenient for members of the group. Topics and resource persons should be selected to meet specific needs of the members as expressed by them.

Transportation

Transportation To and From the Center. Travel to and from the center may be provided by use of public transportation, by families or caregivers, or by the center. Families or caregivers and other alternate methods should be used whenever possible to alleviate transportation problems for the center and to reinforce independence in participants. Those participants able to use public transportation or who can be trained and assisted to do so should be encouraged to travel by this means, for the same reasons.

Outings and Field Trips. Outings and field trips should be planned as a regular part of the program, since participation in these activities provides opportunities for social interaction, education, and community involvement. Outings might include visits to local points of interest such as factories, parks, churches, and historic sites. Specific activities include picnics, bowling, horse-back riding, fishing, etc. Outings to participate in a community event, such as political rallies, educational seminars, and celebrations are also recommended.

Life Sustaining Travel. Life sustaining travel includes trips for grocery shopping and shopping for other necessities, transportation to medical and therapy appointments, to social services, and to meet other critical needs. Availability of transportation is likely to be limited. Providers must decide whether to plan transportation as a part of service delivery or to seek alternate solutions. Providers should conduct research to learn which method best fits their needs and their budget. The answer is often to use a combination of center transportation and other methods.

Program Methods and Content

Balance in a number of areas is the key to designing a successful adult day care program.

Balance Between Large Group, Small Group, and Individual Activities

While the primary mode of the program is that of the group process, provision must be made for individual activities and services as well. Some participants, especially those who are new to the program or who are suffering from mental or emotional impairments, may not adapt well to groups. They may be drawn into the group eventually, but until that time, quiet activities and those involving only one or two people must be planned for them.

Large group activities include parties, quilting, craft classes, cooking demonstrations, educational events, bingo, and group discussions. Small group activities include sewing, cooking, gardening, checkers and other games for two or three, and small conversation groups. Individual activities include reading, embroidery, knitting, training in activities of daily living (ADLs), therapies, listening to music or talking books, and walking.

Balance Between Activities Which are Active or Noisy and Those Which are Quieter and More Relaxing

Walking, shuffleboard, exercise sessions, horse shoes, bowling, parties, rhythm, singing, and swimming are considered active. Checkers, reading, sewing, rest period, movies or slides, educational classes, and painting are quiet.

Balance Between Activities Which are Routine and Those Which are Special Events

Routine activities would include daily exercises, snack and meal time, group conversations, craft and educational classes. Special events are holiday and birthday celebrations, community outings, visits from public dignitaries and other visitors, visits to participants who are ill, and services for the death of a participant.

Balance Between Activities Which are Highly Structured and Those Which are More Open

Structured activities include exercise sessions, classes, outings, therapies, ADL training, group craft projects, and parties. Those less structured include walks, rest or quiet time, small group conversations, and individual activities such as sewing or gardening, reading, bird feeding or watching, and individual crafts. If participants engage in unstructured activities on an individual basis, the staff has a responsibility to monitor them to be sure that safety practices are observed. If walking alone, an individual must not be allowed to leave the building or grounds; and if exercising, should not go beyond advisable limits, etc.

A Balance in Meeting the Varying Needs of Participants, Based Upon Characteristics of the Program Population: Age, Sex, Religion, Ethnic Background, Interests

While stereotyped sexual roles have become blurred in recent years and tend to become less distinct with age, many men will not want to engage in activities which they consider to be feminine in nature, such as sewing, cooking, and cleaning. Conversely, many women will not be interested in woodworking, fishing, or leathercraft. Caution must be taken that no assumptions are made about respective interests of men and women, but where such feelings exist, they must be respected.

Similarly, any ethnic differences must be respected. There may be interest in different kinds of music, religious observances, food, activities for parties, etc. If the program population is made up of more than one ethnic group, program planning must consider the interests of each such group. The same consideration applies to religious differences: blessings at meals, services in observation of a death, and other religious differences may be carried out differently by different religious groups. The adult day care climate can assist participants to accept individuals who are different from themselves. By the same token, however, beliefs of all participants must enter into program planning and respect must be maintained for refusal to participate in any given event.

If the group contains individuals from widely varying social backgrounds, their interests and lifestyles are likely to demonstrate this. Activities must be planned to accommodate such differences. While some participants may enjoy checkers, others may prefer bridge; classes in current events may be of interest to some, bible studies to others. Having participants help in the planning process should reveal their personal interests. Asking them to fill out a questionnaire or engaging them in conversations to discuss activities which they enjoy are other methods for obtaining this information.

As the group membership changes, interests may also change. Because of this, efforts to learn about interests must be ongoing.

Interests and skills developed over a lifetime of living should also be considered. Individuals who have spent time learning a hobby such as photography, painting, gardening, growing herbs, or story-telling, should be encouraged to continue with this if functional abilities permit. In some situations where the interest is no longer pursued due to disability, creative adaptation by staff may encourage a rekindling of interest. Participants who possess particular skills of this nature should be encouraged to share them with other participants. This serves to motivate the individual and adds variety to the program.

A Balance Among Activities Which are Carried Out in the Center by Center Personnel and Those Which Either Use Outside Resource Personnel or Take Participants to Events in the Community

As a general rule, activities provided by center personnel will be more focused upon improving capacity for self-care and learning skills to occupy leisure time. Those utilizing outside resources may also accomplish these goals, and will in addition provide opportunities for social and community activities, broadening horizons and capacity to participate in the greater community.

Activities in the center include group conversations, games, ADL training, counseling, nursing services, crafts, gardening, singing, parties, etc. While there will be overlapping between the two, activities involving community resource people coming into the center may include classes in any subject of interest to participants, speakers, counseling, crafts for which staff have no skills, open house in the center, slide shows and movies. Participants may go on outings to view autumn foliage to musical programs and plays, or to participate in picnics, swimming, and fishing.

Balance Between Those Activities and Services in Which Participants are Recipients and Those Offering Them Opportunities to Give of Themselves

Given the fact that participants attend adult day care because they have unmet needs and must receive care, it is likely that most activities will be planned to provide the care and meet the needs. However, a need for most people is that of being able to give rather than always taking. Activities which meet this purpose include making toys for the Christmas toy shop, stuffing envelopes for charitable organizations, visiting in nursing or convalescent homes to entertain with a dramatic presentation or rhythm band, visiting or telephoning participants who are ill, visiting a school or kindergarten to share life experiences or stories, teaching a skill to a staff member or another participant, making tray or table decorations for a hospital, helping to make crafts for a sale to benefit the center, helping with chores in the center, sweeping, and washing dishes.

Insofar as Possible, Activities Should Balance Indoor and Outdoor Functions

If space is available, outdoor activities could include walks, eating meals or snacks outside, bird watching, rhythm band practice, balloon volleyball, dramatics, discussion groups, or just sitting outside to enjoy spring or fall weather. Outings can be planned to take place in parks or other outdoor areas if space is not available at the center, or can be in addition to basic outdoor activities. Additional activities may include fishing, picnicking, walking, photography, or swimming.

The Planning Process

The process of planning the program must include consideration of program capacity in all the areas which have been discussed in previous chapters.

Availability of Equipment and Supplies

If funds are not budgeted to purchase supplies and equipment to carry out desired services and activities, substitutions must be planned or creative canvassing of the community must take place to obtain what is needed.

Staff Skills and/or Availability of Needed Talents and Skills From the Community

Given the wide variety in participant needs and interests, it is unlikely that the program staff will possess capability to plan and carry out a program to satisfy all needs. Program plans should include use of staff abilities and talents, with research to locate and arrange for supplementary skills and services.

Program Space

Planning for specific activities will depend upon whether sufficient space is available or can be adapted to accommodate the activity. Space needs may include:

- A large space for large group activities such as parties and dances
- An area where active, noisy activities can take place without disturbing others: singing, sports, hand clapping, those involving a lot of movement
- Areas for quiet, private activities: counseling, small group conversations, individual activities
- Areas to provide medical, nursing care, or therapies, if these are to be offered on-site

- Areas where messy activities can be carried out. This is preferably in an area which does not have to be used for other purposes, so that clean up does not have to be done after each working session
- Space for outdoor activities
- Isolation areas for participants who become ill: a rest area with a bed and comfortable lounge chairs
- Space for holding meetings. If a family support group is to be included in the program, there must be space to hold meetings. This space will also be needed for staff meetings
- Community facilities which can be used for program activities outside the center: swimming pools, bowling alleys, picnic spots, etc.

Needs of Individual Participants

Specific needs of individuals as determined in service plans must be a major factor in overall program plans. For example, some individuals may need activities to encourage eye-hand coordination; others may require training in some aspects of ADLS; others need training in socialization skills or memory training. All of these needs must be worked into the total program plan; the staff must be skillful at fitting individual needs into plans for the entire group.

Time

Scheduling of activities for the time of day or week should be done with consideration of the following:

- When energy levels of participants are at a peak
- Participant preferences for doing certain activities at certain times of the day: perhaps an inclination for group exercise early in the morning; a need for unstructured time just after lunch, etc.
- Scheduling concurrent activities for participants with differing needs: quiet activities during rest time for those who do not need or want to rest; activities at the center for those who may be unable to go on community outings, etc.
- Planning activities for early morning and late afternoon when there are only a few participants at the center.

When these factors have been recognized and considered, drawing up a daily and weekly calendar for the program is the next step. Much of the daily schedule will be blocked out for routine activities that are a part of each day: snacks, meals, exercise, morning greeting and conversation, preparation for leaving at the end of the day. The amount of time remaining will be what is available for classes, education, training, personal care and special events. Making the maximum use of this time is the crux of planning. Staff will want to ensure the time is used to provide services and activities to achieve care goals.

Once the time has been scheduled, additional planning must take place to be sure that all aspects of each activity are prepared for. Necessary supplies and equipment must be purchased or arranged for and be in place in time for the planned event. The individual to be in charge of each event must be familiar with what is to be done, what specific care goals the event is to support, and what instruction and assistance will be needed. Space to be used must be prepared: tables, chairs and any other equipment should be in place and supplies easily available (placed so that participants can help themselves, if feasible).

Staff/Participant Partnership

The program staff has a responsibility to create an atmosphere within the program which encourages and supports participant involvement. It should help participants to communicate their needs and to make suggestions for activities and services which they believe are beneficial and which are of interest to them. Furthermore, the staff is responsible for translating suggestions into action, for obtaining resources, and for planning experiences which embody the needs of participants and address concerns voiced by them. The staff must demonstrate to participants a desire to utilize participants' knowledge and talents as a resource, helping them to make whatever contributions they are able in order to create a dynamic and therapeutic program.

Staff and participants are working toward the same goals: improvement of functioning and of quality of life for participants. These goals cannot be achieved without the full partnership and cooperation between participants and staff. Adult day care programs with staff who understand this and are able to bring participants into the partnership will be programs where activities are truly goal-oriented and where participants are provided opportunities for growth and improvement.

Summary

Adult day care programs should be much more than a place where someone watches the old folks (Padula 1983, 47). Every activity, service, and experience of each day should be planned to achieve a purpose and be used to work toward the overall goals of care. It should be understood that those events which are called "the program" constitute only a small part of what takes place in the center during each day. Rather, every action in which participants are involved, from time of leaving home to returning in the afternoon, should be considered a part of the daily program. Traveling to and from the center, sharing meals, conversations, and other unstructured time are experiences which should be considered program events, in that they are valuable times for socialization and skill renewal or development. To this end, staff must be available and serve as guides, helping each participant to be involved and to benefit from these situations.

Likewise, program planning cannot be viewed as the time when staff sits down together (perhaps with one or two participants) and decides upon the schedule for each day. The planning process consists of planning how every happening of the day can be managed so that participants benefit fully from the event, and how events can be fitted together to form a complete structure, the total adult day care program.

References

Atchley, R.C. 1977. Social forces in later life. Scripps Foundation Gerontology Center, Miami University. Belmont, CA: Wadsworth Publishing Co., Inc.

National Institute on Adult Daycare. 1984. *Standards for adult day care.* Washington, DC: National Council on the Aging, Inc.

Padula, H. 1983. *Developing adult day care for older people, a technical assistance monograph.* Washington, DC: National Council on the Aging, Inc.

20 Working with Functionally Impaired Participants

Introduction

Because adult day care is not a specialized service, the range of health impairments among participants will cover a broad spectrum. Staff members must be familiar with the symptoms of impairments which are likely to be most prevalent and develop effective helping techniques for working with impaired participants. They must learn to address the total well-being of participants within the helping mode of the service.

Health impairments can be categorized as being either physical or mental/emotional.

Physical Impairments: Sensory Loss

Learning to adjust to physical impairments can be among the most traumatic of human experiences. Successful adjustment to such losses may be largely dependent upon the quality of help the individual receives with learning to understand the degree of impairment and with developing compensatory and coping skills.

Almost inevitably, the aging process is accompanied by some gradual sensory loss. Although these impairments are not limited to the aging, it is likely that 100 percent of this population will experience diminished capacity in use of at least one of the five senses.

Vision Loss

Causes of Lost or Diminished Eyesight. A gradual loss of vision takes place throughout the life span. By age 60, 51 percent of the population has experienced some degree of loss. Typical impairments are that the near point of vision moves away from the eye; the far point moves closer. The eye fails to open and close quickly in response to light level. The pupil does not contract and expand as rapidly. Ability to distinguish colors declines.

There is also an increased percentage of vision loss among the aged due to other causes, including glaucoma, macular degeneration (loss of central vision), cataracts (the most common vision disability among the aged), high blood pressure and other diseases. Other causes include retinal detachment, diabetes, cancer, infections, and injuries.

Results of Vision Loss. The individual may lack adequate vision to perform all tasks and to care for self adequately. Independence is lost due to inability to drive, shop, write, etc. Freedom to pursue leisure activities, such as reading, movies, television, and handcrafts is also lost. As a result of so many activities being curtailed, the individual may become depressed and withdrawn, or refuse to cope with the limitations.

Symptoms of Vision Loss. As a result of vision loss, the individual may walk with an awkward, shuffling gait and may appear to be tense and hunched. Walking may be done close to a wall, with disorientation resulting from attempts to walk away from the wall. The individual may attempt to compensate for loss of peripheral vision by tilting the head from side to side in an effort to widen the field of vision. The visually impaired individual may comment that the room appears dark, may change the position of a chair to follow the light, may hold printed materials at arm's length, and may ask for more light. The staff should be alert to these indicators of an uncorrected vision problem. Staff may also notice that an individual is unable to see or read materials which are easily read or seen by others.

Helping Techniques for Vision Loss. First, the degree of vision loss and its causes should be assessed, and the participant referred for professional treatment to correct the loss or to treat underlying problems. The participant should be offered help with locating and utilizing resources, such as Services for the Blind, Lions Clubs, talking books, sensory devices (beepers, etc.) and seeing eye dogs. Vision aids that optimize existing vision should be made available. These aids include optical lenses, magnifiers, felt pens, line guides, large print, reading stands, use of dull-finish paper, proper illumination, and non-glare lighting.

In designing communications for the visually impaired, an attempt should be made to simplify the field of vision. This entails avoidance of unnecessary clutter and use of contrasting colors (black, blue, green, or red on white; white on these colors, yellow on red, green on red, red on green, blue on red, etc.). Communication can also be enhanced by the use of touch. Taking the person's hand or patting a hand during conversation will provide reassurance that the person is being listened to.

Assistance with walking should be provided if needed: the helper should offer an arm just above the elbow for the individual to hold on to and should walk a half-step ahead. When entering a new environment, the helper should offer an explanation of the circumstances, including what the scenery or room is like, who is present, and where people are located.

In general, regular activities should be adapted to suit the abilities of the visually impaired participant.

Hearing Loss

Loss of hearing is potentially the most serious of sensory impairments. About her deafness, Helen Keller said:

> I am just as deaf as I am blind. The problems are deeper and more complex, if not more important than those of blindness. Deafness is a much worse misfortune. For it means the loss of the most vital stimulus—the sound of the voice that brings language, sets thoughts astir, and keeps us in the intellectual company of man . . . (quoted in Buckley 1969)

Approximately 30 to 50 percent of all older people suffer a significant hearing loss which affects their ability to maintain relationships and communicate with others. Men experience a greater percentage of hearing loss than women.

Types of Hearing Loss.

Conductive Loss. With conductive loss, sound waves are not properly conducted to the inner ear. All sounds seem muffled. Some causes of this type of loss can be corrected: an accumulation of wax in the ear, blockage caused by swelling or other obstruction, etc. Most often, however, the problem is in the middle ear.

Sensory-Neural Loss. With sensory-neural loss, sound waves reach the inner ear, but are not properly converted into a message that can be passed on to the brain. The person generally hears low-pitched tones but loses high frequency sounds, or hears them as being distorted. Vowels are easier to hear since they are low-pitched; consonants such as th, s, sh, f, and p are high-pitched and therefore more difficult to hear. The person has difficulty distinguishing similar sounds, and this results in difficulty following a conversation. The individual may hear:

dead—for bed
choose—for juice
sixty—for fifty
fill—for pill
fifty—for fifteen

The loss of hearing is one which adults are often reluctant to admit; the victim may not be aware of the disability or may not recognize the degree of loss.

Results of Hearing Loss. Hearing loss results in isolation, anxiety, and depression. Even a slight loss can interfere with watching TV or movies and with correctly understanding family or friends. Conversation is difficult and tiring. If hearing loss occurs in conjunction with other sensory loss or other age-related losses, the adjustment to both the loss of hearing and to the other losses becomes more difficult.

Symptoms of Hearing Loss. Unlike the visually impaired, the individual with hearing loss does not carry obvious visual clues to this impairment: white canes or thick glasses, or those with mobility impairments who use walkers or canes. Adult day care staff must become sensitive to evidence that the hearing impaired person is experiencing difficulty. Cues will include frequent requests to have conversations repeated, complaints that the TV is not loud enough, indications that communication has been missed, failure to react to sounds which everyone is hearing, and cupping a hand behind the ear in an attempt to "catch" sounds.

Helping Techniques for Hearing Impairment. Participants should be observed for signs of loss. When hearing loss is detected, the participants should be screened and, if necessary, referred for treatment by professionals. Hearing aids should be prescribed, if indicated, and the participant should be properly trained in their use.

For communicating with the hearing impaired, amplified sound should be used, if indicated and possible, or written communication should be used.

Shouting should be avoided. The staff should make a practice of forming words with distinct lip movement to facilitate lip-reading by the impaired participant. Use of basic language can also facilitate conversation, i.e., answer questions with "yes" or "no." Always make sure that these individuals are listening before speaking and direct speech toward their "good" ear, if hearing is better in one ear than the other. The speaker should sit or stand in front of the person and from the same level. Choose words and sounds which are more easily heard and understood.

To facilitate vocal communication, keep background noises to a minimum, and avoid constant noises such as excessive playing of radio or TV, which will compete with conversation and interfere with efforts to hear. Also, avoid lights which shine directly into the face of those who are hard of hearing.

Finally, speakers should refrain from use of gestures behind the back of the individual, and refrain from any exhibit of impatience when directions have to be repeated. Always ask questions to make sure that the person has heard accurately. In general, help should be offered in ways which enable the individual to retain their dignity and pride.

Loss of Speech

Causes of Loss of Speech. Speech loss can be caused by loss of hearing, which affects the ability to speak clearly; aphasia, caused by stroke; memory loss; stuttering; cancer of the tongue, mouth, or throat; or injury.

Results of Speech Loss. Speech loss can result in the inability to speak or great difficulty in expressing thoughts and ideas, causing the individual to experience a high level of frustration and anxiety. Depression and/or withdrawal can result.

Helping Techniques for Speech Loss. Professional speech therapy and memory training can be effective. The individual can be encouraged to use singing rather than talking (singing is easier for some persons who are speech impaired). The individual can also be taught to use pre-arranged signals, finger movements, or eye blinks as communication methods.The use of written communication when speech becomes too difficult or tiring can also be encouraged.

Staff should refrain from talking *for* the individual, unless indications are given that this is desired. However, hints can and should be offered to help the individual remember the needed word. Always listen attentively, looking directly into the eye of the person who is talking.

The staff should make a habit of reading and talking to the vocally impaired; they miss being able to use language, and hearing other talk helps to alleviate this. Finally, the staff should offer strong encouragement of efforts to re-learn speaking; such positive reinforcement includes demonstrations of patience for efforts and allowing the individual plenty of time to speak.

Loss of Taste

Causes of Loss of Taste. With age, the number and sensitivity of taste buds decrease. Usually, no serious diminishment of tasting ability occurs until the seventh decade of life. However, after fifty, ability to perceive the four taste sensations (sweet, sour, salty, bitter) declines. This loss is more serious for some than others. Sweet and salty flavors are usually affected first, the taste buds which sense bitter and sour usually function into old age.

Use of dentures and excessively dry mouth which sometimes accompanies diseases or chronic poor health can also interfere with the tasting sensation.

Symptoms of Loss of Taste. The individual will complain that food does not taste "right"; a loss of interest in food will be observed. The individual may display an excessive desire for sweet or salty foods. Where dry mouth is part of the cause, there may be difficulty in chewing and swallowing.

Results of Loss of Taste. Loss of taste can result in:

- Loss of appetite
- Malnutrition
- Eating excessive amounts of sugar, salt, or seasonings
- Failure to prepare adequate diets by those with low energy levels or those living alone.

These problems may be worsened by vision problems which make identification of foods difficult, or by being on restricted diets, low salt or bland. These cause further loss of appetite and contribute to malnutrition.

Helping Techniques for Loss of Taste. First, individuals should be referred to professionals for good dental care, and trained both in mouth hygiene and in nutrition. Those who prepare their own meals should receive assistance with meal planning to find foods which appeal to the appetite. Those unable to prepare their own food should be assisted in finding sources of meals, such as meal sites, home-delivered meals, etc. The program should try to serve foods with distinct flavors and varied textures, colors, and temperatures. Such variety aids in identification of different foods and contributes to food enjoyment. Mixing foods together should be avoided because this allows the individual to distinguish flavors and to better enjoy tastes. Finally, both for home-cooked meals and in program food services, use of spices to enhance flavors should be encouraged.

Loss of Smell

Causes of Loss of Smell. Studies indicate that the sense of smell may be the earliest of the senses to decline with age, beginning as early as the late thirties or early forties. Some diseases also cause loss of smell.

Symptoms of Loss of Smell. Symptoms of loss of smell include failure to detect odors to which others are reacting; failure to identify food or other substances by smelling; and complaints about not being able to smell.

Results of Loss of Smell. Because two thirds of the taste sensation depends upon the ability to smell, loss of smell may further depress the appetite or interest in food, possibly causing malnutrition. The individual may fail to detect odors in the home or on their person which may be offensive to others. Also, there may be failure to detect odors which may signal danger, such as smoke, gas or spoiled food.

Helping Techniques for Loss of Smell. The individual should be referred for professional care to alleviate conditions which may be treatable. For protection, training in methods of and sensitivity to food spoilage should be provided. Also, smoke and fire alarms should be installed in the home. If all smell ability has not been lost, artificial odors, which help to stimulate appetite, can be added to food. (Manufacturers of artificial odors are Furmenich, 277 Park Ave., NY, NY; International Flavors & Fragrances, 1515 Highway 56, Union Beach, NJ.)

Tactile Loss

Causes of Tactile Loss. As with the other senses, the skill of touch or feeling with the skin becomes less acute with age. Other causes include diseases and injuries.

Results of Tactile Loss. The individual experiences a decrease in ability to perceive heat and cold, pressure, and pain. The ability to feel pain is usually least affected, although there is an increase in the pain threshold. Balance and coordination may become affected, due to loss of sense of vibration in the legs and feet, and it becomes more difficult to distinguish textures and objects on the basis of touch alone. Injuries may result from declining ability in this area. The individual may experience burns because of an inability to feel the temperature of bath water or heating pads or suffer cuts from sharp utensils because of insensitivity to pain.

Helping Techniques for Tactile Loss. The individual should first be referred for professional care to alleviate any conditions which may respond to treatment. Training should be provided in safety measures, such as lowering temperatures of bath water, use of heating pad on low only, use of a thermometer to check temperatures, and testing of water temperature with elbow, hands, or feet (the sense of touch remains more acute in these spots). Training in safe handling and storage of knives and other tools should also be included.

The staff should use a great deal of touching as a form of communication. This helps to make up for loss of other senses, reduces anxiety, and provides comfort. It should be remembered that touching should be done with respect for the private space of the individual and with sensitivity to background, culture, and personal preferences. Hugs or other close touching should not take place unless it is clear that they are welcome. Caring and warmth can be communicated by use of handshakes, pats on the back, and taking the other person's hand.

Physical Impairments: Loss of Mobility

Causes

Loss of mobility can be caused by strokes, amputation, diseases such as polio, arthritis, Parkinson's, poor circulation, spastic condition; paraplegia; injuries; and blindness.

Results

With loss of mobility, to whatever degree, the participant experiences limitations in movement, and difficulty and/or insecurity in walking, as well as the inability to perform ADLs. The individual also experiences isolation and inability to travel by normal methods.

Helping Techniques

As always, a participant with apparent loss of mobility should be referred for professional treatment. Training will be needed in the use of aids and prosthetic devices, as well as in safety measures and in the overall process of adjustment and adaptation.

Staff should provide assistance in learning about and utilizing community resources, such as chore services, homemaker/health aides, use of transportation system for elderly/handicapped, protective services, etc. Therapies or exercise deemed beneficial, and any needed assistance in ambulation should be provided. The staff should strongly encourage afflicted individuals to use remaining abilities to the fullest extent possible.

Physical Impairments: Stroke

One of the leading causes of impairment among the aged, strokes are also among the most debilitating of impairments, leaving the victim with a wide range of injuries and traumas.

Causes

Leading causes of stroke are: atherosclerosis or blockage of the artery wall; high blood pressure; and embolism or aneurysm. The incidence of stroke is increased by diabetes, obesity, high blood lipids, and smoking.

Results

Strokes can occur on either the left or right side of the brain; injuries differ according to the side on which the stroke occurs.

Left Brain Injury. The most visible evidence that a stroke has occurred on the left side will be paralysis on the right side of the body. Strokes on the left side may result in difficulties speaking and using language (aphasia). The person may also be left with a tendency to be slow and cautious; there may be exhibitions of disorganization and anxiety when confronted with unfamiliar situations.

Right Brain Injury. Any paralysis will be on the left side of the body. Strokes on the right side may cause difficulty in judging distances, rate of movement, form, and relationships of parts to the whole. Right brain injury leaves individuals with more difficulty learning self-care techniques than does left brain injury. Evidence of right brain damage:

- Missing the edge of the table with a cup
- Confusion of the right and left side
- Difficulty reading and using figures
- Missing buttons when buttoning clothes
- Difficulty estimating distances from distant objects
- Difficulty knowing whether standing upright or leaning

- Tendencies to be impulsive and too fast
- Inability to judge own abilities.

Strokes in General. In general, the stroke victims will lack the ability to check their own behavior, to be sure that the right thing is being done at the right time. Changes will be exhibited in attitude toward personal appearance: the person who has been fastidious may become sloppy and care little about grooming. There may be a tendency to say inappropriate things, to perform inconsistently, and to make errors on tasks usually performed well. Changes in personality may be exhibited: shy persons may become immodest or quiet persons noisy. Typically, a loss of emotional control may be observed; and evidence of depression. Excessive crying is another common symptom. Crying may take place because of grief over perceived losses or may be symptomatic of the brain damage. Crying may become prolonged and not easy to interrupt.

Techniques for Helping Stroke Victims

Staff should make sure that the individual receives professional treatment for all causes and symptoms which are treatable. Prescribed therapies and exercise should be pursued regularly. The individual should receive training to overcome, adjust, or adapt to impairments. Staff should assist with locating and utilizing all needed community resources.

Helping Aphasiacs. A normal tone of voice should be used when speaking to the individual. The staff should have an accurate assessment of the participant's ability to speak and receive messages. Staff should be trained to allow the use of incorrect terms or words in situations where attempts to find the right word become stressful.

Helping Those Who are Slow and/or Disorganized. Staff should provide constant feedback for correct performance, and should offer encouragement and praise when a task is completed.

Helping Those With Difficulty Judging Distances. The staff can help break tasks into small steps and then offer abundant feedback as steps are completed. At all times, observers should ensure that safety is maintained. It is best to use verbal, not hand or gesture directions or clues to guide the individual. Staff can facilitate the individual's efforts by minimizing clutter and avoiding rapid movement.

Helping Those With Visual Impairments Due to Stroke. Check which way the individual is facing: keep the unimpaired side of vision toward where action is taking place. Staff should avoid placing participants in a confined environment, and provide frequent clues to aid orientation.

Helping Those With Confusion. Staff should be sensitive as to whether the participant needs increased stimulation, or whether too much will be overwhelming. The individual can be taught to use memory aids, such as reminders, written notes, and schedule cards. When teaching new tasks, staff should use familiar objects and old associations to build upon past strengths and learning.

Helping Those With Depression or Excessive Crying. Staff can help these participants to gain control by leading them to become involved in an activity or conversation. Emotional support should be provided to help the individual work through the grief process. The program should provide or refer the individual for in-depth counseling if this appears indicated.

Participants who have experienced strokes will need great understanding and support from the adult day care staff, especially when the stroke has been recent and the process of adjustment is still taking place. Opportunities to verbalize feelings about the losses, and help with learning new skills or re-learning old ones will reinforce the individual's ability to believe that impaired abilities will be regained and that life will again become meaningful.

The individual should not be presented with too many new ideas or activities at one time. New information should be presented one step at a time, with short messages phrased in familiar words. Encouragement and praise for progress should be provided in generous amounts, with sensitivity for the feelings of helplessness and dependency to which most stroke victims are subject.

Physical Impairments: Incontinence

Probably the most embarrassing impairment for any individual, incontinence often causes the victim to become a recluse, not venturing out for fear of having accidents.

Causes

Incontinence is usually related to to other problems: memory loss, Alzheimer's disease, loss of muscle tone, and kidney or bladder failure. It can also be due to infections, multiple sclerosis, and injuries.

Results

The individual loses bladder/bowel control and will soil clothes and furniture and have bathroom accidents. The resulting embarrassment and humiliation will often cause isolation and withdrawal. Depression is also a consequence of incontinence.

Helping Techniques

As with other impairments, professional treatment should always be sought initially. The individual should receive training in memory techniques and also periodic reminders.

The staff should schedule frequent visits to the bathroom. The individual should feel that the staff is there to help participants assume responsibility for control. In some cases, devices such as the catheter (only with medical prescription and surveillance) or diapers may be used. The individual should also receive training in muscle control techniques.

All participants in adult day care should have a change of clothing kept at the center; participants suffering from incontinence should perhaps have more than one.

The staff must work with the individual, using acute sensitivity for the dignity and self-esteem of the person and treating the problem in ways which help to avoid embarrassment and loss of self-confidence and self-respect.

Other Physical Impairments

Epilepsy

Causes. Epilepsy is a disease of the nervous system: a temporary disturbance of the brain impulses.

Results. The word epilepsy means a seizure. These seizures may be minor or major. If minor, the seizure takes the form of a brief clouding of consciousness, with some purposeless movements and brief periods of forgetfulness. Major seizures will result in the victim falling to the floor, perhaps foaming at the mouth, with compulsive shaking movements.

Helping Techniques. Professional treatment should of course be sought.

In the event of a seizure occurring at the center, the person should be lowered to the floor. The head sould be turned to one side to prevent choking or obstruction of the airway by the tongue. There should be no attempt to force the mouth open; the staff should wait for a relaxation of the jaws. No foods or liquids should be offered until the attack is over. A time for rest should be allowed after the seizure. If the individual has a series of seizures, one after the other, medical help is recommended.

Epilepsy has often been looked upon as affecting the intelligence of the affected person; this is not the case. The adult day care staff should be aware of this fact, and understand that the individual may be normal and function normally in every way except for having seizures.

Individuals with epilepsy are subject to feelings of fear and anxiety; the staff must be aware of these and exercise sensitivity and tact to help relieve them and to demonstrate acceptance of the individual. The staff must be aware of and be able to recognize symptoms of oncoming seizures so that it is able to respond promptly and appropriately. Seizures sometimes take place suddenly, with the individual becoming unconscious without warning, they also may be preceded by some twitching, by the eyes becoming fixed, or by complete stillness.

Alcoholism/Substance Addiction

If participants suffering from these addictions are admitted to the adult day care program, their illness must be under control to the degree that they can be assimilated into the program without being disruptive.

Helping Techniques. Professional treatment, counseling, and therapies should be pursued. Community resources should be used to the fullest extent possible: Alcoholics Anonymous, drug control agencies. The individual should receive maximum support to maintain control of the addiction.

Adult day care is frequently not successful with alcoholics or those addicted to drugs unless the addiction has been overcome or is under control to the point that the individual is able to function within the adult day care setting as a member of the group. Unless the individual is at this stage of recovery, it is often more appropriate to refer the person to other, more intensive methods of treatment.

Obesity

Causes. Obesity is caused by overeating, inactivity, poor diet or eating habits, or a malfunction of the endocrine system.

Results. Obesity may be defined as being more than 20 percent over normal weight. This condition may cause several physical and mental or emotional consequences. Premature death due to cardiovascular disease, fatty liver disease, or stroke are very dangerous potential consequences of obesity. The obese individual frequently lacks self-confidence and self-esteem and can easily become depressed. The individual almost inevitably becomes sedentary, thus losing the good effects of activity and exercise.

Helping Techniques. Obesity may be the result or the cause of the individual's experiencing depression and loss of self-worth. In either case, if the individual wants to work toward weight loss, the staff may help by providing a referral for professional treatment if this seems indicated or by helping the person to enroll in a weight control program. The staff may want to start such a program at the center. All individuals who participate in the program must be examined by a doctor first to be sure that they can engage in the program safely. The staff can also provide education in healthy eating habits and regular exercise activities. Appropriate diets should be provided at the center. Individuals struggling with obesity should receive support and encouragement to work toward attaining appropriate weight.

Parkinson's Disease

There are 25,000 to 43,000 new cases of this disease reported every year, making it a major cause of poor functioning among the elderly.

Causes. Parkinson's disease is a chronic, progressive disease of the nervous system caused by a deficiency of dopamine, a chemical which is important to the transmission of nerve impulses in the brain.

Symptoms. Early symptoms of Parkinsonism include diminished blinking, reduced spontaneity of facial expression, stiff posture, difficulty in changing from sitting to standing or vice versa, and a tendency to remain in a single position for a long period of time. Later in the progress of the disease a shaking tremor of the hands, uncontrollable tremor of the body, and muscle weakness will be observed; speech is frequently affected.

Helping Techniques. The Parkinson's sufferer should of course be referred for professional treatment. Symptoms of the disease may be controlled to varying degrees and for varying lengths of time by medication. The individual should be allowed plenty of time for completion of tasks, and activities should be adapted to the abilities of the individual. Staff can encourage use of shorter sentences and a reduced rate of speaking. Time for the individual to start speaking to compensate for his difficulty in beginning speech should be allowed.

Persons with Parkinson's disease are often self-conscious about their ability to control body tremor. They must receive support and encouragement to enroll in the adult day care program and to participate in activities.

Diabetes

Causes. The causes of diabetes are largely unknown. Genetic factors are considered to play a role; and some doctors believe that it is caused by a fault in the immune system.

Symptoms.

excessive, insatiable thirst
frequent urination
hunger
loss of weight
feelings of weakness
mood swings
slowness to heal
fatigue
blurred vision
ketoacidosis (fruity, sweet odor of the breath)
dryness of skin
nausea/vomiting

Results.

increased susceptibility to infection
vision problems/possible blindness
increased risk of heart attack, strokes, and high blood pressure

slowed reflexes

circulatory disorders

kidney failure

pain/diabetic comas

emotional stress

Helping Techniques. The suspected diabetic should always be referred for professional treatment. Once diagnosed, the individual will need assistance with treatment: adjusting diet and exercise; taking insulin and other needed medications; and also with the prevention of diabetic comas. Appropriate diet must be provided. The individual will need support to deal with a changed life style and the effects of the disease.

Cancer

Causes. The causes of cancer are largely unknown.

Symptoms. Symptoms of cancer differ according to the location of the cancer. Common warning signs are:

- Change in bowel/bladder habits
- Sore which does not heal
- Unusual bleeding or discharge
- Thickening or lump in breast or elsewhere
- Indigestion or difficulty in swallowing
- Obvious change in wart or mole
- Nagging cough or hoarseness.

Results. Results vary with location and types of cancer; the disease of course may be fatal. Depression or anger are common consequences of a cancer diagnosis. The victim experiences severe pain with some types of cancer.

Helping Techniques. If symptoms of a form of cancer are observed, the individual should be referred immediately for professional diagnosis and treatment. Support for coping with symptoms and depression is likely to be needed. The individual may also need support for dealing with the effects of any chemical or radiation therapy which may be needed. Help with locating and utilizing appropriate community resources: social services, nursing services, hospice, etc. should be provided. In general, this individual should be encouraged to continue living as normally as possible.

Mental or Emotional Impairments: Problem Behaviors

Cognitive impairments are common among the older population; at least 20 percent of those over age 80 experience this problem in some form.

Causes

The causes of mental or emotional impairments are not always known. Among possible causes are:

Alzheimer's disease	need for attention
brain injury	malnutrition
stress	reaction to medications
depression/grief	arteriosclerosis (hardening of the arteries)

Symptoms

Cognitive impairments can be exhibited in a number of problem behaviors, which must receive special attention within the adult day care program.

Wandering. Wandering is usually connected with Alzheimer's disease and is caused by the confusion and disorientation brought on by this disease. Wanderers can be categorized as falling into one of three patterns: 1) intentional wandering; 2) confused wandering; and 3) periodic wandering.

Intentional Wandering. With intentional wandering, the individual makes a constant effort to leave the program and go to another place. This impulse may sometimes fade when the environment of the adult day care program becomes familiar. If this situation does not improve, however, and efforts to leave are active and determined, the program may be unable to continue caring for this individual, since doing so will take so much time that it may detract from the time needed by other participants. On the other hand, if the facility is designed so that the individual can be kept within the building or grounds, and safety is assured, the situation may be manageable. The director will have to assess each situation and make a decision based upon these factors.

Wandering Caused by Confusion. Confused wandering creates a somewhat different situation from determined wandering. The person may try to leave the program simply because the surroundings are unfamiliar and cause feelings of insecurity. With much support and reassurance from the staff, this individual can often adjust to the new environment.

Periodic Wandering. Even after adjustment has been made to the new situation, some participants with a high level of confusion may make periodic attempts to leave. This often takes place after lunch or close to time to go home. They may also attempt to walk away if they become bored or have no activity to keep them occupied.

Activities should be planned to keep these individuals busy during those times when they are most likely to become restless. Coats and other articles associated with going home should be placed in coat closets or other places where they cannot be seen. If they are in view of the participants, they serve as a reminder of going home.

Plenty of space for walking during restless periods should be provided, preferably in long corridors or outside areas. For some reason, walking in a circular pattern appears to meet the need to pace better than do straight patterns. Comfort may be provided to participants who become agitated by having a staff member walk with them, offering reassurance that they will be going home at the regular time. Remember that the need to pace may be compulsive and beyond the control of such individuals. Insisting that they remain still will only serve to increase the compulsion and may result in hostility from the participant.

Suspicion or Paranoia. Suspicion or paranoia may be caused by an injury to the brain, by drug or substance abuse, or by organic brain disorders. Working with individuals exhibiting this symptom requires special care. The staff must make sure that suspicions do not have a legitimate cause: that the individual is not being treated unfairly or having money or belongings taken from them. When there seems to be no legitimate cause, the staff members must work to develop a trust relationship with the individual if they are to help them. The following principles should be kept in mind.

- Promises which cannot be kept must not be made
- There must never be any whispering or appearance of secretiveness in the presence of the individual
- Responses to accusations must be made calmly and not defensively
- Confrontations must be avoided
- Attention should be distracted from the problem
- The individual should never be surprised or rushed
- All procedures should be explained and explanations repeated as needed
- Reassurance should be constant; the participant should be helped to believe that everyone present is friendly and concerned.

Catastrophobic Reaction. Catastrophobic reaction appears often among brain damaged persons, and is usually caused by the individual's being overwhelmed or overstimulated by a situation. There may be frustration caused by a lack of abilities, or the individual may be affected by misunderstandings or by internal discomfort. This reaction may cause the person to refuse to engage in activities or to appear stubborn, mean, or withdrawn.

Individuals who become agitated should be removed from the situation if possible; however, neither force nor restraints should be used. Constant, gentle reassurance should be offered.

Continuity is important for the affected individual; plans must not be changed unexpectedly and the individual must not be rushed to make decisions.

It is helpful to engage the individual in an activity which is familiar, quiet, and soothing. Arguing or explaining should be avoided; time must be allowed for the reaction and feelings to go away. If it appears indicated, the person may be held and rocked, patted, or stroked. Reassurance provided by touch rather than by talking is often more effective.

Attempts must be made to determine what triggers the reaction and efforts made to avoid such situations. Individuals subject to having catastrophic reactions will function better in small groups with close supervision. Staff who work with them must become skilled in recognizing situations likely to cause the reaction, and they should attempt to change the circumstances causing the problem.

Aggressive or Hostile Behavior. Aggressive or hostile behavior is usually caused by fear; the behavior is exhibited as argumentativeness and sometimes as threatening behavior.

The staff must never react with fear and must not argue when a person becomes hostile or threatening. Instead, they should demonstrate a friendly attitude, while working to turn the attention of the individual from the source of anger. If possible, the person should be removed from the situation. If there is a refusal to leave, other members of the group should be removed; the presence of an audience may worsen the situation. If knowledge of the person indicates that humor may get a response, reacting with some humor will often defuse the situation. Extreme naivete may also be used as an appropriate tactic with some persons. When the person has calmed down to some degree, a safe environment for working through remaining feelings of hostility should be provided.

Activities requiring the use of sharp tools, small heavy objects which can be thrown, or other objects with the potential for being used as weapons must be avoided with these participants.

Anxiety. Anxiety is usually a neurotic symptom, occurring when there is nothing to justify anxiety; the person with this problem is anxious most of the time. It is exhibited as a feeling of apprehension or dread that something awful is about to happen. The person may also suffer from headaches, chronic fatigue, dizziness, or lack of appetite.

Attempts must be made to learn what the person is feeling anxious about, and efforts made to discuss the problem. The staff must demonstrate a calm attitude, with continuous assurance that the dreaded event will not take place. A trust relationship must be developed with the individual, one inspiring confidence. These participants must be continuously monitored to be sure that they are not suicidal or likely to harm themselves.

Withdrawal. Individuals suffering from withdrawal may avoid being with others, preferring to remain alone. Or they may be with others, aware of what is taking place around them, but appear oblivious. These individuals should never be discussed in their presence, even though they appear not to be listening. They must be coaxed out of their withdrawal gradually. If they can be persuaded to enroll in adult day care, they must first be engaged in individual activities at the center. When they indicate some willingness to be involved in group activities, they must be allowed to move into the group gradually, one step at a time. If anxiety occurs at any point, they must be provided with a means to withdraw and spend some time alone.

Regression. Regression is exhibited as inability to cope with current reality; the person is emotionally exhausted. All coping or adapting abilities have been exhausted or have failed; the individual abandons all effort and retreats to a level of primitive functioning.

Symptoms of this condition may include disorientation; delusions; return to childish behavior (including incontinence); increased dependency; and inability to make decisions, accept disappointments, or tolerate anxiety.

If the individual suffers from this impairment to the degree that behavior is completely anti-social or there is no ability to control basic impulses, the person is not likely to be an appropriate candidate for adult day care. Until such individuals have received treatment and have reached a stage of recovery allowing them to function in the group setting, they will probably need more intensive treatment than most adult day care programs can provide.

When they are admitted, they should be assigned simple chores requiring little or no concentration: mechanical jobs such as sweeping, sanding blocks, etc. They must be provided with a secure environment and helped to become involved with the group, even if they only participate as listeners in the beginning.

The regressed individual requires much patience and reassurance. Calmness and a peaceful atmosphere are needed. If the person is using denial as a coping device, this method of coping should be respected. It may be the only way for the person to avoid a reality which is unbearable at this time. The staff should never argue with these individuals; any subject which becomes controversial should be dropped.

Depression. Depression is the most prevalent of emotional disorders among the elderly. It is caused by emotional problems, usually associated with losses: spouse, relatives, friends, health, looks, meaningful roles, economic problems, fear of death, etc. Depression is serious and should receive careful attention. The afflicted individual may require psychiatric treatment, treatment with medications, counseling, or a combination of these. Adult day care staff must be able to recognize limitations in their skill for working with severely depressed participants and refer them to other sources for professional treatment if this seems indicated.

Symptoms of depression include the following:

- dejection
- loss of energy
- loss of interest in activities
- loss of interest in friends
- loss of appetite
- anticipation of failure
- restlessness
- crying spells
- suicidal tendencies

Although depression causes loss of interest in activities, depressed persons should be encouraged to keep busy. It is the responsibility of the adult day care staff to help them become involved in activities to take their mind off the depression. They need new experiences and help with setting new goals and establishing new roles.

Caring support should be provided and reinforcement that the participant is cared for as an individual. Demonstration of flexible and positive attitudes with commendation of progress should be offered to the participant as a part of their plan of care in the adult day care program.

Inappropriate Sexual Behaviors. Individuals with sexual behavior problems fixate on sexual desires. They may make inappropriate advances or attempt to touch inappropriately. Techniques for working with such individuals within the adult day care environment include refraining from over-reaction: they should be spoken to in a matter-of-fact voice and informed that their behavior is inappropriate. Opportunities for physical contact must be avoided, and efforts should be made to keep their attention focused on something else. Any stimulation of sexual interest should be avoided, including physical contact and conversations with sexual overtones. Efforts should be made to prevent the individuals from embarrassing themselves or others. They should be referred for professional help if this seems indicated.

Adult Day Care Staff Skills for Working with Functionally Impaired Participants

Staff methods for working successfully with all adult day care participants, and especially the severely functionally impaired, include training for both staff and participants, as well as strong staff efforts at communication and motivation.

Self-Training for Staff

The first goal for adult day care staff is that of learning to accept all participants as individuals who are experiencing a need for help, but who must not be judged or condemned for the problem, or be seen as a problem themselves. Rather, the staff must convey to participants a recognition of their dignity and worth, including them as a

Exhibit 20-1 Do's and Don'ts in the Treatment of Participants

Do

- Recognize the ability to change
- Show genuine concern for the individual
- Strive to create an atmosphere of warmth and acceptance
- Try to instill trust and confidence in participants
- Demonstrate knowledge and skill in helping
- Be consistent
- Refrain from feelings of anger, pity, or frustration
- Reserve judgement about an individual who arouses feelings of hostility
- Recognize cultural and value differences with acceptance for each individual's set of values
- Recognize any feelings being experienced which are negative to the participant: prejudice, intolerance, frustration, anger, etc.
- Recognize the parameters of the job.

Don't

- Makes promises which cannot be kept
- Offer help which will diminish the ability of the participant to help themselves
- Be persistent in ways which are intrusive or annoying when offering help
- Criticize, nag, or preach to participants
- Discuss controversial subjects: religion, sex, money, politics, etc., unless the participant indicates a desire to do so or unless there is a problem with one of these which must be dealt with.

partner in the process of making decisions about the care they are to receive in the program. Important do's and don'ts for the adult day care staff in this regard are listed in Exhibit 20-1.

The relationship between participants and staff should be viewed by the staff as a partnership; progress will demand full participation and cooperation of the participant. Participants must be encouraged to become involved in decisions such as goal setting and action process to the fullest extent possible. The staff must work with all participants to learn whether they really have a desire to work toward resolution of the problem; and whether they realistically grasp the problem (i.e., whether they view the situation as it really is). The staff should ascertain what outcome each individual wants to bring about.

Communicating

The staff of an adult day care program must possess and use extraordinary skills in communication in order to work effectively with the highly impaired adults in the program.

Good communication entails the following principles.

1. Understanding of what the person is saying and empathy for how feelings are being expressed.
2. Listening for hidden agendas: are verbal communications a true expression of feelings?
3. Acceptance of what the person is saying.
4. Offering of appropriate responses, by body language (conveying a listening attitude), head nods, facial expressions, and voice intonation.
5. Checking periodically to make sure that perception is accurate.
6. Use of phrases: "I heard you say," "as you said," etc., to relay feedback so that the individual feels his or her messages are being received.
7. Letting individuals know that they are cared about, that what they are saying is important to the listener.
8. Clarifying any misunderstandings which may occur.
9. Promoting a trust relationship.

Goals of Communication. The goals of effective communication are as follows:

- To learn what the participants are feeling
- To learn what they perceive as the problem
- To learn what they want to do about it
- To learn what their needs are
- To discover strengths, weaknesses, feelings, relationships, etc.

Staff Communication with the Participants. The staff should try to communicate:

- Feelings which are positive and supportive
- Feelings that there is plenty of time for the individual
- Reassurance that participants have the staff's undivided attention

- Feelings that emotional support is available for whatever they wish to accomplish
- Respect for the individual; this may be expressed by calling the person by name, by refraining from asking embarrassing questions, by a lack of over-solicitousness and demonstration of prejudice, etc.
- Friendliness: laughing with the participant, sharing of feelings and life outside the program
- Recognition of the feelings aroused by the participant's being dependent upon others: fear, anxiety, loss of control, fear of rejection or being humiliated, shame, anger, resentment, or guilt
- The knowledge that this is an atmosphere where it is safe to ask for help and to communicate feelings about the program with honesty: what the individual sees, hears, and feels about the program.

Educating Participants

A preliminary step in helping participants act to resolve their problems is that of helping them to increase their understanding of the parameters, causes and effects of the problem(s). The staff can help them define the strengths they possess to work toward resolution. Among these may be: freedom of choice; freedom from duty or responsibility to others; freedom to use their energies to pursue their own goals and interests; knowledge gained over their lifetime; life experience and abilities; coping and adapting skills developed from years of living and solving problems; and survival skills gained from years of overcoming crises. They also need to define what constitutes realistic goals for them, the ways in which they may learn to accept new roles and methods of achieving goals, and also how they may develop new skills.

Working within the environment of the adult day care center with participants can accomplish much toward achieving desired goals; however, to be wholly successful, the staff must work to educate not only participants, but their families and caregivers. Support within the home environment is essential if goals are to be carried out. Families must be helped to develop a new set of expectations of the participant, and develop coping skills for living with the dependent member. They must be shown how to provide support to the participant in efforts to resolve problems and establish new roles within the family unit, and how to provide continuity of care by working toward goals of care within the home environment.

Motivating Participants

Using the methods outlined above, the staff will work to motivate participants to achieve the following.

- Develop latent strengths and abilities
- Use all existing abilities
- Learn new coping skills through reaching out and expressing feelings
- Accept necessary help
- Work toward developing decision making skills, thereby lessening dependency
- Work toward developing positive feelings, understanding that life can still be worthwhile and satisfying
- Learn that there are new and different ways to accomplish desired goals, and new ways of relating and being.

If participants are to be motivated to achieve, the adult day care environment must be one which contributes to their motivation. It is the responsibility of the staff to bring about such an environment. A good environment will have the following attributes:

- All barriers to freedom of movement have been removed including all clutter
- The center is properly lighted
- There is space to establish smooth traffic patterns
- Encouragement to use remaining sensory and other abilities is provided by use of large visuals, non-glare surfaces, written reminders of activities, clocks, calendars, etc.
- Opportunities are provided to express feelings in a non-threatening atmosphere, by means of group conversations, and acting-out activities: drama, role-playing, role reversal, etc.
- Activities are provided which will help to increase functional abilities: regular exercise, games to develop hand-eye coordination; and to supply mental stimulation; educational activities are provided to increase awareness, etc.
- An atmosphere is created which is free of conflict: staff attitudes toward participants are friendly and helpful; potential for conflict among participants is controlled; the program operates in an orderly and organized—but not rigid—manner; staff attitudes toward each other are friendly and cooperative
- Activities are planned to challenge participants, not overwhelm them
- Activities with increasing levels of challenge are provided as progress is made
- Necessary resources are provided: tools and equipment, time and expertise, access to needed auxiliary services
- Participants are encouraged and assisted to do everything possible for themselves: planning, making decisions, caring for their own needs

- Activities are provided which fully utilize strengths of participants
- The staff members understand their roles as: co-planner, advisor, coordinator of resources, evaluator of progress, supporter, friend
- Preventive measures are a part of the program: encouragement to obtain regular medical examinations and get needed treatment
- Close observation of the participants' physical and behavioral actions and attitudes is carried out to detect clues of any potential problems
- The staff is alert to identify problems and get all needed help.

Summary

The challenge to the staff from the wide variety of participant impairments and problems will be great. If these challenges are to be met successfully and participants are to benefit from enrollment in the program, staff members must be knowledgeable about and possess skills to work with impairments and problems of each participant; they must also maintain an awareness of the total needs of each individual and work to ensure that all attempts to help are carried out with this in mind. Among these needs, which are universal:

- The need for love: access to family and friends; satisfying relationships
- The need to feel safe: lack of fear from crime; from being victimized or hurt
- The need for an environment conducive to enhancement of functioning ability and within which physical needs are satisfactorily met
- The need for self-esteem and feelings of self-worth through participation in creative and productive activities; for useful occupation and use of skills to make contributions and experience growth.

Reference

Buckley, I. 1969. *A few do's and don'ts to talk with the hard of hearing*. Raleigh, NC: North Carolina State University. Reprinted with permis-

21 Using Community Resources

Introduction

In addition to the use of contractual arrangements, consultants, and volunteers to supplement staff skills and knowledge and to expand program capability, a more informal method of supplementation is to fully use the resources available within every community. It is important that the staff becomes familiar with what is available to the program and how to use resources for the benefit of participants and the program. As with other supplementary services and persons, using community resources will enhance program ability to meet participant needs and achieve goals of care.

Identifying Community Resources

Adult day care staff should conduct research in the community to locate the resources which constitute the helping network and which can be used by the program. Components of the network can be categorized as "formal" or "informal." Investigation will reveal the information needed by the staff to identify each network and how to use it.

Knowledge of formal resources is usually to be found through basic research.

Local Telephone Directory

Many phone companies include a listing of human services agencies and organizations in a special section of the book. Additional listings of resources of interest to the program may be found in the yellow pages. Headings to look for include the following.

Services for the Aging

Social Services

Mental Health Services

Clinics/Hospitals

City/County Services

Religious Organizations

Fraternal Organizations

Services for Veterans

Labor Organizations

Senior Citizen Organizations

Volunteer Organizations

Charitable Organizations

Social/Benevolent Clubs and Organizations.

Information and Referral Agencies

It is the business of these agencies to be knowledgeable about what is provided within the community. Much research will have gone into compiling information about resources so that those needing the service can be helped to locate and learn what is available and how to use the resources. A call or visit to this agency will pay well in knowledge gained.

Agency and Organization Directories

Many private, nonprofit, public and private organizations compile service directories for their use and use by other agencies serving similar populations.

Chamber of Commerce. The Chamber usually publishes a directory of civic groups, volunteer and fraternal organizations. The name of a contact person for each listing and a phone number and mailing list are included.

Council on Aging. The Council on Aging compiles a directory of services within the community for the aging. Entries include the name of a contact person, along with information about eligibility requirements for use of the service of each agency: age, cost, level of impairment, etc.

Counties. Counties publish a directory of county services. The directory includes information about how to use the service.

Social Services Departments. Social Services publishes a directory of divisions within the department. The directory includes names and phone numbers of personnel in each division.

Religious Associations. A directory of churches and synagogues within the community can be found as well as some information about their services.

Staff members conducting the research will look for answers to the following questions:

- What is the agency affiliation?
- Where is the agency located and what is the phone number?
- What are the agency's purposes?
- What population is served?
- What services are offered?
- What are the eligibility requirements?
- What are the costs of services?

- What information is needed about the applicant?
- Who should be contacted for more information or to apply for services?

Adult day care staff will need answers to these questions about any services they plan to use within the program and about those to which participants are referred.

Information not included in directories or other easily available sources can be obtained by a phone call or visit. A visit to other community services is recommended in any event; useful knowledge not obtainable from printed information or from a phone call is likely to be gained.

Extending invitations to representatives of each agency to visit the adult day care program is also recommended. The collaborative relationship needed between agencies within the community service network is best established by personal contact among staff members.

Adult day care staff will do well to compile the results of their research on community resources into a directory of resources for the center. This puts the data at their command and prevents having to duplicate the effort each time they need to use the resources. The directory should be updated as new information is obtained and if changes take place.

Often adult day care staff are inclined to use only those services well known to them, without spending the time necessary to determine whether a particular service is the most appropriate resource for the specific need to be addressed. All available services should be considered to decide what will work best in the given situation and what will come closest to meeting the identified need. Where there are discrepancies between what is needed and what is available, the staff must be creative in adapting what is obtainable and looking for additional resources to fill gaps.

Frequently, more informal resources can be used to fill the need and in some situations may be preferred over more structured services.

Informal Resources

Characterized as non-bureaucratic in nature, informal resources usually offer assistance to the recipient because of a personal interest in or concern for the individual. There are no definite parameters for this helping network; almost any individual or group within the community can be included when a need arises which may be filled by them. Obvious components include:

- Family or other caregivers
- Neighbors
- Friends

- Groups in which the participant is or has been involved: work/professional associations; church, civic, and fraternal organizations; neighborhood groups or organizations; educational organizations
- Delivery services: postal carriers, meter readers, newspaper carriers, neighborhood stores, etc.

A number of studies have shown that families are the primary source of care for older people and that they will go to great lengths to help care for an impaired member. Public resources are usually not called upon by those in need of help until the informal system becomes overwhelmed. A cooperative effort between caregivers and the service network is less likely to result in a breakdown of the helping effort and more apt to work for a longer period and come closer to meeting outstanding needs. By cultivating and using the total helping network, adult day care programs are more likely to be successful in their efforts to help participants maintain or improve capacity for independence.

A second benefit of using the informal network is that the individual or group offering assistance because of their concern for one participant will often become supportive of the total program and will become involved in other ways: for example, as volunteers and goodwill ambassadors in the community. The program staff should encourage such involvement by:

- Contacting individuals and groups who are likely sources of such assistance and making specific requests for needed help
- Providing them with information about the program and the need which they are being asked to fill
- Working cooperatively with the individual or group, encouraging and supporting their helping efforts
- Providing any needed orientation and training to help maximize abilities to provide assistance
- Providing recognition: making the helpers aware of the value of contributions they are making
- Maintaining contact, keeping the helping network updated about results of care being provided.

Using Community Resources

There are basically two methods of using resources of the community to enrich and assist the adult day care program: 1) providing more complete services to individual participants and 2) obtaining equipment, supplies and personnel to expand program capability and stretch program funds.

The helping network can be used to supplement program efforts to work more effectively with participants and is essential in bringing about desired outcomes. Components of the helping network fall into five basic categories; health care, social care, legal assistance, economic and educational needs. Defining needs of each participant and seeking help needed to address specific problems is a practical approach for utilizing network components.

Health Care Needs

Medical Care.

physicians
physicians' assistants
public health department
visiting health nurse
medical volunteers
home health aides
home health agencies
clinics: hospital and community
adult day care staff

Health Monitoring.

visiting nurse service
family/caregivers
health aides
neighbors/friends
adult day care staff

Nutritional Needs.

Provision of Meals.

adult day care program
home delivered meals program
family/caregivers
neighbors/friends
church

Dietary Supervision/Counseling.

adult day care staff
home extension agencies
nutritionist/dietician
family/caregivers
physician
nurse

Physical Activity.

- adult day care staff
- physical therapists
- YW/YMCAs
- swimming pools
- bowling alleys
- dance instructors
- recreation therapists
- city/county recreation departments

Rehabilitation.

- physical therapists
- occupational therapists
- Vocational Rehabilitation Department
- Cancer Society
- Heart Society
- Alcoholics Anonymous
- Stroke Association
- Diabetes Association
- Services for the Blind
- Ostomy Association
- Mental Health Department
- visiting health nurse
- adult day care staff

Activities of Daily Living.

- homemaker aides
- chore workers
- community action agency
- volunteer agencies
- home health agencies
- family/caregivers
- visiting nurses
- volunteers
- occupational therapist
- physical therapist
- adult day care staff

Transportation for Health Care.

- community transportation
- churches
- volunteers
- public transportation
- adult day care staff

Home Safety Training.

- police
- fire departments
- home extension agencies
- family/neighbors
- social services
- volunteers
- community action agencies
- adult day care staff

Mental Health Care.

- mental health department
- mental health professionals
- ministers
- pastoral care organizations
- home extension agencies (programs on mental health)
- families/friends
- adult day care staff

Social Care Needs

Social Activities.

- senior citizens' clubs
- youth organizations
- church groups
- drama/music therapists and teachers
- recreation department and therapists
- occupational therapists
- social clubs
- family/caregivers
- neighbors/friends
- adult day care staff

Leisure Activities.

- arts and crafts teachers and organizations
- drama/music/art therapists, teachers, clubs
- community college
- students
- dance clubs
- home extension agencies
- agricultural agencies
- community social clubs
- senior citizens' clubs
- parks
- YW/YMCA
- libraries
- churches
- family/caregivers
- neighbors/friends
- volunteers
- adult day care staff

Community Involvement.

churches
community service organizations
political organizations
volunteer agencies
senior citizens' clubs
civic groups and organizations
schools
hospitals
charitable organizations
adult day care staff

Friendly Visitor/Telephone Reassurance.

volunteer agencies
senior citizens clubs
postal carriers
police
churches
libraries
neighbors/friends
family/caregivers
fraternal organizations
adult day care participants
adult day care staff

Home Maintenance.

Council on Aging
community action agency
churches
youth groups
schools and colleges
volunteer agencies
family/caregivers
neighbors/friends
individual volunteers

Shopping Assistance.

church groups
homemaker/chore service
volunteers
neighbors/friends
family/caregivers
adult day care staff

Legal Assistance.

- Legal Aid Society
- County Bar Association
- volunteer attorneys
- consumer protection agency
- small claims court
- social services protective services division

Educational Needs

- community colleges
- libraries
- home extension agency
- Services for the Blind
- National Retired Teachers Association
- financial planning services of banks
- consumer protection agencies
- Social Security Department
- Social Services Department
- YW/YMCA
- volunteers
- police/fire departments
- ministers
- adult day care staff

Economic Needs

Income Supplement.

- Social Services Department (income supplement, food stamps, Medicaid)
- Social Security Department
- Veterans Administration
- churches
- Salvation Army
- Goodwill Agency (clothes, household equipment)

Budgeting Assistance.

- Social Services Department
- Consumer Credit Association
- Consumer Protection Agency
- home extension agencies
- adult day care staff

Other Community Resources

Personnel

In addition to volunteers, consultants, and contractual services and components of the helping network, adult day care can extend the capacity of the staff by taking advantage of other resources which may be available to help stretch program funds.

Title V Employees. The area Agency on Aging should be contacted to learn whether funds are available for employment of older adults through this program. Depending upon the amount of funds, this can be an excellent method for supplementing the staff.

Community Colleges. Instructors from community colleges can be invaluable to the adult day care program. They can be used to teach classes on topics of interest to participants or meeting their needs. Classes may be from two to four hours in length; this time free from attending the participants can be utilized by staff for program planning or other purposes. Some community colleges will supply a part-time staff member for a special purpose or to fill a particular need in the adult day care program. These special needs include teaching adult basic education, teaching families how to care for dependent members, etc.

Adult Basic Education Program. This program can supply an instructor to the program for up to six hours per day to instruct participants in issues of basic education. The program's interpretation of basic education can be broad, covering topics such as re-learning money management skills or memory training.

Youth Summer Employment Program. Young people can add a valuable dimension to the adult day care program. Summer youth employment programs are often searching for organizations willing to offer job training to help the young adults develop or improve job skills. The employees are usually eager to learn and to develop special relationships with participants. They can be used as program or office aides.

Public Health. The public health department will usually arrange to have a visiting nurse come to the program to provide for a specific health care need for a participant, e.g., help with an ostomy or dressing a wound. Some departments will also provide a nurse to visit the program on a regular, periodic basis to do blood pressure checks and to perform health checks to detect any need for additional care or treatment.

The department should be contacted to learn under what terms these services may be made available to the program.

Chore Services. In some locations, adult day care programs receiving social services' funds may arrange to have a chore worker assigned to the program. The duties of this worker include visiting homes of participants absent due to illness and providing any needed care or assistance. The individual receiving this help must meet all eligibility requirements normally required to qualify for chore service.

Equipment

Program and administrative equipment are often available to the adult day care program at minimal or no cost from various sources in the community. Counties or cities often own desks, chairs, tables, and office machines which are in storage because they are not currently needed. These are usually in good condition and can sometimes be borrowed by community service agencies which are nonprofit. The loan is usually for long periods, and possible permanent.

Businesses buy new furniture and equipment on a regular basis and will often dispose of the old by giving it away or selling it for small amounts. Nonprofit agencies will be more likely to benefit from this, but for-profits may also be able to purchase equipment this way.

A listing of program needs in newspaper columns devoted to this purpose in many communities will often elicit donations of many items: desks, typewriters, chairs, tables, piano, and tools. Again, donations are more likely to be available to nonprofit programs, but for-profits on a small budget and providing a recognized service to the community may be able to request and receive donated equipment.

Program Supplies

Many, many items which can be used in adult day care to carry out program activities can be obtained within the community for the asking. A list of such needed supplies should be posted in the center, made available to the staff, board members, volunteers, families, and other visitors to the center.

Requests to churches, schools, and civic groups to collect these items for the program are usually effective in obtaining almost any needed item.

Department stores and manufacturers are also potential sources for supplies. Department stores discard many items such as yarn, sewing materials, and display articles and are often receptive to requests from such programs as adult day care to call the program when these are to be thrown away.

Manufacturers of wood, fabric, paper, and plastic items will have throw-away materials which can be put to good use by the program. Contacting the manufacturer and asking to be notified when materials are discarded will often result in the program's being placed on a list to be called on a regular basis.

As projects are planned in the program, notations should be made of needed supplies, and research conducted to learn whether they can be obtained in this way.

Summary

Thoughtful planning and creativity are the keys to the adult day care program taking full advantage of the plentiful resources available in every community.

Staff must be willing to spend some time in researching to learn what is available. Additional time will be needed to make the necessary contacts, to make program needs known, and to meet any requirements imposed by the agency or donor before obtaining the desired resource. However, the time spent will be as cost effective as any spent by the staff. The dividend gained in terms of savings to the program and provision of better and more complete services to participants are immeasurable.

Appendix A: Sample Job Descriptions

Job Description: Program Director

Salary Range:

Responsible to:

Qualifications:

1. *General:* Shall be at least 21 years of age. Shall provide a written statement from a physician certifying good health, including freedom from communicable disease.
2. *Training and Experience:* Shall have a master's degree in gerontology, counseling, or other health related field or

   Shall have a bachelor's degree in gerontology, counseling, or other health-related field and have had at least one year of professional experience working with elderly and/or impaired adults in a supervisory, administrative capacity, or

   Shall have had at least 2 years of formal post-secondary education from an accredited institution of learning and a minimum of 5 years experience working with elderly and/or impaired adults in a supervisory administrative capacity.

   Shall have completed or renewed training in standard First Aid within the last two years. Shall have completed or renewed training in cardiopulmonary resuscitation within the last year. CPR training must be renewed annually.
3. *Abilities:* Ability to make decisions and set goals; ability to exercise good judgement; to work with people in a variety of settings; to work independently; to understand needs of aging and/or disabled adults, including recognition of the role adult day care should play in contributing to independence and autonomy; leadership, management and planning; marketing and selling abilities.
4. *Personal Characteristics:* Creativity; flexibility; emotional stability; acceptance of people; non-judgemental; non-prejudicial; highly motivated.

Duties and Responsibilities

1. Administrative: Implement program policies and procedures.
   - Ensure compliance with all existing health, safety and programmatic standards and regulations applying to adult day care in the State of ___________________.
   - Prepare reports and provide information as required by the Board of Directors/Governing Body, committees of that body, funding bodies, regulatory agencies, referral agencies, and others.
   - Oversee and supervise office routine.
   - Maintain (supervise maintenance of) record and document system as required by sound administrative practices.
   - Manage program budget.
   - Carry out sound fiscal management practices within the program.
   - Work with Board/Advisory Committee to plan and carry out a public relations campaign within the community.
   - Serve as liaison between the program and the community, working to develop cooperative relationships with other community service agencies and organizations.
2. Personnel: recruit, hire, and manage program staff.
   - Plan/provide/oversee staff orientation and ongoing staff development.
   - Recruit, train, and supervise (or oversee) program volunteers.
3. Program: Oversee and supervise program provision.
   - With other program personnel, plan and carry out a program of services and activities to achieve program goals and meet needs of participants.
   - Carry out ongoing efforts to recruit and enroll participants.
   - Coordinate and oversee admissions and discharge procedures.
   - With other program staff, review information about individual participants and, working with members of the care team, design a plan of care for the individual.
   - Maintain (cause to be maintained) appropriate records and documents for participants.
4. Other related duties as required for effective discharge of the position of director.

Signed: ____

Date ____

Job Description: Nurse

Salary Range:

Responsible to:

Qualifications:

1. *General*: Shall be at least 21 years of age. Shall provide a written statement from a physician certifying good health, including freedom from communicable disease.
2. *Training and Experience:* Shall be either a registered nurse or licensed vocational/practical nurse, with valid state credentials. Shall have had at least one year experience working with elderly or chronically impaired adults.
3. *Abilities:* Ability to make decisions, to work independently, to exercise good judgement; to understand needs of aging and/or chronically impaired adults and to work with them in ways which increase/maintain functional independence.
4. *Personal Characteristics:* Flexibility; emotional stability; acceptance of people; non-judgemental; non-prejudicial; highly motivated.

Duties:

1. Conduct health assessment of each participant; set up and monitor health care plans.
2. Administer medications (or supervise taking of medications) and monitor response to medications.
3. Work with each participant to achieve and maintain optimum health through health education and counseling.
4. Consult with dietetic staff regarding diet needs of participants, including therapeutic diets.
5. Work with other program staff to ensure that program environment and activities are safe for participants.
6. Maintain First Aid kit; maintain emergency information on participants; set up and train staff in emergency procedures.
7. Maintain contact with families of participants and work with them to carry out health education and practices with participants.
8. Maintain communication with participants' physicians and other health care providers to ensure continuity of care.
9. Refer participants and families to appropriate community health care sources; act as liaison with these.

10. Work with other program staff to plan and carry out individual care plans for each participant. Accept responsibility for health care aspects of plans.
11. Coordinate personal care activities for participants; oversee other staff members in carrying out personal care.
12. Make home visits as required.
13. Other duties as assigned.

Signed: ______________________________

Date ______________________________

Job Description: Program Assistant/Activities Leader

Salary Range:

Responsible to:

Qualifications:

1. *General:* Shall be at least 21 years of age. Shall provide a written statement from a physician certifying good health including freedom from communicable disease.
2. *Training and Experience:* Shall have a combination of training and work experience as will have provided knowledge and skills (as judged by program interview committee) needed to carry out position duties.
3. *Abilities:* Ability to make decisions and set goals; to exercise good judgement, to work with people in the adult day care setting; to work independently and as a team member; to understand needs of aging and impaired adults, including helping them to participate in services and activities to maintain/increase functional ability.
4. *Personal Characteristics:* Creativity; flexibility; emotional stability; acceptance of people; non-judgmental; non-prejudicial; highly motivated.

Duties and Responsibilities:

1. With other program staff formulate individual plan of care for each participant and assist in carrying out plans.
2. Plan and implement activities designed to help participants achieve goals of care plan.
3. Participate in periodic review and revision of care plans.
4. Provide participants with any assistance needed in activities of daily living or supervise aides in provision of such assistance.
5. Recruit, provide orientation for, assign, and supervise volunteers. Maintain volunteer records.
6. Participate with other staff in the maintenance of a safe and healthful environment in the center.
7. Maintain communication with families on progress, problems, and needs of participants in order to ensure continuity of care.
8. Be aware of emergency practices and procedures.

9. Work with director and other staff members to identify staff training and development needs and help to plan/carry out educational activities to meet needs.

10. Other related duties as assigned.

Signed: ____

Date ____

Appendix B: Sample Program Evaluation Plan and Forms

I. *Evaluation Objectives*

An internal evaluation will be conducted annually with these objectives:

1. To measure effectiveness of present service delivery methods.
2. To determine whether service is appropriate for participants being served.
3. To analyze what services and activities have proven successful in helping participants to maintain/improve functional capacity.
4. To analyze gaps/deficiencies of services which may have contributed to failure of participants to maintain or improve.
5. To determine whether direct services are being provided in accordance with stated program goals.
6. To learn whether indirect services are being provided in accordance with goals.
7. To learn whether the program is fulfilling its proper role in the community continuum of care.
8. To measure impact of service upon participants and families.
9. To determine whether program resources are being used efficiently.
10. To learn whether community resources are being utilized to the fullest to enhance and expand program capability.
11. To determine whether program administration is functioning effectively and fulfilling assigned roles and responsibilities.

II. *Evaluation Methods*

The evaluation process will involve:

1. The Board of Directors: questionnaires
2. Director: questionnaires, data report
3. Staff: questionnaires, data report
4. Participants: those able will complete participant Evaluation Form (#6); others will have questionnaire administered by a volunteer recruited for the purpose.

5. Families/Caregivers: questionnaire to be mailed or handed to individual. Assistance offered upon request. Forms returned by mail to insure anonymity.
6. Department of Social Services, other community agencies/ individuals who make referrals or who are involved in some part of service delivery: questionnaire to be mailed.

III. *Steps in Evaluation*

Evaluation will take place in four phases:

1. Development of evaluation instrument.
2. Collection of information as outlined above.
3. Interpretation of data.
4. Use of data.

IV. *Evaluation Codes*

Forms 1-5 will be completed using the following codes:

1 = Excellent

2 = Fair

3 = Satisfactory

4 = Needs Improvement

5 = Unsatisfactory

Forms 6-8 will be completed by marking appropriate answer. Forms 9-11 will be completed by filling in numbers as indicated. Form 11 will be completed after others so that information from these will be available.

V. *Evaluation: Program Performance*

Form 1. Board of Directors

(To be conducted as internal evaluation and completed by board members and by the director. Outside evaluation consultants may be used if deemed appropriate.)

Based upon your knowledge of the board and from your perspective, please answer the following questions.

Number of years association with program __________ Date _________

____ a. Board members as a unit possess qualifications needed to carry out duties. List skills you believe are missing ________________

____

___ b. Membership of the board is representative of the community. Any population not represented ______________________

___ c. Leadership is effective, handles decisions well and able to motivate board to carry out action plans.

___ d. Board is in compliance with all legal requirements which apply.

___ e. Necessary documents are adequately maintained and accessible when needed.

___ f. Board is familiar with program policies and examines them periodically to be sure that they continue to reflect program goals and plans.

___ g. Personnel policies and job descriptions are current and work well.

___ h. Organization is financially stable; there is ongoing funding and financial records are current and accurate.

___ i. Annual audits are conducted by an outside auditor; findings indicate satisfactory financial management.

___ j. Board is actively involved in ongoing public relations and has demonstrated success in gaining community support: material and supply donations, financial support, volunteers. Gaps __________

___ k. Board engages in both short- and long-term plan development.

___ l. All board members are active in work of board and carry out their assigned role on the board.

___ m. Board meetings are well attended; a quorum is always present.

___ n. Committees are functional, responsibilities are carried out within reasonable time limits, and appropriate reports are given to the board.

___ o. All board members have participated in orientation and engage in available training as needed to maintain and improve skills.

___ p. All board members understand and support the adult day care philosophy.

___ q. Board is organized so that routine tasks (signing checks and documents or making purchases) can be easily handled. Improvements needed ______________________________

___ r. Board is organized so that it is responsive to crisis situations. Improvements needed ______________________

___ s. Board engages in regular, periodic self-assessment to determine how effectively responsibilities are being discharged.

___ t. Board is satisfied with the way director discharges responsibilities. Improvements needed __________________________________

___ u. Board is responsive and supportive of the director and is accessible for consultation when needed.

___ v. Board and staff relationships are well defined; board does not interfere with day-to-day management of the program. Improvements needed __________________________________

V. *Evaluation Instrument: Management*

Form 2. Director

(To be completed by the director and board members, staff members as deemed appropriate.)

Based upon your knowledge of the work of the director and from your perspective, please answer the following questions.

___ a. Director possesses qualifications needed to discharge position responsibilities and duties.

___ b. The director engages in professional training opportunities to maintain and improve knowledge and skills.

___ c. The director exhibits an understanding of the philosophy of adult day care and demonstrates this in program management.

___ d. The director understands the working relationship between the board and staff and works to maintain an effective relationship.

___ e. The director understands the separate responsibilities of the board and the director and discharges those of the director's position.

___ f. The director reports to the board are submitted as appropriate and are accurate, inclusive, and current.

___ g. The director works to help educate the board about program goals, participant needs, and program service methods.

___ h. The director carries out fiscal control practices in the program to achieve fiscal accountability and maximum use of program resources.

___ i. The director acts as a bridge between the board and staff.

___ j. The director is effective in daily program management.

___ k. The director functions effectively in the role of staff manager, utilizing staff for maximum benefit to the program.

___ l. The director is effective in projecting the desired program image to the community.

___ m. The director is knowledgeable about characteristics peculiar to the population to be served by the program and keeps admissions within this group.

___ n. The director is effective in overseeing service planning, making sure that participants are receiving the care appropriate for them.

___ o. The director maintains enrollment and daily census numbers within the range stated in program goals.

V. *Evaluation Instrument: Management*

Form 3. Staff

(To be completed by director, staff members, board if appropriate.)

Based upon your knowledge of staff performance and from your perspective, please answer the following questions.

___ a. The staff as a whole demonstrates understanding and support of the adult day care philosophy.

___ b. The staff possesses qualifications needed to provide services and activities needed by and appropriate for the population served in the program.

___ c. The staff engages in regular training and development to maintain and upgrade skills and knowledge.

___ d. The staff functions as a team to plan and provide services.

___ e. The staff recognizes each participant as an individual with unique characteristics, abilities, and needs.

___ f. The staff plans services and activities and helps participants achieve and maintain maximum functional independence.

___ g. Interaction among the staff and between staff and participants is warm, open, and constructive.

___ h. The staff interacts in ways which allow participants to voice needs, feelings, and responses to treatment.

___ i. The staff communicates any problems or changes in direction in participant treatment to families and caregivers.

___ j. The staff adequately documents actions to facilitate review and revision of program plans.

V. *Evaluation Instrument: Management*

Form 4. Facility

(To be completed by board, staff, participants, appropriate members of the care team.)

Based upon your knowledge of the program facility and from your perspective, please answer the following questions.

Position of person completing questionnaire: ____________________

___ a. Facility is in a safe location.

___ b. Facility is located so that it is easily accessible to participants.

___ c. The facility is within comfortable distances to other community services.

___ d. The facility meets zoning and other codes applying to such programs.

___ e. All systems—plumbing, electrical, heating/cooling—are in safe working condition and are adequate for the number attending the program.

___ f. The amount of indoor space is adequate for the number of participants and staff and for provision of needed services and activities.

___ g. There is adequate storage space for program materials and for participants to store personal possessions.

___ h. Program space is arranged to facilitate good traffic patterns.

___ i. Space arrangements accommodate both large and small group activities and allow for participants to withdraw from the group.

___ j. The space is free from architectural barriers and allows freedom of movement.

___ k. Space and furniture are arranged to provide safety of movement.

IV. *Evaluation Instrument: Management*

Form 5. Program Resources

(To be completed by board, director, staff, others as deemed appropriate.)

Position of person completing questionnaire ____________________

Based upon your knowledge of the program and from your perspective, please answer the following questions.

___ a. Funds are adequate to provide services and activities needed by and appropriate for the population being served.

___ b. Funds appear to be well managed, with little or no obvious waste.

___ c. Supplies and equipment are adequate for activities and numbers being served.

___ d. Supplies are available as needed.

___ e. Supplies are placed so that participants can help themselves when practical, fostering independence.

___ f. Staff numbers are adequate to numbers being served.

___ g. Staff members utilize resources wisely and without waste.

___ h. Volunteers are utilized to enhance the program.

___ i. Volunteers are well trained to carry out program policies and support the adult day care philosophy.

___ j. The staff is knowledgeable about and provides assistance in use of community services needed by participants.

V. *Evaluation: Program Performance*

Form 6. Participant Evaluation

(To be completed by present participants and those who have left the program during the period, if deemed appropriate.)

Participant Profile: Age ______ Sex ______

How long in program __________

Reason for enrolling ____

1. Do you believe that, in general, you have benefited from coming to the program?

   A lot ______ A little ______ No change ______
   Worse off ______ Not sure ______

2. Can you name ways in which you are better or worse off?

3. Has your outlook on life changed since coming to the program?

   Improved a lot ______ A little ______ No change ______
   Worse ______ Not sure ______

4. Can you name ways in which your outlook has changed?

5. Has your physical health changed?

   Improved a lot ______ A little ______ No change ______
   Worse ______ Not sure ______

6. Can you name changes which have taken place?
7. Has there been any change in your ability to care for yourself?

   Improved a lot ______ A little ______ No change ______
   Worse ______ Not sure ______

8. If there have been changes, can you name them?
9. Have there been any changes in your relationships with your family since coming to the program?

   Improved a lot ______ A little ______ No change ______
   Worse ______ Not sure ______

10. Has there been any change in your ability to get along with people?

    Improved a lot ______ A little ______ No change ______
    Worse ______ Not sure ______

11. How are any changes demonstrated?
12. Have you learned or improved any skills which help you to occupy yourself?

    A lot ______ Some ______ Not many ______
    None ______ Not sure ______

13. Name any skills you have learned.
14. What skills would you like to learn but haven't had the opportunity?
15. Do you believe the program offers ample social opportunities?

    Plenty _____ Some _____ Few _____ Not many _____
    None _____ Not sure _____

16. What are those offered?
17. What would you like to see added?
18. Does the program offer opportunities to learn things which interest you?

    A lot _____ Some _____ Few _____ Not many _____
    None _____ Not sure _____

19. What are some things you have learned?
20. What would you like to learn but haven't had the opportunity?
21. Have you enjoyed working on group projects at the center?

    A lot ______ Some ______ Not usually ______
    No ______ None offered ______ Not sure ______

22. What group projects would you like to see offered?

23. Have you enjoyed working on projects by yourself?

    A lot ______ Some ______ Not usually ______

    No ______ None offered ______ Not sure ______

24. What are projects you would like to do?

25. Do you feel free to refuse to engage in any activity at the center?

    Completely free ______ Sometimes ______
    No, I feel pressured ______

26. Do you like the mixture of activities at the center: active, quiet, crafts, classes, outings, etc.?

    Just right ______ About right ______ Needs change ______
    No ______

27. What changes would you like to see made?

28. Do you enjoy the food at the center?

    A lot ______ It is O.K. ______ Sometimes ______
    Needs improvement ______ No ______

29. How would you like to see it changed?

30. Does the staff seem to care about you as a person?

    A lot ______ Mostly ______ Sometimes ______
    Not usually ______ Never______

31. Do you believe they respect your dignity as an individual?

    A lot ______ Mostly ______ Sometimes ______
    Not usually ______ Never______

32. Do you receive adequate attention when you do not feel well?

    Plenty ______ Mostly ______ Sometimes ______
    Not usually ______ Never______ Not sure______

33. Are there changes you would like to see made in the way staff relates to participants?

34. Do you look forward to coming to the program each day?

    Always ______ Mostly ______ Sometimes ______
    Not usually ______ Never______

35. Can you give reasons for your feelings?

36. Are you satisfied with the way transportation is carried out?

    Always ______ Mostly ______ Sometimes ______
    Not usually ______ Never______

37. Any changes you would like to see made?
38. What would you miss most about the program if it were to close?
39. What are the most important services you receive at the program?
40. What activities do you most enjoy?
41. What about the program do you dislike or would like to see changed?
42. How much do you pay for attending the program?________________
43. Is that affordable?________________________________
44. What is the primary reason you come to the program?
45. How did you spend your time before coming to the program?
46. Do you feel safe in the center?

    Always ______ Mostly ______ Sometimes ______
    Not usually ______ Never______

47. Do you feel at home at the center?

    Always ______ Mostly ______ Sometimes ______
    Not usually ______ Never______

48. Can you give reasons for your feelings?
49. Do you feel that space, furnishings, and equipment are adequate and appropriate for the program and participants?

    Yes, just right ______ Mostly right ______ Some ______
    Needs improvement ______ Not adequate ______
    Not appropriate ______

50. Could you suggest any needed changes?
51. Would your life be affected if the center were to close?

    Life would be: Better ______ Little change ______
    Worse ______ Not sure ______

52. What would you do if the center were to close:

    Stay home with relative ______ Home alone ______
    Home with other help ______ Go into residential care ______
    Other ______ Not sure ______

53. How did you learn about the center?
54. Would you recommend the program to others?

55. Taking everything into consideration, how would you describe your feelings about the program?

    It is: Very satisfying ___ Somewhat satisfying ___
    Sometimes satisfying ___ Not very satisfying ___
    Not at all satisfying ___ Not sure ___

56. In general, do you feel that

	Never	Sometimes	Most of the time	Always
a Things get worse as you get older?				
b. You feel worse as you get older?				
c. You feel sad and lonely?				
d. Things bother you?				
e. You would like more time with family and friends?				
f. You find it hard to sleep?				
g. You worry a lot?				
h. You feel that life is no longer satisfying?				
i. You are less useful as you get older?				
j. You are less happy as you get older?				
k. It is hard to make decisions?				
l. You need more to do?				
m. You miss the"old days"?				
n. Your mind is less clear than it used to be?				
o. You get tired for no reason?				
p. You prefer being by yourself?				
q. Life is hard for you?				
r. You feel pessimistic about the future?				

57. Thank you for your help. The information will be used to try to improve the program so that it is better able to meet your needs. We would be interested in any additional comments/suggestions you would like to make.

    Comments:

V. *Evaluation: Program Performance*

Letter to accompany questionnaires to families and professional caregivers.

Date

Dear ________________,

In order to evaluate effectiveness of program services and to learn how well the program is meeting desired objectives and goals, the ________________ ____________________ Adult Day Care Center is conducting an annual evaluation of all phases of its operation.

As a (*family member of a participant; professional caregiver; participant,* etc.) we need your help in evaluating our program's benefits to our participants.

Your cooperation in completing the enclosed questionnaire would be greatly appreciated. Your information will be anonymous unless you choose to sign the form, and all replies will be treated as confidential.

Please consider each question and answer to the best of your ability. You may feel that some questions do not apply to your situation; if this occurs, just skip that question and mark it NA ("not applicable").

We would like to request that you complete the form and return it to us by *(date)* in the enclosed envelope.

If you have questions, or need more information or need assistance in completing the questionnaire, please call the center and ask for *(Staff Member)* *(phone number)* They will be glad to answer questions or provide you with a volunteer who will give the necessary help.

Thank you for your assistance in our evaluation; we hope to use this information to continue to improve our services to participants, families, and the community.

Sincerely,

Program Director

V. *Evaluation: Program Performance*

Form 7. Family Evaluation

(To be completed by family/caregivers of present participants and any who have left during the period, if deemed appropriate.)

Relationship to the participant ____________________ Date ____________

Participant Profile: Age ____ Sex ____ How long in Program ________

Primary reason for enrolling ____

1. Do you believe that, in general, the participant has benefited from their attendance in the program?

   A lot ______ A little ______ No change ______
   Worse off ______ Not sure ______

2. How does this demonstrate itself to you?

3. Has attendance in the program made any change in participant's outlook on life?

   Improved a lot ______ A little ______ No change ______
   Worse ______ Not sure ______

4. What evidence is there of changes?

5. Has participant's physical health changed since coming to the program?

   Improved a lot ______ A little ______ No change ______
   Worse ______ Not sure ______

6. What is evidence of these changes?

7. Has there been any change in participant's ability to perform self-care?

   Improved a lot ______ A little ______ No change ______
   Worse ______ Not sure ______

8. How is this demonstrated?

9. Has there been any change in participant's relationships with family?

   Improved a lot ______ A little ______ No change ______
   Worse ______ Not sure ______

10. How does the change show itself?

11. Has there been any change in participant's social skills?

    Improved a lot ______ A little ______ No change ______
    Worse ______ Not sure ______

12. Name ways changes are demonstrated?

13. Has the participant learned or improved any skills which help to occupy time?

    Many _____ Some _____ Few _____ Not many _____
    None _____ Not sure _____

14. Can you name skills which have been learned?
15. What additional skills do you believe participant needs to learn?
16. Do you believe the program offers ample opportunities for social activities?

    Plenty _____ Some _____ Few _____ Not many _____
    None _____ Not sure _____

17. Would you name those you know to be offered?
18. What would you like to see added?
19. Does the participant look forward to coming to the program?

    Always ______ Mostly ______ Sometimes ______
    Not usually ______ Never______ Not sure______

20. What reasons does the participant give for this?
21. Can you suggest ways in which the program could help participant to be more eager to come?
22. Does the participant prepare for the day by getting up on time and getting ready to come?

    Always ______ Mostly ______ Sometimes ______
    Not usually ______ Never ______ Not sure______

23. Can you give reasons for this?
24. Do you believe that program services meet outstanding needs of participant?

    All needs _____ Most _____ Some_____ Few_____
    Outstanding needs not met _____

25. Would you name needs which you think the program is meeting?
26. Needs not being met?
27. What do you believe to be the most important service the participant receives?
28. Are there additional services you would like to see offered?
29. Are you satisfied with the way program staff relates to participant?

Always ______ Mostly ______ Sometimes ______
Not usually ______ Never______ Not sure______

30. How does this manifest itself?

31. What would you like to see changed?

32. Has enrollment of the participant benefited your life in any way?

    A lot ______ A little ______ No change ______
    Worse off _____ Not sure ______

33. Can you give reasons for this?

34. Has your outlook on life changed since enrollment?

35. Can you give reasons for this?

36. Has your relationship with the participant changed since enrollment?

    Improved a lot ______ A little ______ No change ______
    Worse ______ Not sure ______

37. Can you give reasons for this?

38. Have relationships within the family unit changed?

    Improved a lot ______ A little ______ No change ______
    Worse ______ Not sure ______

39. Are there reasons for this which are connected with participant's enrollment?

40. What method of care would be provided for participant if day care were not available?

    Remain at home with family member ______ Home alone ______
    Home with employed help ______ Full time residential care ______
    Other ______ Not sure ______

41. Does participant's enrollment mean that you have more time for yourself?

    A lot ______ A little ______ No change ______
    Less time ______ Not sure ______

42. If you have more time, how do you use it?

    Outside employment ______ Care for family ______
    Personal needs ______

43. Have you experienced any lessening of stress since enrollment of participant?

    A lot ______ A little ______ No change ______
    More stress ______ Not sure ______

44. Can you give reasons for this?
45. Are operating hours such that they meet your needs?

    Yes ______ No ______ Changes needed ______
46. Are you satisfied with the way staff members related to you/family members?

    Very satisfied ______ Mostly ______ Sometimes ______
    Needs improvement ______ No______
47. Can you give reasons for your feelings?
48. Do you feel satisfied with communication: do you receive all information needed to let you know what is going on with the participant?

    Very satisfied ______ Mostly ______ Sometimes ______
    Needs improvement ______ No______
49. Can you give reasons?
50. Are you encouraged to participate in planning and carrying out care plans for participant?

    Always ______ Usually ______ Sometimes ______
    Not usually ______ Never______
51. How would you like to see this changed?
52. If you participate in a family support group at the center, are you satisfied with the group?

    Very satisfied ______ Mostly ______ Sometimes ______
    Needs improvement ______ No______
53. What changes would you like to see?
54. What topics or information would you like to have which has not been offered?
55. How did you/participant first learn about the program?

    Doctor ______ Social worker ______ Relative ______
    Brochure ______ Radio/TV ______ Other ______
56. Who recommended enrollment for the participant?

    Participant ____ Family member ____ Doctor ____ Other ____
57. Do you feel that the participant is in a safe environment while in the center?

    Always ______ Mostly ______ Sometimes ______
    Not usually ______ Never______ Not sure ______

58. Reasons for feelings?

59. Do you feel that space, furnishing, and equipment are adequate and appropriate for the program and participants?

    Yes, just right ______ Mostly right ______ Somewhat ______
    Needs improvement ______ Not adequate ______
    Not appropriate ______

60. Could you suggest any needed changes?

61. What factors made you believe that adult day care would be the best method of care for the participant?

62. How much does it cost for the participant to come to the center?

63. Is this affordable?

64. What is the most important service you/family receive from the program?

65. Taking everything into consideration, how would you describe participant's satisfaction with the program?

    Very satisfied ______ Mostly satisfied ______ Sometimes ______
    Not satisfied______

66. Taking everything into consideration, how would you describe your own and your family's satisfaction with the program?

    Very satisfied ______ Mostly satisfied ______ Sometimes _____
    Not satisfied______

67. If the center were to close, how would participant's life be affected?

    Would be: Better ______ Little change ______ Worse ______
    Not sure ______

68. How would your own and your family's life be affected?

    Would be: Better ______ Little change ______ Worse ______
    Not sure ______

69. If adult day care were not available, what care would your doctor or other medical care provider recommend? (Based upon their statements.)

    Home, with family ______ Home alone ______
    With employed help ______ Residential care ______
    Other ______ Not sure ______

70. Thank you for your help. Please feel free to add any comments or suggestions which you believe were not covered by questions in the form.

V. *Evaluation: Program Performance*

Form 8. Professional Caregiver Evaluation

(To be completed by doctors, nurses, therapists, social or mental health workers, etc. [Any professional who makes referrals, is involved with care or otherwise familiar with the program.])

Profession ____________________

Relationship to Participant/Program ____________ Date ________

If relationship is to a participant, what is participant's: Age _____ Sex _____

How long in program ____________________

What was primary reason for enrolling ____________________

Based upon your knowledge of the program/ participant(s), please answer the following questions. Information will be used to analyze program effectiveness. Information will be confidential.

1. Do you believe that, in general, participants benefit from attendance in the program?

   A lot ______ A little ______ No change ______
   Worse off ______ Not sure ______

2. Do you believe that attendance has any effect upon mental health of participants?

   Improves a lot ______ A little ______ No change ______
   Worse ______ Not sure ______

3. Would you state any evidence you have of such changes?

4. Does attendance affect physical health?

   Improves a lot ______ A little ______ No change ______
   Worse ______ Not sure ______

5. State evidence of such changes.

6. Is mental health affected?

   Improves a lot ______ A little ______ No change ______
   Worse ______ Not sure ______

7. State evidence.

8. Does attendance affect family relationships?

   Improve a lot ______ A little ______ No change ______
   Worse ______ Not sure ______

9. Any evidence?

10. Does attendance affect participants' ability to care for themselves?

    Improve a lot ______ A little ______ No change ______
    Worse ______ Not sure ______

11. Evidence?

12. Any effect upon social/communication skills?

    Improves a lot ______ A little ______ No change ______
    Worse ______ Not sure ______

13. Evidence?

14. Does attendance affect participants' ability to occupy their time?

    Improves a lot ______ A little ______ No change ______
    Worse ______ Not sure ______

15. Evidence?

16. Do you believe the program meets outstanding needs of participant(s)?

    All needs ______ Most ______ Some ______ Not many ______
    Outstanding needs not met ______

17. What is the evidence of this?

18. Can you suggest ways in which the program could improve in this?

19. What do you believe to be the most important service participant(s) receive?

20. Are there additional services you believe should be offered?

21. In your experience with program staff, do you believe skills to be adequate to provide services to population being served?

    Skills are: Excellent ______ Satisfactory ______ Fair ______
    Needs improvement ______ Unsatisfactory ______

22. Can you state reasons for your belief?

23. Can you suggest ways in which staff skills need to be changed or improved?

24. Have you referred participant(s) to the program?

25. If yes, how would you rate the care they have received?

    Excellent ______ Satisfactory ______ Fair ______
    Need improvement ______ Unsatisfactory ______

26. Any recommendations for change or improvement?

27. If no, would you make referrals to the program?

28. Why, or why not?

29. If you have made referrals, what factors led you to believe that adult day care was the best method of care for the participant?

30. If you have made referrals or are a care provider for a participant, what do you think would happen to the participant if the center were to close? They would:

    Remain at home with family ______ Be at home alone ______
    At home with employed help ______ Other ______
    Enter full time residential care ______ Not sure ______

31. What characteristics do you believe would be typical of an individual who could be appropriately served in adult day care?

32. Characteristics of an individual who would not be best served?

33. Taking everything into consideration, what is your opinion of the program?

34. Additional comments.

V. *Evaluation Instrument: Program Performance*

Form 9. Direct Services

(To be completed by the director and appropriate staff members.)

Position of person completing questionnaire ____________ Date _________

Based upon your knowledge of the program, please answer the following.

___ a. Total number of participants served over the time period.

___ b. Average daily attendance.

___ c. Number of service inquiries received.

___ d. Number processed.

e. Percent of participants with:

Physical Impairments: Sensory Loss:

Vision _____ Hearing _____

Speech _____ Taste _____

Smell _____ Touch or Feeling _____

Loss of mobility _____ Stroke _____

Hypertension _____ Arthritis _____

Parkinson's disease _____ Atherosclerosis _____

Incontinence _____ Cancer _____

Alcoholism/Substance Abuse _____

Obesity _____ Diabetes _____

Other ___________________________

Mental/Emotional Impairments:

Alzheimer's disease _____

Depression _____ Brain Trauma/Injury _____

Wandering _____ Paranoia _____

Hostility _____ Acute Anxiety _____

Withdrawal _____ Regression _____

Acting Out _____ Sexual Fixation _____

Grief _____ Other ____________________

f. Percent of participants provided with:

Social Services _____ Medical Care _____

Mental Health Care _____

g. Services and activities. Number of social interaction activities (parties, volunteer activities, drama, music, etc.) ________________

Total number of participants engaging in these ________________

Number of leisure time activity classes offered ________________

Number of participants ____

Number of classes/sessions in skill training/re-training __________

Number of participants ____

Community Outings________ Participants ________________

Community Involvement Activities _____ Participants ________

Personal Assistance Activities/Training ____ Participants _______

Provision/Training in ADL __________ Participants ________

Number of trips for life sustaining purposes _____ Participants____

___ h. Number of home interviews conducted with prospective participants.

___ i. Number of present participants.

___ j. Number of prospective participants visiting the program.

___ k. Number admitted during the period.

___ l. Number of participants discharged during the period.

V. *Evaluation Instrument: Program Performance*

Form 10. Direct Services: Impact

(To be completed by director and appropriate board/staff members.)

Position of person completing questionnaire____________ Date ________

Based upon your knowledge of the program, please answer the following.

___ a. Number of participants who have moved into a lesser level of care.

___ b. Number who have maintained functional level.

___ c. Number who would have to enter full-time care without enrollment in adult day care. (Based on family, doctor, etc. statements.)

___ d. Number who have had neglect or self-abuse remedied or avoided.

___ e. Number of participants referred to other services by the program.

___ f. Number of participants participating in planning their own care.

___ g. Number of participants participating in planning program activities.

___ h. Number of family members participating in planning care.

___ i. Number of professional care providers. (In addition to program staff.)

___ j. Number of participants who have achieved some goals of care.

___ k. Number who have been unable to achieve goals.

___ l. Number of participants who function more independently in the home environment since enrollment in the program.

___ m. Number functioning about the same.

___ n. Number functioning less well.

___ o. Number who state that adult day care meets their need for care.

___ p. Number who state that the program fails to meet needs.

___ q. Number of families/caregivers offered relief from full-time care of participant.

____ r. Number of family members/caregivers freed for employment.

____ s. Number of family members stating that their needs are met through enrollment of the dependent family member.

____ t. Number stating that needs of participant are being met.

____ u. Number stating needs are not met

____ v. Number of participants who show evidence of positive change due to their use of the service.

____ w. Number who do not demonstrate positive change.

____ x. Number of families stating improvement in family situation from enrollment in adult day care.

____ y. Number stating no improvement.

____ z. Number of working relationships established/maintained with other community agencies/service providers.

____ aa. Number of participants moving into a more intensive method of care.

____ bb. Number who have left for other negative reasons.

List reasons ____________________

____ cc. Number of applicants denied admission to the program.

Reasons: ____________________

V. *Evaluation Instrument: Program Performance*

Form 11. Indirect services

(To be completed by the director, staff members, board members.)

Position of person completing questionnaire ____________ Date ________

____ a. Number of families receiving counseling services.

____ b. Number receiving other supportive services.

List ____________________

____ c. Number of information/referral services provided to participants.

To what services ____________________

____ d. Number of information/referral services provided to families.

List services ____________________

____ e. Number of referral services provided to persons outside the program.

List services referred to: ____________________

___ f. Number of staff members engaging in outside training/development events.

List topics of training ______________________

___ g. Number of staff engaging in training/development events inside the center.

List topics ______________________

___ h. Number of staff/board/volunteers/others to whom orientation has been provided.

___ i. Number of outside resource persons providing training.

___ j. Number of staff members providing training.

___ k. List benefits to program from training.

___ l. List training needs which have not been met.

___ m. Number of volunteer recruitment efforts carried out.

___ n. Number of volunteers recruited in the period.

___ o. Total number of volunteers serving in the program.

List services provided by volunteers ______________________

___ p. Total number of volunteer hours.

___ q. Number of community events in which staff/board members served as a resource person. List topics presented ______________________

___ r. Number of persons reached through these efforts.

___ s. List benefits to program ______________________

___ t. Number of public relations efforts planned and carried out.

List purposes ______________________

___ u. List benefits to program ______________________

___ v. Number of fund-raising events carried out.

Name them ______________________

___ w. Amount of money realized from these.

___ x. Number of events held for purposes of educating families/caregivers.

___ y. Number of persons participating.

___ z. Number of staff members serving as resource person.

____ aa. Number of outside resource persons used.

____ bb. Number of groups/individuals visiting the program.

Reasons ____

____ cc. Benefits to program ________________________________

Appendix C: Sample Enrollment and Discharge Forms

Participant Enrollment Application

Applicant's full name ______________________ Birthdate ______________

Address ______________________________ Phone ______________

______________________________ Sex ______ S.S. # ____________

Personal Data

Reason for applying for adult day care ______________________________

____

____

Any prior experience in adult day care? Yes ___ No ___ If yes, where ________

Marital status ____________ Present living arrangements ______________

____

Nearest responsible relative ______________________________________

Address ____________________ Daytime phone # ____________________

____________________________ Relationship ______________________

Emergency Care Information

Names of two persons who can be contacted (in addition to one above)

Name ______________________________ Phone ______________

Address ____________________________ Relationship ____________

Name ______________________________ Phone ______________

Address ____________________________ Relationship ____________

Physician ___________________________ Phone ______________

Hospital of choice ____

Dentist _____________________________ Phone ______________

Services

Transportation will be provided by: ________________________________

Days of attendance ____

Special dietary needs ____

Limitations on activities ____

Any other special conditions _____________________________________

Participant Discharge Form

Name ______________________ Date of birth ____________

Address ______________________

Date of enrollment ______________________

Reason for enrollment ______________________

Type of discharge ______________________

Specific reasons for discharge ______________________

____

Person making decision to discharge ______________________

If participant will move into other care, what kind? ______________________

____

If not, what other arrangements will be made? ______________________

____

Family/caregiver input into decision ______________________

____

Is participant likely to need adult day care again in the future? ____________

Will re-admission be considered? ______________________

Reasons for this ______________________

____

How does participant feel about discharge ______________________

____

How much notice was given participant? ____________ Family? ____________

Was this ample time to make other arrangements if needed? ____________

Additional comments ______________________

____

Signed ______________________ Date ____________

Position ______________________

Appendix D: Sample Functional Assessment Forms

Adult Day Care Functional Assessment

Program Name____________________ Date____________________

Interviewer____________________ Position____________________

I. *Participant Profile*

Name____________________ Phone____________________

Address____________________ Birthdate____________________

Sex________ Race____________ Religious preference____________

Marital status____________________ Living arrangements____________

Family members at home:

Name Relationship

____

____

____

Past work experience______________________________

____

Educational background______________________________

Special skills/interests______________________________

____

II. *Social Resources/Needs*

1. Family members with whom participant has supportive relationship

____

2. Family members living nearby:______________________________

____

3. Frequency of contact: By phone________ Visits participant________

Participant makes visits______________________________

4. Neighbors/friends who are supportive ____________________
____
____

5. Social/conversational skills:
Initiates/engages in conversation: ____________________
Maintains social contacts: Neighbors ____________________
Church ____________________ Friends ____________________
Other ____________________

6. *Seeks needed help or assistance:*
Assistance requested ____________________
From ____________________

7. Has someone to confide in *(Name)* ____________________

8. Has someone who will provide necessary help in event of sickness:
(Name) ____________________

9. Has meaningful role in family ________ Neighborhood ________
Social group ____________ Church ____________ Other _____

10. Social support system appears: Very supportive ____________
Adequate ______ Inadequate____ No social support system ________

11. Interviewer's comments ____________________
____
____

12. Social Needs ____________________
____
____

III. *Physical Resources/Needs*

1. *Ambulation:* Walks without assistance ____________________
Needs help with:
Stairs ____ Carpeted floors ____ Uneven terrain ____
Walks with assistance of: Support of another person ____
Cane____ Tripod____ Walker ____ Wheelchair____

2. Any Paralysis: __________ What part of body __________________

3. Any difficulty with motor control __________________________

4. Any sensory loss ____________________________________

   Describe ____

5. Any speech impediment/aphasia ____________________________

6. Any loss of bowel/kidney control ___________________________

   Describe ____

7. Condition of teeth and gums ______________________________

8. Weight problem ________ Evidence of malnutrition ______________

9. Therapeutic diet ______________________________________

10. Acute health problems __________________________________

    ____

11. Chronic health problems ________________________________

    ____

    ____

12. Prescribed medications: For:

    ____

    ____

13. Non-prescription drugs: For:

    ____

    ____

14. Can take own medications ______ Needs supervision ______________

    Medications must be administered ____________________________

15. Any history of alcoholism ________________________________

    Other substance addiction ________________________________

16. Days of illness during last 6 months (unable to carry out normal activities)____

17. Number of days spent in hospital/nursing home/rest home in last 6 months ________ For: ____________________________________

18. Able to participate in physical activities:

    Walking ______________ Swimming ______________________

    Exercise sessions _______ Outside games (croquet, etc.) __________

19. Any prescribed therapy or activity ______________________

    ____

20. Any supportive devices being used:

    Leg brace ______ Artificial limb ______ Hearing aid ______

    Glasses ______ Contact lens ______ Dentures ______

    Colostomy equipment ______ Catheter ______

    Kidney Dialysis ______ Other ______

    Any special instructions/assistance needed with these

    ____

21. Interviewer's comments ______________________________

    ____

    ____

22. Needs not presently being met: ________________________

    ____

    ____

IV. *Mental/Emotional Resources/Needs*

1. Any diagnosed mental/emotional illness or problem ____________

   ____

2. Any observed indications/symptoms of mental/emotional disorders:

   Depression _____ Anxiety _____ Withdrawal _____

   Paranoia _____ Hypochondria _____ Confusion _____

   Sense of helpfulness/uselessness _____ Disorientation _____

   Memory loss ___ Hallucinations _____ Acting out _____

   Wandering _____ Self-neglect/abuse ____ Sexual fixation _____

   Hostility _____ Anger _____ Aggressive behavior _____

   Other ____

3. Describe symptoms ______________________________
____
____

4. Able to express self verbally ______________________________
5. Exhibits understanding of others ______________________________
6. Appears able to make decisions ______________________________
7. Exhibits evidence of independence ______ Dependence ______________
   Describe ______________________________
   ____

8. Evidence of self-motivation ______________________________
9. Appears to maintain healthy relationships ______________________________
10. Copes well with problems ______________________________
11. Manages personal affairs _____ Another person manages affairs _____
12. Shows common sense in making judgements ______________________________
13. Exhibits ability to adapt to new circumstances/situations ______________
14. Demonstrates ability to adjust to any loss of function/changes in roles
    ____

15. Finds use for leisure time ______________________________
    List activities ______________________________
16. Appears to find life: exciting ____ enjoyable ____ satisfactory ____
    unsatisfactory ____ dull and routine ____ depressing ____
17. Interviewer's comments ______________________________
    ____
    ____

18. Needs not presently being met ______________________________
    ____
    ____

V. *Economic Resources Needs*

1. Monthly income _______ Sources ___________________________
2. How many live on income ___________________________________
3. Own home _____ rent ________ other _______________________
4. Adequate medical insurance __________ From _________________
5. Income adequate to provide:

   Adequate housing ______ Furnishings ______ Food ______

   Clothing ______ Utilities ______ Medical care ______

   Medications ______ Transportation ______ Extras ______

   To meet emergencies ____________________________________
6. Any income supplements received:

   Family contributions ______ Food stamps ______

   Medicare/Medicaid ______ Income supplement ______

   Heating assistance ______ Other ______________________
7. Any noted deprivations ___________________________________
8. Interviewer's comments ___________________________________

   ____

   ____
9. Unmet needs ____

   ____

   ____

VI. *ADL/IADL Resources/Needs*

1. Cares for personal grooming: Well ______ Adequately ______

   Inadequately _____ Has help _____ Describe __________________

   Grooming not cared for _______________________________

2. Is able to care for personal needs: (Insert code below: 1 = Without assistance; 2 = Supervision needed; 3 = Assistance of equipment; 4 = Assistance of a person; 5 = Assistance of equipment and a person; 6 = Unable to accomplish; 7 = Not observed).

	Code	Comments
1. Eating		
2. Meal preparation		
3. Toileting		
4. Dressing/undressing		
5. Bathing		
6. Getting in/out of bed		
7. Household chores		
8. Shopping		
9. Laundry		
10. Manages finances		
11. Manages household		
12. Takes own medications		
13. Driving		
14. Uses public transportation		
15. Uses telephone		

Appendix E: Sample Plan of Care Form

Adult Day Care: Participant Care Plan

Participant name ____________________ Age ______ Sex ______________
Marital status ______________________ Living arrangements ______________
Reasons for enrollment in adult day care ______________________________
____

Problems/Needs:
Physical ____
____

Mental/emotional ____
____

Social ____
____

Economic ____
____

Highest priority needs ____

Possible options for resolution ______________________________________
____

Care Goal: Maintain present functional level in ___________________________

Demonstrates improvement in ____
____

Discharge plans ____
____

Adult Day Care: Participant Care Plan (Page ________)

Participant name________________________ Date____________ Nature of need: Physical ___ Mental ___ Social ___ Economic ______

Care team members____

Specific problem to be addressed__________________________________ Goal of plan ______________________________

Barriers to resolution	Resources to be used/including strengths-skills of participant	Specific actions to be taken and responsible party	Expected result and time for accomplishment

Date for plan to be reviewed________________________ Results of review ______________________________

Progress notes______________________________

____

______________________________ Revised Goal ______________________________

Recorded by ______________________________

Bibliography

Arling, G. and M. Romaniuk. 1982. *The final report from the study of adult day care programs in Virginia.* Richmond, VA: Virginia Center on Aging, Virginia Commonwealth University.

Atchley, R.C. 1977. *Social forces in later life.* Scripps Foundation Gerontology Center, Miami University. Belmont, CA: Wadsworth Publishing Co., Inc.

Austin, M.J. et al. 1982. *Evaluating Your Agency's Programs.* Beverly Hills, CA: Sage Publications.

Bachner, J.P. and E. Cornelius. 1978. *Activities coordinator's guide to long-term care services.* Department of Health, Education, and Welfare. Washington, DC: United States Government Printing Office.

Baldwin, B.A. 1985. *The dynamics of delegation, sharing responsibility.* Piedmont Airlines Magazine. June.

Belkner, L.B. 1978. *The First Time Manager.* AMACOM. division of American Management Association. New York: American Management Association.

Brill, N. 1969. Basic knowledge for working with the aged. *Gerontologist.* 9, Autumn.

Brodowski, B. 1981. The state of the art: The design of assessment instruments in long-term care. From: *Working with the at-risk older person.* Washington, DC: National Council on the Aging, Inc.

Buckley, I. 1969. *A few do's and don'ts to talk with the hard of hearing.* Raleigh, NC: North Carolina State University. Reprinted with permission from *Geriatric Care.* 1(12).

Collins, M.A. and J.E. Mills. 1979. *Boards and advisory councils: A key to effective management.* Washington, DC: National Council on the Aging, Inc.

Cooperative study of older adults in Winston Salem/Forsyth County. 1985. Conducted by the Area Agency on Aging, West Piedmont Council of Government, Forsyth Council for Older Adults, and United Way of Forsyth County, Winston Salem, NC.

Craig, R. and L.R. Bittell (Eds.) 1967. *Training and development handbook.* American Society for Training and Development. New York: McGraw Hill.

Duke Center for the Study of Aging and Human Development. 1978. *OARS training program in techniques of adult day care assessment.* Durham, NC: Duke Center for the Study of Aging and Human Development.

Ernst, M. and H. Shore. 1978. *Sensitizing people to the processes of aging, The in-service educator's guide.* Denton, TX: Dallas Geriatric Institute, Center for Studies in Aging, North Texas University.

Fallcreek, S. and M. Mettler. 1984. *A Healthy Old Age: A Source Book for Health Promotion.* Seattle, WA: School of Social Work, Center for Welfare Research, University of Washington.

Fear, R. 1978. *The evaluation interview.* New York: McGraw-Hill.

Goldston, S.M. 1982. *An adult day care study of the Richmond metropolitan adult day care centers,* prepared under a grant from Aetna Insurance Co. Foundation. Unpublished.

Hall, N.M. 1975. *Social action outreach skills, A training manual.* Prepared for the Governor's Coordinating Council on the Aging, University of North Carolina, Extension Division. Chapel Hill, NC: University Press.

Jacobs, B. 1981. *Working with the at-risk older person: A resource manual.* Washington, DC: National Council on the Aging, Inc.

Johnson, A.M. 1976. *Community resources for day care,* paper presented at the Adult Day Care Conference, Duke University. Durham, NC.

Larmer, K. et al. 1986. *Adaptive re-use of buildings for adult day care,* paper presented at the National Council on the Aging, Inc. Conference. Washington, DC.

Leanse, J., M. Tiven, and T. B. Robb. 1979. *Senior center operation: A guide to organization and management.* Washington, DC: National Council on the Aging, Inc.

McKenzie, A.R. 1972. *The time trap.* New York, NY: AMACOM, a division of the American Management Association.

Meinke, G., C. Murphy, and R. Von Behren. 1984. *On Lok senior health services, Staff training manual for adult day care programs.* San Francisco, CA: On Lok Senior Health Services.

Myers, J. E., P. Finnerty-Fried and C. Graves (Eds.). 1981. *Counseling older persons. Vol. I, Guidelines for a team approach for training.* Washington, DC: American Personnel and Guidance Association and Administration on Aging, National Project on Counseling Older People.

National Council on the Aging. n.d. *Media relations handbook.* Washingon, DC: National Council on the Aging, Inc.

National Institute on Adult Daycare. 1986. *Marketing adult day care: A packet of ideas.* Washington, DC: Publications and Research Committee, National Institute on Adult Daycare, National Council on the Aging, Inc.

National Institute on Adult Daycare. 1984. *Standards for adult day care.* Washington, DC: National Council on the Aging, Inc.

National Institute on Aging. 1980. *Our future selves.* Department of Health, Education, and Welfare. Washington, DC: Government Printing Office, NIH Pub. No. 80-1096.

North Carolina Department of Human Resources. 1981. *North Carolina adult day care services: standards for certification.* Raleigh, NC: North Carolina Department of Human Resources.

North Carolina Office of Volunteer Services. 1981. *Handbook for volunteer services,* Raleigh, NC: North Carolina Department of Human Resources, Office of Volunteer Services.

O'Brien, C.L. 1982. *Adult day care: A practical guide.* Monterey, CA: Wadsworth Health Sciences Division.

Padula, H. 1983. *Developing adult day care for older people, a technical assistance monograph.* Washington, DC: National Council on the Aging, Inc.

Padula, H. 1981. Toward a useful definition of adult day care. *Hospital Progress.* March.

Ransom, B. 1982. *Adult day care centers.* Paper presented to North Carolina Adult Day Care Association, Asheboro, NC.

Rhodes, L.M. 1982. *A Weissert profile and functional task analysis of Vintage, Inc.* Pittsburgh, PA: Vintage, Inc.

Schmall, V.L. 1983. *Growing older, sensory changes.* Pacific Northwest Extension Publication, Oregon State University, Washington State University Extension Service, University of Idaho Cooperative Extension Service, and the United States Department of Agriculture cooperating. Reprinted April 1983.

Schoenberg, R.J. 1978. *The Art of Being A Boss.* Philadelphia: J.B. Lippincott Co.

Silverston, B. and H.K. Hyman. 1982. *You and your aging parent.* New York, NY: Pantheon Books.

Southern Piedmont Health Systems Agency. 1981. *Adult day care guide: How to organize an adult day care program.* Charlotte, NC: Southern Piedmont Health Systems Agency.

Special Committee on Aging, United States Senate. 1978. *Training needs in gerontology, hearing before the Special Committee on Aging.* 93rd Congress. Washington, DC: Government Printing Office.

Subcommittee on Health and Long-Term Care. 1980. *Adult day care programs: Hearings before the Subcommittee on Health and Long-Term Care of the Select Committee on Aging.* 96th Congress. 2nd. Session, April 23, 1980. Washington, DC: United States Government Printing Office, Comm. Pub. No. 96-260.

Syracuse University Gerontology Center. 1977. *Instructor's handbook in the development of a basic course in gerontology.* Syracuse, NY: New York State Office for the Aging.

Trapiano, F.M. 1978. *Initial planning considerations for developing an adult day care center.* Denton, TX: Center for Studies in Aging, North Texas University.

Tsiny, D., E.S. Newman, and R.G. Brockett. 1981. *Basic adult services: A model curriculum.* Albany, NY: Continuing Education Program, School of Social Welfare, The University of New York.

Uris, A. and M. Noppel. 1970. *The turned-on executive.* New York, NY: McGraw-Hill.

U.S. Federal Council on the Aging. 1978. *Assessment and plan of care: Public policy and the frail elderly.* Washington, DC: United States Government Printing Office.

Von Behren, R. and A. Gould. 1985. *Adult day health care: Policies and procedures manual.* San Francisco, CA: On Lok Senior Health Services.

Watson, W.H. 1981. *Aging and social behavior: Introduction to social gerontology,* Monterey, CA: Wasdsworth Health Sciences Division.

Weiler, P.G. and E. Rathbone-McCuan. 1978. *Adult day care: Community work with the elderly.* New York: Springer Publishing Company.

Willard, S. 1980. *Staff development, grantsmanship,* paper presented at Grantsmanship Seminar. Winston-Salem, NC.

Winston, S. 1983. *The organized executive: New ways to manage time, paper, and people.* New York, NY: W.W. Norton and Co.

Index